Building a Trustworthy State in
Post-Socialist Transition

Political Evolution and Institutional Change
Bo Rothstein and Sven Steinmo, editors

Exploring the dynamic relationships among political institutions, attitudes, behaviors, and outcomes, this series is problem-driven and pluralistic in methodology. It examines the evolution of governance, public policy, and political economy in different national and historical contexts.

It will explore social dilemmas, such as collective-action problems, and enhance understanding of how political outcomes result from the interaction among political ideas—including values, beliefs, or social norms—institutions, and interests. It will promote cutting-edge work in historical institutionalism, rational choice, and game theory, and the processes of institutional change and/or evolutionary models of political history.

Building a Trustworthy State in Post-Socialist Transition

Edited by
János Kornai
and
Susan Rose-Ackerman

BUILDING A TRUSTWORTHY STATE IN POST-SOCIALIST TRANSITION
© János Kornai and Susan Rose-Ackerman, 2004

First published 2004 by
PALGRAVE MACMILLAN™
175 Fifth Avenue, New York, N.Y. 10010 and
Houndmills, Basingstoke, Hampshire, England RG21 6XS
Companies and representatives throughout the world

PALGRAVE MACMILLAN is the global academic imprint of the Palgrave Macmillan division of St. Martin's Press, LLC and of Palgrave Macmillan Ltd. Macmillan® is a registered trademark in the United States, United Kingdom and other countries. Palgrave is a registered trademark in the European Union and other countries.

ISBN 1–4039–6448–3

Library of Congress Cataloging-in-Publication Data
    Building a trustworthy state in post-socialist transition / edited by János Kornai and Susan Rose-Ackerman.
        p. cm.—(Political evolution and institutional change)
Interdisciplinary research conducted at Collegium Budapest by invited visiting scholars.
    Includes bibliographical references and index.
    ISBN 1–4039–6448–3
        1. Democracy—Europe, Eastern. 2. Democracy—Europe, Central.
3. Trust—Europe, Eastern. 4. Trust—Europe, Central. 5. Social capital (Sociology)—Europe, Eastern. 6. Social capital (Sociology)—Europe, Central.
7. Political corruption—Europe, Eastern. 8. Political corruption—Europe, Central.
I. Kornai, János. II. Rose-Ackerman, Susan. III. Collegium Budapest. IV. Series.

JN96.A58B84 2004
320.947—dc22   2003066429

A catalogue record for this book is available from the British Library.

Design by Newgen Imaging Systems (P) Ltd., Chennai, India.

First edition: June, 2004
10 9 8 7 6 5 4 3 2 1

Printed in the United States of America.

Transferred to digital printing in 2006

CONTENTS

LIST OF TABLES AND FIGURES

Tables

Figures

CONTRIBUTORS

Bruce Ackerman is Sterling Professor of Law and Political Science at Yale University. He is the author of more than a dozen books, including *Social Justice in the Liberal State* (1980) and *We the People* (1991, vol. 1; 1998, vol. 2).

Georgy Ganev has a Ph.D. in Economics. He is the program director for economic research at the Centre for Liberal Strategies in Sofia, Bulgaria, and an assistant professor at Sofia University. His research interests include macro and monetary theory and policy, political economy, and new institutional economics. His recent publications include *Transmission of Monetary Policy in Central and Eastern Europe* (2002) and "The Bulgarian Currency Crisis of 1996–1997" (2003).

Russell Hardin is Professor of Politics at New York University. His Ph.D. is from MIT. He is the author of *Collective Action* (1982), *Morality Within the Limits of Reason* (1988), *One for All: The Logic of Group Conflict* (1995), *Liberalism, Constitutionalism, and Democracy* (1999), *Trust and Trustworthiness* (2002), and *Indeterminacy and Society* (2003).

Joel Hellman is currently Senior Adviser on Governance in the East Asia and Pacific Region at the World Bank based in Jakarta, Indonesia. Previously, he held senior positions on governance and political affairs in Eastern Europe and the former Soviet Union at the World Bank and the European Bank for Reconstruction and Development. He has taught political science at Columbia University and Harvard University.

Cynthia M. Horne is an assistant professor at the John C. Whitehead School of Diplomacy and International Relations at Seton Hall University. Her research and teaching center around international and comparative political economy issues. She is especially interested in questions related to the economic and political transitions in former socialist countries. She received her Ph.D. from the Department of Political Science at the University of Washington.

Daniel Kaufmann is the Director of Global Governance at the World Bank Institute (WBI). Regarded as a leading expert and advisor in the field of governance, he has published widely on academic and policy issues, pioneering new empirical and survey methodologies with colleagues at the

World Bank. He leads a team supporting countries on good governance and anticorruption programs and on capacity building. He has previously held positions as manager and lead economist at the World Bank in Washington, DC; as the first Chief of Mission to Ukraine, and as Visiting Scholar at Harvard University. A Chilean national, he received his M.A. and Ph.D. in Economics at Harvard University.

János Kornai is Allie S. Freed Professor of Economics, Emeritus at Harvard University and Permanent Fellow Emeritus at Collegium Budapest. He is the author of many books including *Anti-Equilibrium* (1972), *Economics of Shortage* (1980), and the *Socialist System: The Political Economy of Communism* (1992). He is an honorary doctor of several universities and has been a visiting professor at the Yale, Princeton, Stanford, and Stockholm universities, and the London School of Economics. He is an honorary member of the American Academy of Arts and Sciences and the American Economic Association, and foreign member of numerous academies and other scholarly associations. Currently he serves as the president of the International Economic Association.

Ivan Krastev, a political scientist, is the Chairman of the Board of the Centre for Liberal Strategies in Sofia, Bulgaria and research director of the project "Understanding Anti-Americanisms in the World" coordinated by the Central European University, Budapest. He has been visiting fellow at Oxford, the Woodrow Wilson Center in Washington, Wissenschaftskolleg, Berlin, the Institute of Federalism, University of Fribourg, and the Institute for Human Sciences, Vienna. His recent publications include "De-Balkanizing the Balkans: The State of the Debate" (2000), "The Balkans: Democracy Without Choices" (2002), and *The Anti-Corruption Trap* (2004).

Margaret Levi is Jere L. Bacharach Professor of International Studies in the Department of Political Science, University of Washington, Seattle. She received her Ph.D. from Harvard in 1974. Her books include *Of Rule and Revenue; Consent, Dissent, and Patriotism;* and the coauthored *Analytic Narratives*. She is the general editor of *Cambridge Studies in Comparative Politics* and coeditor of the trust series for the Russell Sage Foundation. She is a member of the American Academy of Arts and Sciences, a Guggenheim Fellow, and President-Elect of the American Political Science Association.

John Mueller holds the Woody Hayes Chair of National Security Studies, Mershon Center, and is professor of Political Science at Ohio State University. He has published widely in the fields of national security and international relations. His most recent books are *Policy and Opinion in the Gulf War* (1994), *Quiet Cataclysm: Reflections on the Recent Transformation of World Politics* (1995), and *Capitalism, Democracy, and Ralph's Pretty Good Grocery* (1999). Mueller is a member of the American Academy of Arts and Sciences, has been a Guggenheim Fellow, and has received grants from the National Science Foundation and the National Endowment for the Humanities.

Dr. Clause Offe, rer. pol., is Professor of Political Science at Humboldt-University, Berlin. Recent book publications include *Beyond Employment, Time, Work and the Informal Economy* (1992), *Varieties of Transition* (1996), *Modernity and the State, East and West* (1996), and the coauthored *Institutional Design in Post-Communist Societies: Rebuilding the Ship at Sea* (1998).

Susan Rose-Ackerman is the Henry R. Luce Professor of Jurisprudence (Law and Political Science) at Yale University. She holds a Ph.D. in Economics from Yale and has held Guggenheim and Fulbright Fellowships. She has been a fellow at the Center for Advanced Study in the Behavioral Sciences and Collegium Budapest and was a visiting research fellow at the World Bank. Her most recent book is *Corruption and Government: Causes, Consequences and Reform* (1999). She has written widely on corruption, law and development, administrative law and regulatory policy, the nonprofit sector, and federalism and urban economics.

András Sajó, a constitutional scholar, is Professor at the Central European University (CEU), Budapest and Global Faculty, New York University Law School. He was the founding dean of Legal Studies at CEU. He has been involved in legal drafting throughout Eastern Europe and advised on the drafting of the Ukranian, Georgian, and South African Constitutions. He has served as Counsel to the president of the Republic of Hungary, and chaired the Media Codification Committee of the Hungarian government. He was the principal draftsman of the Environment Code for the Hungarian Parliament, as well as the founder and speaker of the Hungarian League for the Abolition of the Death Penalty. He is the member of the American Law Institute and the Hungarian Academy of Sciences.

Irina Slinko graduated from Moscow State University, Department of Mechanics and Mathematics, where she specialized in Mathematical Statistics and Probability Theory. She received an M.A. in Economics from the New Economic School, Moscow in 1999. She was a research assistant in RECEP then worked as an economist at CEFIR, Moscow. She started her Ph.D. program in finance at the Stockholm School of Economics in 2001. Her research interests include economics of transition, fiscal federalism, public finance, asset pricing, and mathematical finance.

Alexandra Vacroux is currently completing a Harvard University doctoral dissertation that explores the relationship between regulatory institutions and Russian pharmaceutical companies. She is a Research Associate with the Center for Economic and Financial Research (CEFIR) in Moscow and is affiliated with the Davis Center for Russian Studies at Harvard University. She has lived in Russia since the beginning of the transition from communism, was involved in the implementation of the privatization program, and worked with a local investment bank for several years. She wrote one of the first articles describing the development of Russian financial–industrial groups in 1994.

Evgeny Yakovlev holds an M.Sc. in Mathematics from Moscow State University and an M.A. in Economics from the New Economic School,

Moscow. Currently he works as an economist for the Center for Economic and Financial Research (CEFIR) and is a teaching and research assistant at the New Economic School.

Ekaterina Zhuravskaya received her Ph.D. in Economics from Harvard University in 1999. She returned to Russia to become the first Hans Rausing Assistant Professor of Economics. She is the academic director at CEFIR, Moscow, and a research affiliate of the Center for Economic Policy Research, London. Her research interests include economics of transition, political economy, institutions, fiscal federalism, regulations, and bankruptcy. She has published widely in scholarly journals and contributed volumes. In 1999, she won the Nobel Foundation Young Economist Competition for her work on fiscal federalism. In 2000, the World Economic Forum in Davos named her a Global Leader for Tomorrow.

PREFACE

The problems of dishonesty and distrust are ubiquitous in Eastern Europe and the Soviet successor states. These issues are aired daily in the press and on television and are discussed at home, at work, and among friends. Corruption, deception, lying, and abuse of trust are mentioned more often these days than they were before the change of system. Although distrust and dishonesty permeated social relations before the transition, these problems were concealed, or it was forbidden to talk about them.

Research on honesty and trust is wide-ranging and covers many fields of inquiry. The Collegium Budapest project, Honesty and Trust: Theory and Experience in the Light of Post-Socialist Transformation, aimed to integrate that disparate activity and to draw some lessons for the transition countries. The project sought to foster integration in at least three senses: in research approaches, in international coverage, and in disciplinary reach.

The huge international literature on the subject centers around two major topics. One of these is *trust* and its relation to *social capital*. What is meant by these concepts? What helps or hinders their formation? What are the beneficial or detrimental effects of trust in its various guises, and how is it related to social capital and democratic consolidation? The second is concerned with the *institutional* roots of *dishonest behavior* and with the difficulty of promoting *honesty*. Many authors study various forms of dishonesty: corruption, conflicts of interest, deception of business partners or the state, or the theft of others' property.

In the world of science and scholarship, these two research themes have hardly been cognizant of each other. Exponents of one scarcely ever cite work of the other, let alone attend each other's conferences. The project set out to bring together some prominent representatives of each group and prompt them to exchange and integrate their ideas.

The group was *international*, with over 50 scholars recruited from 17 countries of the "East" and "West." Researchers came from Bulgaria, Canada, China, France, Germany, Hungary, Italy, Mexico, Norway, Poland, Romania, Russia, Sweden, Switzerland, Turkey, the United Kingdom, and the United States. (See the list of participants following the preface.) Some were experts on the post-socialist transition. Others were invited because they showed a willingness to learn and to cooperate with those who specialize in analyzing the post-socialist transition. Most importantly, the members of the group agreed to think seriously about what lessons could be drawn for the post-socialist region from research—both theoretical and empirical—dealing with other parts of the world.

The research was *interdisciplinary*. The disciplines represented were political science, economics, sociology, law, anthropology, and political philosophy. We hope that those who take the baton onward will be able to extend the cooperation further by including history and ethical philosophy.

If those doing research in neighboring topics hardly know each other's work, that was all the more so between different disciplines. The essays that participants submitted when they joined the project tended to cite works within their own discipline, mainly because that was almost exclusively what they had studied. This limitation relaxed somewhat in the course of the project. The personal conversations, seminars, and workshops helped to familiarize members of the group with each other's work and with the approaches, methodologies, methods of argument, and styles prevalent in "neighboring" disciplines.

Interdisciplinary work, apart from being thought-provoking and helping to enrich everyone's set of research tools, also exerts a disciplinary force in another sense. Every field becomes inured to its own, narrowly employed and narrowly understood jargon. Interdisciplinary discourse obliges people to talk and write in a way comprehensible to a wider intellectual circle. This also forces people to clarify their ideas.

Within each discipline, there is general acceptance of certain simplifying assumptions, abstract schemata, and accepted criteria for a convincing argument or a valid defense of a statement. As one climbs out of one's disciplinary bunker, it immediately becomes clear that such "generally accepted" abstractions, simplified assumptions, or techniques of argument are by no means self-evident or convincing to exponents of another field. Interdisciplinary confrontation did indeed prompt the members of the group to explain themselves, revise lines of argument, and reappraise assumptions.

The purpose of the project was not to arrive at a uniform point of view. This was not a "task force" exercise designed to produce a joint report. On the contrary, it was designed to stimulate debate, and there were several important problems on which no agreement was reached. Respecting each other's points of view, the participants cooperated and differed in a friendly manner. That is natural enough in democracies with a long history behind them, but far from common in the post-socialist region of the world, where the academic world all too often reflects the impatience and antagonism of political divisions.

When a research group assembles to examine a big subject, there are a number of organizational principles to choose from. One possibility is to draw up in advance, plainly and accurately, a limited number of questions and designate clearly which members are expected to respond to which questions. If answers to one question are expected from several researchers, prior agreement is reached on methodological principles as well, so that the responses become comparable. The upshot of collective work organized in such a decisive, even strict, fashion will be a publication whose parts constitute a coherent, rigorously structured whole. Equally likely is a collection that is artificial and uninteresting.

The project directors were aware of this organizational strategy and its inherent advantages. Nonetheless, it was deliberately set aside in favor of a different course. Pursuing the integrating purpose outlined earlier meant drawing the members of the group from a very wide area. Recruiting leading researchers from different disciplines and countries meant allowing each to write on a subject of his or her own choice. The members could not be confined to a Procrustean bed of compulsory, previously formulated questions. The most important thing was to build on their individual initiatives and ideas to produce essays that spoke to the broad themes of our project.

Given the integrating objectives already described, it is hard to imagine a more favorable organizational setting than Collegium Budapest. This institution, founded in 1991 during the post-socialist transition's first great burst of organization and creation, belongs to a genus of scientific institutions usually referred to (after the original institute at Princeton) as "institutes for advanced study." Others include the Palo Alto Center for Advanced Study in the Behavioral Sciences, the Wissenschaftskolleg in Berlin (which initiated the foundation of Collegium Budapest), and similar bodies in the Netherlands, Norway, Romania, Sweden, and elsewhere. There is no teaching in such institutions, only research. Each operates with a small permanent staff, and most of the researchers are guest fellows invited for a year or less. Each institute is international and interdisciplinary in its makeup.

The fellows invited to Collegium Budapest pursue their research individually. But it has become a tradition to have one or two "focus groups" each year in which a number of scholars approach a specific theme. The project on Honesty and Trust was such a focus group, and it was the largest focus group in the Collegium's history.

Many of the authors of the studies in this book and its companion volume, *Creating Social Trust in Post-Socialist Transition*, spent shorter or longer periods as fellows or visiting scholars at the Collegium. The interaction among them was not confined to a brief conference but lasted for weeks or months. The fellows had lunch together every day, and each author led an intensive seminar on his or her own research. Furthermore, there were many informal discussions that provided opportunities for exchanging views or debating about each other's ideas and writings. In addition, three workshops, each of two days, were organized at Collegium Budapest for fellows in residence along with invited experts. These larger gatherings were also attended by group members unable to spend an extended period at the Collegium. Results and findings were posted on the Internet (http://www.colbud.hu/honesty-trust) as working documents while the research continued.

The most tangible products of this project are these two volumes—
Building a Trustworthy State in Post-Socialist Transition (edited by János Kornai
and Susan Rose-Ackerman) and *Creating Social Trust in Post-Socialist
Transition* (edited by János Kornai, Bo Rothstein, and Susan Rose-
Ackerman). In addition, many members of the group will subsequently
publish articles and books begun in Budapest. However, the success of the
project should not be measured simply in terms of published pages.
Another important product of the project was the discourse and the intellectual influence that members exerted on each other while at the
Collegium Budapest, housed in a lovely Baroque building in the historic
Castle District of the city. The spirit of that discourse, we hope, was valued
by all participants who will disseminate it in their own environments.

We would like to express thanks on behalf of all group members for the
intellectual inspiration contributed by the rector of Collegium Budapest,
Professor Imre Kondor, the institution's permanent fellows, and the
research fellows whose visits to the Collegium coincided with the project.
We are especially grateful to Katalin Szabó, János Varga, and the Collegium
staff for their manifold kind and attentive help and to Julianna Parti for her
excellent editorial assistance in preparing the manuscript and the indices.
Bo Rothstein, a member of the focus group, assisted us with the editorship
of *Creating Social Trust in Post-Socialist Transition*, and we are very grateful for
his contributions. David Pervin, the books' editor at Palgrave, has been a
great help in shepherding the book through the production process.

We would also like to extend our sincere thanks to the Bank of Sweden
Tercentenary Foundation and the William and Flora Hewlett Foundation
for their generous financial support for the project. Without their support
the project would not have been able to go forward.

September 2003   JÁNOS KORNAI
                                                  SUSAN ROSE-ACKERMAN
                                                       Project Directors

PARTICIPANTS IN THE PROJECT

Bruce Ackerman, Yale University, New Haven CT
Jens C. Andvig, Norsk Utenrikspolitisk Institutt, Oslo
Gabriel Badescu, Babes-Bolyai University, Cluj-Napoca
Ildikó Barna, Eötvös Loránd University, Budapest
Bernard Chavance, University of Paris 7, CEMI, EHESS
Karen S. Cook, Stanford University, Palo Alto CA
Bruno Frey, University of Zurich
Scott Gehlbach, University of Wisconsin, Madison
Russell Hardin, New York University
Joel. S. Hellman, World Bank Institute, Washington DC
Cynthia M. Horne, Seton Hall University, Newark NJ
Rasma Karklins, University of Illinois at Chicago
Daniel Kaufmann, World Bank Institute, Washington DC
János Kornai, Harvard University and Collegium Budapest
Ivan Krastev, Centre for Liberal Strategies, Sofia
Jana Kunicova, California Institute of Technology, Pasadena
Alena A. Ledeneva, SSEES, London
Natalia Letki, Nuffield College, Oxford
Margaret Levi, University of Washington, Seattle
Larissa Adler Lomnitz, Universidad Nacional Autonoma de Mexico
Marie Mendras, CERI, Paris
Julius Moravcsik, Stanford University, Palo Alto CA
John Mueller, Ohio State University
Helen Nissembaum, New York University
Claus Offe, Humboldt-Universitaet, Berlin
Annamária Orbán, Central European University, Budapest
Antal Örkény, Eötvös Loránd University, Budapest
Margit Osterloh, University of Zurich
Katharina Pistor, Columbia Law School, New York City
Vadim Radaev, State University, Moscow
Martin Raiser, World Bank, Washington DC
Susan Rose-Ackerman, Yale University, New Haven CT
Bo Rothstein, Göteborg University

András Sajó, Central European University, Budapest
David Shugarman, York University, North York, Canada
Mária Székelyi, Eötvös Loránd University, Budapest
Piotr Sztompka, Jagiellonian University, Krakow
Davide Torsello, Max Planck Institute for Social Anthropology, Halle/Saale
Eric M. Uslaner, University of Maryland
Alexandra Vacroux, Harvard University and Center for Economic and Financial Research, Moscow
Federico Varese, University of Oxford
Vadim Volkov, The European University at St. Petersburg
Christopher Woodruff, University of California, San Diego
Chenggang Xu, London School of Economics
Ekaterina Zhuravskaya, Center for Economic and Financial Research, Moscow
László Zsolnai, Budapest University of Economic Sciences

Introduction

SUSAN ROSE-ACKERMAN

Trust has two distinct meanings in state–society relations. First, a person may trust that he or she will be favored over others in official dealings. This could occur because one relies on ties of kinship or friendship, or because of bribes or campaign contributions. Second, one may trust in the fairness of the rules and in their impartial application by honest officials in particular cases. This can occur when government justifies its decisions publicly and provides reasons consistent with the evenhanded application of the law (Rose-Ackerman 2001a,b). As Nicholas Luhmann points out, in complex societies the benefits of the second type of trust are large but this type of trust may undermine trust based on family and friends (1988: 99–105). In the post-socialist transition, trust in family and friends retains a hold on the operation of public institutions and may be limiting the success of efforts to implement the laws impartially (Kornai 1992; Miller et al. 2001; Rose 1999).

Honesty is an important substantive value with a close connection to trust (Bok 1978). Honesty implies both truth-telling and responsible behavior that seeks to abide by the rules. One may trust another person to behave honestly, but honesty is not identical to trustworthiness. One may be honest but incompetent and so not worthy of trust. Corruption is dishonest behavior that violates the trust placed in a public official. It involves the use of a public position for private gain (Rose-Ackerman 1999).

The transition in Central and Eastern Europe (CEE) has many distinctive features, but it also has much in common with transitions elsewhere. The Collegium Budapest project, Honesty and Trust: Theory and Experience in the Light of Post-Socialist Transition, attempts to distinguish between these aspects of regime change. This book and the companion volume, *Creating Social Trust in Post-Socialist Transition*, draw on the experience of those who have lived through and studied the transition from socialism; both volumes seek to combine the insights of those scholars with those of others who lack this regional focus.

There are several distinctive features of the transition in CEE. First, the state was viewed as dishonest and untrustworthy by much of the population, and this general distrust of public institutions has continued into the present and made even well-meaning state reform difficult (Kornai 1992: 580; Mishler and Rose 1998). Second, communist ideology had become devalued over the postwar period, and this has given all ideologies a bad name even those directly opposed to communism. Third, on the bright side, the population of most post-socialist states is highly educated, and income was distributed relatively equally at the start of the transition. Some minority groups, such as the Roma and some rural households, suffer from poor economic and social conditions, but, in general, the population is capable of participating in and running a functioning modern state and economy. Fourth, before the fall of many socialist regimes, some reform efforts were begun that attempted to increase the legitimacy of the one-party state by providing oversight and permitting public participation and organization. A complex mixture of continuity and change has marked the transition. The continuity of some institutions and officials made the transition easier, but it also made some aspects of the new regime suspect in the eyes of those most dissatisfied with the previous authoritarian regimes.

The contributions in the present volume explore some aspects of the transition process. They indicate the wide diversity of experience in CEE but suggest that there is a rough divide between countries in the first round of European Union (EU) accession and those in the rest of the region. The EU candidates have problems that do not differ in kind from those facing established market democracies. However, the relative newness of their institutions and the population's lack of experience with constructive political activity create difficulties. These countries need to focus on reforms that will enhance institutional stability and predictability and increase public involvement in political life. The options discussed here—increased public participation in government, neutral institutions, lustration processes, anticorruption policies, and higher levels of civic engagement and public morality—form a selective list that is an artifact of the interests of the project participants. However, they all have in common efforts to create more democratic and effective states.

Russia, and by extension, the rest of the former Soviet Union, face deeper problems. Although both bureaucrats and business people are coping in the face of adversity, dysfunctional state and market institutions raise the risk of a long-term period of weak democracy and inefficient markets. None of the project participants predicts a return to autocratic one-party rule, but the transition remains fragile with even the stability of the basic shift to democracy in some doubt. Reforms such as broadened public participation or reform of particular regulatory agencies will have little impact without a deeper national commitment to democracy in its most basic sense of contested elections with alternations in power.

The volume begins with three chapters that explore alternative ways to enhance government accountability and legitimacy as a supplement to the electoral process. They analyze, in turn, public participation in government policy making, neutral regulatory institutions, and lustration policies designed to deal with the shadow of the past. The next five chapters focus on the way corruption and state capture are affecting business-government relations in the region and point to the difficulties of carrying out robust reform strategies in this area. The volume ends with a debate between three scholars over what one ought to or can expect from democratic government. Are the problems that bother the residents of transition countries inherent features of modern democracies? Are they a cause for concern, or should they just be accepted as the best that can be expected?

The institutional options we consider in the first section of the volume are by no means exhaustive, but they all take as their starting point a functioning electoral democracy. Their basic claim is that the transition to a modern, legitimate democracy requires more than contested elections. Each essay deals with a different type of institutional development. Susan Rose-Ackerman and András Sajó consider the role of public participation and neutral institutions, respectively. They both point to the value of such institutions although they recognize the difficulties of establishing them when civil society is weak and the level of partisanship is high.

The socialist past is still relevant to the current transition process. Cynthia Horne and Margaret Levi discuss the alternative ways in which countries used lustration processes to exclude some members of the previous regime from holding office. All the transition countries are struggling with this issue, and Horne and Levi demonstrate that a range of options is consistent with democratic consolidation.

The issues raised in these essays are particularly salient for the countries in the first wave of EU applicants because they are being asked to implement a range of reforms to bring them into compliance with EU laws. They must choose what institutions to adopt and how to fit them into existing patterns of behavior. Obviously, the basic democratic and market institutions are modeled after the experiences of other countries, but what about particular institutions such as regulatory agencies, central banks, and laws that encourage civil society participation in government? These chapters imply that the transition countries need to develop the independent capacity to react to pressure from the EU for particular types of reforms and weigh the strengths and weaknesses of the options available.

Corruption and state capture are serious problems throughout the region, although the cross-country differences are large—with the Central European countries doing better than those farther to the east (Hellman et al. 2000). Distinguishing between political and bureaucratic corruption, Claus Offe begins the second section by focusing on political corruption. He concludes that changes in both institutions and morals are needed to control the phenomenon.

Joel Hellman and Daniel Kaufmann report on a cross-country survey that shows that there are wide interregional differences in the degree of state capture by oligarchic interests and in corruption. The trend over time is also highly variable across countries. This has implications for future growth prospects and for the consolidation of democratic institutions in the transition countries. Focusing on a specific case, Irina Slinko, Evgeny Yakovlev, and Ekaterina Zhuravskya study rent-seeking activity in the passage of statutes in the Russian regions. They show that within Russia there is a good deal of variation in the power of concentrated interests, and where it is high, overall growth suffers even as large firms benefit from favorable laws. These two chapters reveal the diversity across and within countries and suggest that the disillusionment expressed by many citizens is, at least in part, based on underlying realities.

Bureaucratic corruption occurs everywhere, but tends to be more prevalent in certain sectors including health care, contracting, and tax collection (Miller et al. 2001). Alexandra Vacroux provides some empirical nuance here with her survey evidence on bureaucratic corruption in the pharmaceutical industry in Russia. Both she and Claus Offe argue for the importance of top leadership that sets a moral example. However, recognizing that corruption is a problem is not the same as finding political supporters to carry out an effective policy. Building on the Bulgarian case, Ivan Krastev and Georgy Ganev argue that anticorruption campaigns will be difficult to implement if sitting politicians gain from corruption and the judiciary is weak. Their essay complements Offe's and Vacroux's emphasis on leadership and public outrage.

Finally, what can one learn about the likely trajectory of democratic consolidation by studying the experience of Western Europe and the United States? Russell Hardin and John Mueller provide a valuable counterweight to those who argue that the region is experiencing special problems. Mueller cites data showing that trust in government institutions is low in the United States. Hardin argues that all consolidated democracies are essentially controlled by narrow elites with little claim of popular support. He is critical of this trend but does not see an alternative. Mueller essentially accepts Hardin's factual premises but is rather optimistic, at least with respect to the stability of such democracies. They may not be very appealing when compared with an ideal, but they do not necessarily presage a return to autocratic rule. According to Mueller, one should accept the fact that real democracies cannot conform to an ideal of popular sovereignty. Democracy is, nevertheless, valuable simply because no narrow group can claim a long-term monopoly on power. Bruce Ackerman counters these arguments by claiming that American history contains important instances of mobilized, committed public debate and of leaders inspired by democratic ideals. This conclusion, however, is not necessarily an optimistic one for CEE. It implies that these states need both to provide attractive career paths for potential leaders who aim to do more than play power games and to limit the cynical disengagement of the citizenry from politics.

Building a trustworthy state is difficult and, according to some of the authors included here, it is not a realistic goal. My own view is different. I agree about the difficulty, but I am not as pessimistic as some about the possibility of improving state accountability both in the transition countries and elsewhere. The post-socialist countries are an outstanding example of how a very great deal can change in a very short time. Those who attribute institutional performance to history, ethnic makeup, and religion need to come to terms with the last decade of upheaval in the former communist bloc. True, there are intercountry and interregional differences that arise from historical realities, but the tremendous changes that occurred everywhere as a result of a sharp change in the institutional landscape are strong evidence that institutions matter and that they are subject to change. Furthermore, the transition experience also demonstrates that institutions can be changed in much more subtle ways than simply by overthrowing the old system. Political development in the region is at a critical point where there is openness to reform ideas with the possibility either of institutionalizing or of failing to consolidate recent changes.

The institutional reforms discussed in this volume can never be sufficient taken by themselves, but they can have a marginal impact on state functioning so long as there is an active and organized portion of the citizenry that is concerned with the quality and responsiveness of government. If citizens express skepticism of those in power, that is surely a desirable thing in a democracy (Hardin 1999). However, citizens must care enough not only to express distrust and skepticism in some state institutions but also to seek ways to make the state work better.

References

Bok, Sissela. 1978. *Lying: Moral Choice in Public and Private Life.* New York: Random House.

Hardin, Russell. 1999. "Do We Want Trust in Government?" In M. E. Warren (ed.), *Trust and Government*, pp. 22–41. New York: Cambridge University Press.

Hellman, Joel, Geraint Jones, and Daniel Kaufmann. 2000. *"Seize the State, Seize the Day": State Capture, Corruption, and Influence in Transition.* Policy Research Working Paper No. 2444, Washington DC: World Bank.

Kornai, János. 1992. *The Socialist System: The Political Economy of Communism.* Princeton NJ: Princeton University Press.

Luhmann, Nicholas. 1988. "Familiarity, Confidence, Trust: Problems and Alternatives." In D. Gambetta (ed.), *Trust: Making and Breaking Cooperative Relations*, pp. 94–107. Oxford: Basil Blackwell.

Miller, William L., Åse B. Grødeland, and Tatyana Y. Koshechkina. 2001. *A Culture of Corruption: Coping with Government in Post-Communist Europe.* Budapest: Central European University Press.

Mishler, William and Richard Rose. 1998. *Trust in Untrustworthy Institutions: Culture and Institutional Performance in Post-Communist Societies.* Studies in Public Policy No. 310. University of Strathcylde, Glascow, Scotland: Centre for the Study of Public Policy.

Rose, Richard. 1999. *What Does Social Capital Add to Individual Welfare? An Empirical Analysis of Russia.* Studies in Public Policy No. 318. University of Strathclyde, Glasgow, Scotland: Centre for the Study of Public Policy.

Rose-Ackerman, Susan. 1999. *Corruption and Government: Causes, Consequences and Reform.* New York: Cambridge University Press.

———. 2001a. "Trust and Honesty in Post-Socialist Societies." *Kyklos* 54: 415–43.

———. 2001b. "Trust, Honesty and Corruption: Reflections on the State-Building Process." *Archives Européennes de Sociologie* 42: 526–70.

PART I

Trust and Institutional Reform

CHAPTER ONE

Public Participation in Consolidating Democracies: Hungary and Poland

SUSAN ROSE-ACKERMAN*

Governing politicians in East and Central Europe have often been able to run their governments in extremely partisan ways. This has produced a polarized electorate that only expects good treatment from government if "their" party is in power.[1] To the extent such trends become solidified, they present a threat to the stability and overall accountability of the underlying democratic forms that were welcomed so warmly in 1989.

Accountability that extends beyond partisan attempts to reward supporters means two different things in a democracy. On the one hand, governments should be fair and evenhanded in carrying out the law. On the other hand, they should be accountable to the public in setting policy. The "public" includes those who voted for the current government in the last election, but it also includes those affected by and interested in particular policy choices. My focus in this chapter is on accountability in the second, policy-making, sense. Competitive elections are necessary but not sufficient routes to policy-making accountability. Also important are institutions that provide oversight and control (O'Donnell 1994). However, I go beyond these institutional arrangements to argue that the second type of accountability requires government procedures under which officials consult with nonpartisan groups with a special interest in the matter at hand or with specialized knowledge (Rose-Ackerman 1995). Achieving this type of accountability presents a paradox. How can public bodies be responsive to the concerns of citizens and yet remain insulated from improper influence? How can they perform both as competent experts and as democratically responsible policy makers?

This tension is a fundamental one in the public law of all democratic systems, but it has particular salience as the new democracies of Central and Eastern Europe (CEE) try to create well-functioning states that are accountable to their citizens. These countries inherited top-heavy bureaucratic states that were viewed with hostility and distrust by their citizens. Disillusionment with politics and politicians is widespread, but few people expect or desire a return to authoritarian rule. This chapter is part of a larger project designed to assess and critique the institutions in Central Europe that are assisting in the creation of an accountable and transparent government outside of the electoral process per se (Rose-Ackerman 2005). Both that project and this chapter concentrate on Poland and Hungary, two of the most successful of the transition economies that are poised to join the European Union (EU).[2]

The first section outlines a framework for the analysis of government accountability that shows how citizen participation fits into the overall structure. The central section outlines the policy-making process in Hungary and Poland. The chapter concludes with a discussion of the benefits and risks of participatory processes in present-day Poland and Hungary and includes some suggestions for reform.

Government Accountability: Alternative Frameworks

An idealized model of parliamentary democracy stands behind many discussions of accountability. Under this framework, citizens vote for politicians who represent political parties, and a group of parties forms a government that promulgates policies after consultation with the partisan groups in the legislature. The resulting statutes are administered by an apolitical, professional bureaucracy as a technical, expert exercise that is not influenced by political considerations. In other words, politics and administration operate in separate spheres. The main constraint on self-seeking behavior by politicians is the threat of loss at the polls in the next round of elections.

Under this view, it would be undemocratic and unfair to permit organized groups or individuals to participate in the legislative or the administrative process. Bureaucrats are expected to operate according to technical, legal, and scientific criteria that provide the "right" answers. The civil service follows clear rules that require little discretion, and officials treat everyone evenhandedly. Review is only available to protect individual rights that might otherwise be ignored by bureaucrats focused on general administrative goals. This model is most clearly expressed in justifications for the postwar German state, but even in Germany it both is a poor description of reality and lacks democratic accountability (Rose-Ackerman 1995).

The most basic limitation is the assumption that the political control of the government can be carried out effectively by the parliament. Bureaucrats and executive branch officials perform political/policy-making tasks as they draft statutes and implement imprecise laws, and the governing coalition has little incentive to create independent oversight processes that could interfere with the exercise of its power. As a result, oversight is likely to be weak or partisan, especially for high-level executive policy making. Any independent oversight bodies and participation rights that do exist are likely either to be required by the constitution or to be the result of pressure from politically powerful groups. If some groups, such as labor unions, local governments, the church, or business associations, have power that others lack, this may be reflected both in the substantive laws and in an unbalanced pattern of implementation. At the same time, citizens may play little role in the monitoring of government decisions. A vicious cycle may exist, where the lack of opportunities discourages the formation of just those types of organized, independent oversight groups that could push for change.

Elected representatives, I claim, cannot solve all political or policy issues. Democratic consolidation thus can be aided by oversight and participation from both political and apolitical bodies and groups other than political parties. There are four basic options that will be the focus of my larger work.

The first option is to modify the pure parliamentary structure through the creation of independent agencies. The goal is the same as in the simple model—the insulation of administration from politics. Second, international treaties impose constraints on nation-states. These are not always unwelcome. In some cases, an incumbent government can benefit from tying its own hands through international commitments such as EU access requirements. The third option is delegation to lower-level governments to bring government decision-making closer to the citizens.

The fourth, public participation, alternative embraces, rather than deplores, public influence on national government decisions. It is my focus in this chapter. The drafting and implementation of complex statutes raise political issues, but, unlike the creation of independent agencies, this option accepts these concerns as valid extensions of democratic ideals. The basic problem of executive branch organization is then the incorporation of these political concerns without giving up the benefits of delegation by a democratically elected legislature. This perspective recognizes the objections to participation voiced by supporters of the simple model, with their worries about bias and about the poor information or short-run orientation of the public. However, it sees a corresponding value in incorporating public input into government policy-making processes.[3]

Participatory mechanisms function better if the press is free and if organized private groups exist that are not closely associated with political parties. An important aspect of government accountability is thus the strength and density of independent groups able to participate in the policy-making process. There may be a positive feedback loop here. If organized groups have a function, then individual citizens and businesses have an incentive to organize if the cost is low.

All legislatures pass laws that lack specificity and clarity, but the problem has been particularly acute in CEE during the transition period. Legislatures have been described as "law factories"—producing many laws rapidly in areas where the parliamentarians are uninformed about the technical details.[4] Thus, governments face a major task in putting these laws into force. State building in CEE needs to confront the problem of competently administering statutory policies. This implies more than political party development and the organization of elections, on the one hand, and technical bureaucratic improvements, on the other. Instead, the interaction between policy making and citizens' participation in public affairs needs to be acknowledged. This requires institutions that permit participation while avoiding both confusion or delay and capture by narrow interests.

Public Participation in Poland and Hungary

Public participation outside of elections is not well institutionalized in Poland and Hungary. Although both countries have administrative codes and recognize the need for reasoned decision making within the government, neither requires the publication of draft rules or gives outsiders general participation rights. The Hungarian government is beginning to make some draft rules available on the Internet and to invite comments, but this practice is not universal and is not required by statute.[5] If consultation occurs, it usually involves only a limited number of prespecified groups and individuals who are sent drafts or are consulted as members of official advisory bodies. Formal hearings open to the public are uncommon, and even when they do take place, appear to be of limited importance to the outcome. Both countries require the publication of central government rules with legal force but do not require written justifications. The courts, including the Constitutional Court (Hungary) and the Constitutional Tribunal (Poland), have been of little importance in opening up executive processes to participation and oversight.

The Legacy of the Past

Under the socialist regimes in Hungary and Poland government decrees, not governed by statutes, were a common form of government action. In Hungary the Council of Ministers had broad discretion to enact decrees with legal force when the parliament was not in session. The legislature only met for two periods of two or three days each year. In most years only a handful of laws were enacted by the parliament, mostly concerning budgetary matters.[6]

In Poland the situation was similar although the formal labels were different. The Polish Council of State could issue decrees with the same status as statutes. However, under the Constitution, these decrees needed to be approved by the Sejm (Parliament) at its next session. As a consequence, the Council of State avoided this route and instead issued "independent resolutions" often called "mimeograph laws." These were not formal decrees and so did not need Sejm approval. The Council of State only used its power to issue decrees in 1981 when it declared martial law, presumably because it felt a need both to act quickly and to have the increased legitimacy that Sejm approval could supply.

This history made reformers in both countries skeptical of granting legal force to government pronouncements whatever their name. Although delegation to the government could not, in practice, be avoided, reformers sought to constrain its scope and to strengthen parliaments. As a result, the need to hold the government to account for its remaining discretion was a relatively neglected aspect of the reform process. The primary aim was to limit the government's power, rather than to manage this power in the public interest.

The second legacy is the central planning process itself that involved extensive paperwork and the development of an overall structure of control. However, the planning exercise was internal to the state and was not meant to produce participation and challenges from citizens (Kornai 1992: 47, 411, 425–6). Some traces of this view of rules as internal guides for officials remain in the administrative law systems of both countries and limit the external force of some provisions of their administrative codes.

A final legacy dates from the last decade of the socialist regimes in Poland and Hungary. Political leaders sought to deal with the growing discontent of the citizenry by introducing a number of new institutions and processes designed to increase governmental accountability without dismantling the one-party state. Thus, Poland established the Office of Ombudsman in 1987, strengthened the independence of the Supreme Audit Office (an institution that dates from 1919), and created an Administrative Court in 1980[7] and a Constitutional Tribunal in 1989. Hungary permitted nonprofit organizations to register and operate openly in the 1980s, and Poland allowed ecological groups to organize. In 1987 Hungary promulgated a Law on Normative Acts (XI/1987) that mandated consultation with organized groups for draft laws and decrees. In the area of labor-management relations, the Hungarian government set up a tripartite committee of labor, management, and government that has continued in one form or another to the present.[8]

Forms of accountability and oversight that did not involve competitive elections between candidates from opposing political parties were thus relatively common at the end of the socialist period in Central Europe. Perhaps for that reason, they are sometimes looked on, even today, as of secondary importance or even as cynical attempts to provide the form, but not the substance, of accountability. Given this legacy, efforts to create genuine accountability outside of the electoral process have not been a major focus of democratic reformers.

I turn now to a more detailed overview of the administrative law of public participation in Poland and Hungary. The two countries have many similarities that point to a common set of difficulties and reform opportunities.

Poland

The Polish Constitution of 1997 specifies a closed list of sources of "universally binding" law: the Constitution, statutes, ratified international agreements, and regulations (Article 87). Regulations can only be issued if authorized by statute and only by certain organs specified in the Constitution. That list includes the president, the Council of Ministers, the prime minister, Ministers with Portfolio, and the National Council of Radio Broadcasting and Television (NCRBTV) [Articles 142(1), 146(4), 148(3), 149(2), 213(2)]. The closed list of sources of law and the limited organs authorized to issue regulations are a reaction to the Communist government's use of "independent resolutions" to govern the country.

The blind spot in the constitutional text is a failure to balance the need for legal regularity against the need for flexibility in the administration of the law. This problem has arisen in cases where the Constitutional Tribunal has faced challenges to an agency's regulatory authority. Thus when the Central Bank issued "resolutions" that it sought to enforce as binding law, the Constitutional Tribunal struck down three resolutions claiming that they were de facto "universally binding normative acts" and that the Bank had no authority under the Constitution to issue such acts [judgment of June 28, 2000 (25/99)]. This decision implies that no agency that operates independently of the Council of Ministers, except for the NCRBTV, can issue legally binding norms but must function through case-by-case adjudication and by issuing guidelines with no binding legal force.

The Constitution does not permit open-ended grants of regulatory authority to the Government or to independent agencies. It does not acknowledge that such grants might be counterbalanced by procedural requirements for transparency, public accountability, and judicial review. Under the Constitution there is only one route for public input at the national level—through the election of representatives to the Sejm, which has the power to enact statutes. Regulations can be issued without giving notice, holding a public hearing, or providing reasons. Final regulations must, however, be published in the Journal of the Laws of the Republic of Poland before they go into effect. The only constitutional constraint is the possibility of a referral to the Constitutional Tribunal for a ruling on the constitutionality of the regulation or indeed of any "legal provisions issued by central state organs" [Article 188(3)]. A referral is only possible after the legal provision has been promulgated and can only be made by a limited number of bodies and only so long as the legal act relates to their scope of authority (Article 191). Individuals also have access to the Tribunal to challenge the constitutionality of statutes and other normative acts but only if they believe that a final decision of a public body violates their individual rights. The Code of Administrative Procedure is mainly concerned with the implementation of the law in individual cases and with the operation of the Supreme Administrative Court.[9] It does not apply to the procedures used to issue regulations and guidelines (Galligan et al. 1998: 85–9, 445–6). A few substantive statutes require consultative procedures—for example, with respect to issues affecting labor and business.

Draft rules need not be published, but at the same time, the administrative code requires that drafts must include reasoned justifications that include "an account of the social, economic, and financial consequences" and a report on any "social consultations or social discussions" that took place. However, these documents operate only as internal instructions to the executive branch (Galligan et al. 1998: 446). Of course, consultation does frequently occur, and citizens and organized groups can seek to initiate rule-making processes and express opinions (ibid.: 446, 449–50).

The constitution gives citizens the right to obtain information from the state without having to show that their individual rights have been violated (Article 61). However, until recently, there was no general statute implementing this freedom-of-information provision. In September 2001, an Act on Access to Public Information was adopted (nr. 112, position 1198, minor amendments in 2002). Some claim that the Act is weak and inadequate, and others argue that the Act is stronger than the main alternative draft. The main criticisms are that the Act can be trumped by other laws restricting access in particular situations, that no oversight institution exists so the only recourse is to the overburdened courts, and that the Act is vague, thus giving a good deal of discretion to individual public officials.[10] In contrast, the Adam Smith Research Center in Warsaw, which played a major role in drafting the Act, views it as a strong and effective response emphasizing that it refers to information, not documents, and thus can be interpreted to require that information be provided even if it does not exist as a "document."[11] Beginning in January 2004, the Act (Article 6.1) gives the public access to information about the "intentions" of legislative and executive authorities and the drafting of normative acts (i.e., government regulations and decrees). Of course, the Act only deals with access to information, not process, but once these provisions are in force, they may help open up the administrative process.

In the area of labor-management relations, "tripartite processes" involving labor, management, and the government began in the early years of the new regime. At first, employers' representatives were weak, and the Solidarity labor union was closely tied to the government. However, that did not prevent sharp conflicts between unions and the government, between Solidarity and other unions, and within Solidarity. In 1994 a Law on Negotiated Determination of Average Wage Compensation was passed that established a Tripartite Committee on Social and Economic Affairs. It operated by consensus to set minimum wages and maximum wage increases and to decide other related matters. The wage decisions then became official government policy. If the Committee could not reach agreement, the Council of Ministers made the decision. The Ministry of Labor was also required to consult with national labor and employer groups regarding other policy issues. During this period, the employers' association represented the large state firms and was not a strong counterweight to labor. Between 1997 and 2000 this process of "social dialogue" stopped, but it was revived by the new government under a statute that gave the group similar powers but broadened employer representation to include a more effective group representing private employers. In 2002 unions and employers negotiated on the liberalization of the labor laws with the government acting as a mediator. However, a draft law on revisions in the labor code has led to conflict.[12] The main difficulty with tripartite groups has to do with representation. There are multiple employer and union organizations, and they do not always agree among themselves. Furthermore, only a relatively small share of the workforce is a member of any union so it is not obvious that the interests of nonunion workers are well represented by either unions or the government.[13]

At present, consultation in some agencies takes the form of ongoing institutions that include stakeholders. Thus, the Social Insurance Agency has a Central Advisory Board that includes retirees (50 percent), employers' representatives (25 percent), and Ministry of Labor and voivodeship (regional administrative unit) appointees (25 percent). A similar group exists in the social security area that includes representatives of unions, employers, government, and the disabled. These groups comment on draft normative acts and on petitions to improve regulations, but they are purely advisory bodies.[14] They follow the model of labor regulations discussed earlier where an institutionalized group of stakeholders has a role in the administrative process to the exclusion of others lacking a connection with specified groups.

The government can achieve some flexibility by issuing resolutions and orders, but these are not sources of binding law (Article 93). The Constitutional Tribunal has held that the Constitution permits the Sejm to authorize public entities to issue internal acts and gives public authorities flexibility in the forms these internal acts can take. The list is open, not closed; the "resolutions" and "orders" mentioned in Article 93 are just two possibilities (judgment of December 1, 1998, K. 21/98). In practice, given the limited scope for legally binding regulations, such rules are very important in guiding the administration of laws. This raises questions about the government's freedom to decide what form of executive action to use in particular cases and about citizens' access to such rules if they have not been published. Informal legal norms are a particularly sensitive issue in Poland because they were widely used by the former communist government to compensate for "the incomplete and unsatisfactory condition of legislation" (Galligan et al. 1998: 503). Thus, there is strong support for treating such norms as supplementary rules that are inferior to statutes and formal rules, and this is reflected in the constitutional text (ibid.: 503–4).

Like formal rules, internal acts are subject to no procedural constraints. They are commonly drafted by officials with no mandatory inclusions of citizens or associations (ibid.: 506, 511). Once again, the new Freedom of Information Act may eventually play a role here in encouraging consultation (Article 6.1). Since 2000, such rules must, like formal regulations, be published in the Journal of Laws of the Republic of Poland or in similar journals issued by individual Ministries. This is an improvement over the past when publication was not required (Galligan et al. 1998: 505).

Judicial review of rules and statutes is solely a matter for the Constitutional Tribunal, and only a limited number of institutions, including the President and the Ombudsman, can bring cases. In a 2002 case brought by the President, the Tribunal held that the details of a particular law designed to manage a tax amnesty program were unconstitutional because they violated individual rights and did not satisfy the principle of proportionality.[15] This case suggests that the Tribunal may plan to play a proactive role in reviewing both statutes and the detailed rules used to implement these policies. However, the importance of this ruling for the future depends upon whether the institutions entitled to bring cases act aggressively in the light of this decision.

The Administrative Court hears citizens' complaints of mistreatment, and this will sometimes require the court to judge the validity of a general legal norm as applied in the case at hand. However, although government agencies occasionally do look to the court for guidance in interpreting statutes, the Court's role is limited by its structure. Although reforms are planned for 2004, in 2003 it consisted of a single layer of 300 judges. The Court has no formal means of resolving conflicts or obtaining a ruling with clear national impact. Constitutional questions can be referred to the Constitutional Tribunal, but they only cover a small number of issues.[16] Those who might potentially use the Administrative Court to pressure the government to reform are further hampered by the substantial delays that plague its work.[17]

Hungary

The situation in Hungary is similar to that in Poland in that there are no general, legally enforceable participation rights in the drafting of rules and statutes. The Environmental Act (LIII/1995) and the Regional Development and Country Planning Act (XXI/1996) include some participation requirements, and several statutes provide for advisory committees. Some participants, such as the Ombudsman for Data Protection and Freedom of Information, some legal academics, and several environmental groups have urged more transparent and legally accountable procedures, but, at present, consultation is mainly under the control of the government and can change dramatically when the political coalition in power shifts. The government that came to power in 2002 has made some tentative moves to increase information and access, but these had not been codified into law by the middle of 2003.

The Constitution authorizes the issuance of decrees by the government (i.e., signed by the prime minister), by cabinet ministers, and by local representative bodies. Decrees must not conflict with statutes or with higher-ranking legal norms [Hungarian Constitution, Articles 35(2), 37(3), 44/A(2)]. Sometimes executive power is delegated by statute to self-governing professional associations such as medical and law associations. The courts supervise the legality of government decrees and of any other actions of the public administration as well as the regulatory activities of professional associations.[18]

The Constitutional Court has limited the power of the executive in several ways. In 1991 it held that it was unconstitutional to regulate a fundamental right through an executive decree. Because the regulation of abortion required a judgment on the meaning of the constitutional right to life, legislative action was required.[19] However, the decision accepted the need to use executive decrees in many cases to avoid overburdening the parliament.

A distinctive feature of the Hungarian legal system is the Law on Normative Acts (XI/1987) originally passed at the end of the socialist period. According to that law, the prime minister can only issue decrees that do not conflict with statutes.[20] This was a concession by the socialist government that used degrees extensively. The law also specifies the procedures to be used for issuing decrees although some crucial features are left unspecified. The minister is responsible for promulgating the decree, but "citizens—directly or through their representative bodies—participate in the preparation and creation of legal regulations [i.e., normative acts] affecting their daily life" (Article 19). Furthermore, prior to promulgating a decree, "jurisdictional bodies, social organizations, and interest representative organs have to be involved in the preparation of draft legal regulations which either affect the interests represented and protected by them or their social relations" (Article 20).[21] Jurisdictional bodies are local and regional governments and other ministries that may be involved in implementing a regulation; social organizations include groups such as environmental and women's groups; and interest representative organizations are trade unions and professional associations. Unfortunately, the Act does not specify how the consultation process should be organized or if the results are to be made public. Because draft rules need not be published, the government and its ministers will generally have considerable leeway to manage participation by deciding who is to receive the draft and how much time is allotted for comments.

In its original form the Act contained broad requirements for consultation with social groups and self-governing associations before a law was passed. These provisions were repealed in 1990 by the first democratic government on the ground that they could undermine efforts to create a functioning multiparty democracy. This suspicion of interest-based representation remains in Hungary and surfaces periodically in debates over the role of nonparty groups in political life.

The Law on Normative Acts does not create any rights that can be enforced in the ordinary courts. My interviews suggested that the 1987 law is not important for groups seeking to participate in policy making. Its provisions are essentially internal orders to the bureaucracy and the ministers. The only possibility for judicial review would be to claim constitutional violations. Because Hungary has permissive standing requirements for some kinds of constitutional challenges, such allegations can provide a route to the Constitutional Court.[22]

However, the Court has not been sympathetic to attempts to read consultation requirements into the constitution. One exception concerns consultation with local governments and affected organizations under the Act on Regional Development and Country Planning (XXI/1996). In deciding a challenge to that Act, the Court held that county governments must consult with these bodies before drawing up a plan (Decision 3/1997). In 2001 the Court held that, in spite of the language of the Law on Normative Acts, consultation was not constitutionally required unless the groups to be consulted were explicitly listed in the statute. Unlike the Regional Planning Law, the Law on Normative Acts mentions no specific groups, thus no one could claim a right to be heard (Decision 10/2001).

Instead of open-ended public participation, a number of Hungarian laws call for the creation of advisory committees that review a range of government proposals and sometimes initiate studies on their own. For example, in the environmental area a well-established process exists for government consultation with the National Environmental Council (NEC), an advisory group that includes 21 people from outside government plus the Minister for the Environment. Under the Act on the Environment (LIII/1995, section 45) seven members are selected by environmental groups along with seven scientists and seven representatives of the business community each representing scientific and economic concerns (Commission of the European Communities 2001: 75; Access Initiative 2002: IV.B.1.c). The NEC is not a public forum and is not equivalent to an open hearing process. Rather, those consulted are defined ex ante, not issue by issue. This feature of the NEC is a common characteristic of public participation processes in Hungary as it is in much of Europe.

As in Poland, in other areas as well, advisory committees comment on draft laws and regulations. These committees include representatives from interested state bodies, citizens' representative organizations, and scientists and professionals with expertise on the issue. The required participants are organizations of citizens or other interests; individuals are seldom involved directly (Galligan et al. 1998: 423–5). For example, under the government that lost power in 2002, an advisory economic council included representatives of banks, financial markets, professional associations, and foreign investors as well as trade unions and domestic business associations. In the social welfare area, a number of councils advise the Ministry of Welfare and the government. They include councils for issues affecting the handicapped, the elderly, and social issues in general. However, in many areas active client groups do not exist so that clients are "represented" only by service providers. Consultation is often limited to such councils with little or no opportunity for input from those outside these organized bodies. Even when public participation is mandated, as it was during the reform of the pension system in Hungary, the process may be handled poorly. Leaders of the larger organizations usually do have direct access to ministry officials, but this process seems ad hoc and favors some organizations over others.[23]

In the area of employment and labor issues a tripartite National Council for Interest Reconciliation has existed since the last socialist regime under a variety of different names and with a variety of functions.[24] The council is legally recognized by the Hungarian labor law, but its composition is not codified (Labor Code XXII/1992, sections 16–17, 38, 53, 75, 144). In practice, the council has six trade union representatives and nine employer representatives. If all three parts agree, it can set minimum wages. If they cannot reach consensus, the government sets the level. It also must be consulted on issues affecting labor, such as health and safety regulation. As in

Poland, this group has sometimes suffered from disagreements within the subgroups of labor and business representatives. In addition, the council is the only group that must be legally consulted on many issues even though only about 25 percent of the workforce is in a union (Commission of the European Communities 2001: 60–2; Héthy 2000; interview with László Herczog, Ministry of Economic Affairs).

Civil society groups have tried to use the Act on Protection of Personal Data and Disclosure of Data of Public Interest (1992/LXIII) to increase their influence by pushing for the disclosure of drafts prepared by the government or its various ministries. The Act has an exception in Article 19(5) stating that "Unless otherwise provided by law, working documents and other data prepared for the authority's own use, or for the purpose of decision making are not public within 30 years of their creation. Upon request, the head of the authority may permit access to these documents or data."[25] The paragraph has sometimes been used by the government to limit outside review of draft laws or regulations.

In 2000 a civic organization objected that some ministries sent it drafts of decrees for comment but stipulated that the drafts could not be made public for 30 years. The organization pointed out that this effectively prevented other organizations from participating. It brought its complaint to the Ombudsman who supported the civic organization. He argued that the line between public and private drafts needs to be clarified in light of the public interest in understanding and debating proposed rules and laws.[26] In his advisory opinion he supported a policy of greater openness so that documents would not be circulated only to those with inside connections. Nevertheless, there is, at present, no legal requirement to publish proposed rules and statutes.

Actual practice appears to vary. In the environmental area draft laws and rules are routinely available to the public although this is done on an ad hoc basis, not through publication in the official gazette. For example, the NEC receives draft statutes and rules for review, and some members post all draft laws and rules received on an open website called Green Spider. The Ministry does not object to this practice.[27] In addition, the Aarhus Convention on Procedural Environmental Rights[28] and the EU Directive on Freedom of Information with Respect to the Environment[29] both encourage open treatment of environmental policy making. In this area, a number of fairly well-established private groups monitor the government and are influenced by American and West European models of public involvement.

Notice that in the Ombudsman's case discussed earlier, the petitioning organization attempted to link the provision of information to the possibility of effective participation by outsiders. A next step is to claim not only that the government should provide information, but also that it should facilitate broad public consultation instead of relying only on informal meetings with a few insiders and on advisory committees with fixed membership.

According to one study of participation rights in the environmental area, "in certain laws strong public participation elements do appear sporadically"

(Access Initiative 2002, part I.A.2). The Ombudsman provides a useful overview of the state of the law. Article 93(1) of the general Act on Protecting the Environment (1995/LIII) requires that the Inspectorate conduct a public hearing after receiving an environmental impact assessment on a particular project. After giving notice, the hearing is held in the premises of the local government of the communities most affected and shall include environmental and social organizations (Articles 93[2], [3]; see also Government Decree 152/1995 [XII.12]). Constitutional Court decisions state that the constitutional right to environmental protection can only be carried out through access to information and participation by the "people concerned" (AB 996/G/1990). This is a right that cannot be protected by protecting the individual. Instead, the state must offer "legal and institutional" guarantees (AB 28/1994). A treaty, incorporated in Government Decree 148/1999 (X.13), also provides for public participation if a project has international impacts.[30] Notice, however, that these requirements only refer to the process used to approve particular projects such as a dam or a highway. Even when broad public interest groups are included, the issues involved are local development projects.

In short, mechanisms for consultation exist in Hungary, at least in some ministries. They mostly take the form of consultation committees with an advisory role that are more or less independent insofar as membership is concerned. If they have a statutory basis, then the Constitutional Court has held that they must be consulted (AB 30/2000). On the other side of the ledger, the Constitutional Court has refused to grant constitutional status to statutory participation rights unless specific groups are mentioned, such as the NEC or local governments (AB 10/2001; see also 7/1993, 16/1998, 50/1998, 39/1999). The court also makes a distinction between "social organizations of public authority" and "interest organizations." The former have been established by law and include such bodies as the Academy of Sciences, the association of medical doctors, and local governments. Consultation rights are frequently incorporated into their founding statutes, and these have been upheld by the Constitutional Court. In contrast, the latter includes civil society or interest groups with no official status and no legal right to be heard.

Judicial review of executive policy making is limited except where constitutional rights are at stake. Although the Constitutional Court has decided a number of important cases, it has not provided much guidance on judicial review of "the legality of decisions of public administration" (Article 50[2]) that involve conformity with statutory schemes rather than asserted violations of constitutional rights.[31]

The government elected in 2002 has made a few moves in the direction of openness. The Ministry of Justice published a draft law on minorities on its website and invited comments. It is also encouraging other ministries to publicize draft laws and regulations and accept comments. The Ministry of Welfare has begun a process of broader consultation although there are limits to the role of consultation for programs that serve the poor, the infirm, and the handicapped. In addition, proposals to pass a substitute for the Law on Normative Acts have been made.[32]

Conclusions

Both Poland and Hungary have requirements for consultations under some conditions, but the statutory language does not always translate well into the day-to-day practices of the government branch. Groups and individuals that want to participate in the policy-making process can seldom assert the right to be consulted. Instead, they need to argue that it is politically expedient for them to be heard or that their involvement will produce more effective programs. In general, the only groups with a right to be consulted on issues of concern to their members are labor unions, business associations, and professional chambers in such areas as law and medicine. Some permanent advisory committees have broader membership and must, by law, be consulted, but their effectiveness varies widely. They are often the only route for input from nongovernmental groups. The effectiveness of consultation processes is not subject to challenge because there is little judicial oversight of the operation of the government as it makes policy under existing statutes or as it proposes new laws.

Private groups concerned with government accountability and policy making are relatively weak and poorly funded. In both countries, independent groups exist staffed by committed and professional individuals, but the number of effective groups is small and overburdened. For example, in the environmental area a small number of groups play important roles in the policy-making process. Far from complaining about not being consulted, the leaders of these groups feel overwhelmed with paper and swamped by the large number of proposals they are asked to review and the short time they are given to review them.[33]

Problems and Prospects

Both Poland and Hungary have rejected the simple model of government accountability that concentrates only on elections to constrain government. As a consequence, both countries face the complex problem of creating internal and external monitoring institutions and of developing routes for participation in government decisions by individuals and organized groups. At present, there appear to be five different problems with the expectation that nonpartisan, governmental organizations can help produce a more accountable administrative process by participating in the administrative process.

First, a history of cynicism and alienation from politics continues to limit the development of civic organizations (Howard 2002; World Bank 2000: 198). The empirical issue here is whether the alienation that people express is an ingrained character trait or is a reasonable response to reality that will change when the situation changes.[34] On the positive side, one study suggests that new private associations in Poland are being used to exert pressure on the government (Wieczorkowska and Burnstein 2001: 160), and my interviews suggest that this is happening in Hungary as well (Rose-Ackerman 2003). Furthermore, the sheer number of NGOs has grown tremendously over the last decade although only a few have policy advocacy as one of their goals.

Second, the nonprofit sector is only beginning to become conscious of itself as a collection of organizations with a special role to play in a democracy (Salamon et al. 1999). Although many new organizations have been created, many are small, locally based, and poorly institutionalized (Wygański 1998; Karatnycky et al. 1997: 180–2). At the other extreme are self-governing bodies such as labor unions and business chambers and those established by statute to regulate professions such as law or medicine. These groups do have a strong institutional presence, but their lobbying activity is quite different from organizations that further broad public goals.

Third, the independence of some of the more established nonprofit organizations may be in doubt because they frequently receive funding directly from the government budget. Some established NGOs have implicit or explicit political party allegiances and benefit from patronage in the form of subsidies and contracts when their party holds power (Hryniewicz 2001). Nevertheless, independence is possible. In Hungary, Katy Pickvance's case studies (1998: 76–107, 143–58) and my interviews found that most environmental organizations had an explicit policy of avoiding partisan entanglements.

Fourth, the state does not always facilitate participation in government policy making and implementation. Freedom of information requests may be given low priority, and agencies seldom organize open hearings. Even when consultation does occur, the agency may only consult a prespecified set of groups, such as members of the NEC or the Social Council in Hungary or particular labor unions and employer groups. Furthermore, the consultation process itself may mean little if the government gives the advisory body or the public only a few days to respond to complex and difficult policy issues. This means that those who really want to have influence need to do so informally at an earlier stage, leaving the way open for insider deals.

Fifth, existing organized groups cannot claim to represent all the conflicting and crosscutting interests of the public in areas such as environmental protection or labor/business relations. The EU expects the governments of the acceding countries to cooperate with nonprofits in a number of specific areas by creating partnership groups. This process does not always work effectively either because the groups have not been created or are not representative. For example, tripartite groups that consist of representatives of business associations, labor unions, and government may do a poor job of representing the interests of the 75–85 percent of the workforce that is not unionized in Poland and Hungary. The problem is twofold. The government has little incentive to strengthen the voluntary sector, and the sector itself is full of small organizations without any coordinating mechanisms. However, recently some umbrella organizations have been created so the EU process itself may be having an impact on the efficacy of the sector as a part of the functioning of democracy.[35]

Some claim that the focus should be on strengthening political parties, not overcoming the problems listed earlier. However, political parties, even the multiple parties produced by a proportional representation system, are not a good substitute for independent civil society organizations. Parties represent a conglomeration of interests and are focused on winning elections, not mastering the details of policy. The governing coalition supports broad statutory mandates that it then implements through the bureaucracy. In doing so, it must have the ultimate authority to issue decrees with force of law, but if it is to do this competently and responsibly, it needs to listen to organized groups and citizens who are informed about and concerned with the policy. These groups need to be able to seek court review of any alleged irregularities in the process.

Although there may be some trade-offs between the development of strong parties and the establishment of well-institutionalized nonparty groups, Hungary and Poland appear to have room for both. Too strong a move to incorporate independent groups under political party labels could produce a system of rotating coalition governments that govern for limited periods of time without considering the interests of those who are associated with other parties. In practice, both Poland and Hungary have few formal requirements for civil society participation in executive policy making, and the current strength of independent NGOs varies across policy areas but is overall rather weak. Nevertheless, there seems no reason, in principle, why public participation could not be strengthened. To do this, participation rights need to have legal status and be open to judicial review, and organized groups need to be strengthened.

Better administrative processes can give officials information about the costs and benefits of particular programs in both technical and political terms. The goal is to permit them to make more competent and politically acceptable decisions. To do this, they need to interact with groups that operate independently of political parties and concentrate on issues of interest to their membership, be they feminist causes, environmental harms, or burdensome business regulation. The available evidence suggests wide imbalances among groups reorganized out of old official groups, chambers representing economic and professional interests, and new groups with public or foreign foundation support, on the one hand, and a large fringe of small, poorly institutionalized groups with few financial resources, on the other. In short, there is some urgency in creating an environment in which public participation can function well without officials seeing it as merely a nuisance to be contained and marginalized.

A two-pronged strategy is needed—both a move to more open and accountable processes in the executive branch and a policy of supporting the creation and consolidation of independent NGOs (Howard 2002).

The former option requires both an openness to comments and testimony from those outside of the narrow circle of organized groups and efforts to expand the membership of permanent advisory committees to better reflect those concerned with policy outcomes. The latter strategy implies that the government funds used to support civil society groups should be provided in a way that does not undermine the groups' independence. Matching funds based on membership numbers are one option, and tax checkoffs are another. However, in Hungary where 1 percent of an individual's taxes can be earmarked for charity, taxpayer participation is low, and most money is channeled, not to advocacy organizations, but to those providing services such as education and health care often to members of one's own family (Kuti 2000). Another option is direct support through grants to cover the marginal costs of informed participation. These funds would have to be disbursed without making judgments on any group's substantive positions.

The problems of democratic consolidation in Hungary and Poland are the problems of countries that have democratic structures, secure borders, no organized violence, and a functioning private sector. They are not different in kind from those facing democracies with much longer histories than those in Central Europe. The scale of the difficulties is larger for some issues, and the existing institutions in the public and the private sectors are fragile and untested, but none of these problems suggests an imminent breakdown of the state. This observation means that Central Europe can learn from experiences elsewhere, both success stories and obvious failures. Its politicians and policy makers can be in a productive dialogue with those in wealthier, more established democracies as the region seeks ways to create more accountable government institutions that can garner popular support.

Notes

* I am very grateful to Katalin Füzér, Ania Horolets, Csilla Kalocsai, Maciej Kisilowski, and Aleksandra Sznajder for help with research and translations and to János Kornai, Margaret Levi, and Elizabeth Barrett for very helpful comments. This essay is part of a larger project (Rose-Ackerman 2005) begun at the Center for Advanced Study in the Behavioral Sciences, Stanford CA, and further developed at Collegium Budapest. I am grateful for the financial support of the Center, Collegium Budapest, and the Yale Law School.

1. See Vachudova on the Czech Republic (2001: 337) and Cook and Orenstein on Russia, Poland, and Hungary (1999).
2. According to Grzymala-Busse and Jones Luong, they are "nearly consolidated democratic states" (2002: 544). This is a category in which they also place the Czech Republic, Slovenia, and the Baltic States.
3. Compare Esty (2002) who makes similar argument for mandating participatory processes at the World Trade Organization.
4. Several of my interviewees mentioned the volume of legislation produced since the regime change. A representative of an environmental organization working on water issues described it as "a flood." The "factory" imagery came from a professor of constitutional law.
5. Interviews with István Somogyvári, Administrative State Secretary, Ministry of Justice, December 2002, and Botond Bitskey, Head of Department, Constitutional and Legal Department, Office of the President, fall 2002.
6. Interview with Dr. Géza Kilényi, D. Sc. Professor, Pázmány Péter Catholic University, Budapest, former member of the Constitutional Court.

7. A commemorative volume published on the twentieth anniversary of the Court describes it as being rushed into existence "by awesome murmurs coming from various environments" (Supreme Administrative Court 2000: 188).

8. A system of tripartite governance (government, labor, management) was established in Hungary in 1988 under the last socialist government (Héthy 2000: 30; interview with László Herczog).

9. Gazette for Current Law 80 (4): position 8; 80(9): pos 26 with amendments. The Administrative Code is at http://www.rp.pl/prawo/doc/Kpa.html.

10. Teresa Górzyńska quoted in Żaneta Semprich "Jawność—zasadą, tajność—wyjątkiem" (Openness—the rule, secrecy—the exception), *Rzeczpospolita*, July 26, 2001; Andrzej Rzepliński, "Opinia o ustawie z dnia 25 lipca 2001r.o dostępie do informacji publicznej (dla Senackiego Biura Informacji i Dokumentacji" (Opinion on statute of July 25, 2001 on access to public information for the Senate Bureau of Information and Documentation), Warsaw, July 30, 2001.

11. Interview with Andrzej Sadowski, director of the Adam Smith Research Center, and material supplied by Wojciech Przybylski of the Center.

12. Interview with Irena Wóycicka, Institute for Research on the Market Economy, Warsaw, and advisor and then deputy minister at the Polish Ministry of Labor, 1989–94, 1997–2001, December 2002; Galligan et al. (1998: 451–2, 458).

13. Irena Wóycicka estimated that union membership is about 20% of the workforce and is falling. Earlier estimates of trade union membership place it at 30–40% of the workforce, but the difference may simply represent a trend over time (Karatnycky et al. 1997: 181, 283). In contrast, in Sweden where tripartite groups have a long history, labor union membership is over 85% of the workforce; see Rothstein (1998).

14. Interview with Irena Wóycicka; Galligan et al. (1998: 511).

15. K41/2002, November 20, 2002 available at http://www.trybunal.gov.pl.

16. Interview with Roman Hauser, President of the High Administrative Court, December 2002.

17. The Court's Annual Report documents the growing backlog. Incoming complaints increased from 55,000 to almost 76,000 between 1999 and 2001 and the backlog increased from 53,500 to 70,000 (Supreme Administrative Court 2002: table 1; see also table 18).

18. The associations' rules can be nullified by the minister in the appropriate subject area, but the associations can appeal such decisions to the courts. Interview with Professor Antal Ádám, School of Law, University of Pécs, October 2002.

19. Decision 64/1991, December 17, 1991, on the Regulation of Abortion, excerpted in Sólyom and Brunner (2000: 178–99).

20. The Act attempted to put some order into the chaotic state of legal rules and decrees that characterized the late socialist period. Interview with Prof. Dr. József Petrétei, November 15, 2002; Galligan and Smilov (1999: 117); Galligan et al. (1998: 421).

21. Based on translations by Katalin Füzér and Csilla Kalocsai. Interview with Professor Petrétei. See also Galligan et al. (1998: 423).

22. Interview with Professor Petrétei. "Anyone" can ask the court to rule on the constitutionality of legal rules, adjudicate alleged violations of constitutional rights, or seek to eliminate unconstitutional omissions (Hungarian Constitution, Articles 33–6, 51). However, many cases remain unresolved for years.

23. Interview with Kinga Göncz, Political State Secretary, Ministry of Welfare, December 2002. On pension reform, I am relying on Eszter Kósa who wrote a CEU doctoral dissertation on the topic. Robert Jenkins studied the Social Council, at the Ministry of Welfare that was created by decree in 1990 (1990/1060). He argued that the Council was not central to social policy formation (Jenkins 1999: 189–91).

24. Compare Rothstein (1998) who outlines a history of corporatism in Sweden, which shows that it developed 20 years before the working class obtained voting rights.

25. http://www.obh.hu/adatved/indexek/AVTV-EN.htm.

26. 2000 Annual Report of the Parliamentary Commissioner for Data Protection and Freedom of Information, Hungary, http://www.obh.hu/adatved/index/2000.

27. Interview with Sándor Fülöp, director, Environmental Management and Law Association (EMLA), October 29, 2002.

28. The text is at http://www.unece.org/env/pp.

29. See 90/313/EEC, 1990 Official Journal (L 158) at http://europa.eu.int/smartapi/cgi/sga_doc?smartapi!celexapi!prod!CELEXnumdoc&lg=en&numdoc=31990L0313&model=guichett.

30. See http://www.obh.hu/adatved/indexek/2000/text4.htm.

31. The Hungarian EMLA has been involved in over 300 cases but most seek to involve the courts in oversight of the administrative process at the level of individual projects, not strategic planning and rulemaking. See http://www.emla.hu.
32. Interviews with Kinga Göncz and István Somogyvári.
33. Based on interviews I conducted in fall 2002 with representatives of several major environmental organizations in Hungary (Rose-Ackerman 2003, 2005). See also Pickvance (1998) on environmental groups in Hungary and Howard (2002) on the relative weakness of civil society in general.
34. For a discussion of this issue and references to the survey evidence see Rose-Ackerman (2001).
35. See the report on cooperation of NGOs with public administration in the process of integrating Poland with the EU at www.fip.ngo.pl.

References

Access Initiative. 2002. *Hungarian Report*, Parts I and II. http://www.accessinitiative.org/hungary.html.

Commission of the European Communities. 2001. *2001 Regular Report on Hungary's Progress Towards Accession*. SEC (2001) 1748, Brussels, November 13. http://europa.eu.int/comm/enlargement/report2001/hu_en.pdf.

Constitution of the Republic of Hungary. 1998. http://www.ekormanyzat.hu.

Constitution of the Republic of Poland. 1997. http://www.sejm.gov.pl/english/konstytucja.

Cook, Linda J. and Mitchell A. Orenstein. 1999. "The Return of the Left and Its Impact on the Welfare State in Russia, Poland, and Hungary." In L. J. Cook, M. A. Orenstein, and M. Rueschemeyer (eds.), *Left Parties and Social Policy in Postcommunist Europe*, pp. 47–108. Boulder CO: Westview Press.

Esty, Daniel C. 2002. "The World Trade Organization's Legitimacy Crisis." *World Trade Review* 1: 7–22.

Galligan, Denis J., Richard H. Langan, and Constance S. Nicandrou. 1998. *Administrative Justice in the New European Democracies: Case Studies of Administrative Law and Process in Bulgaria, Estonia, Hungary, Poland and Ukraine*. Budapest: Open Society Institute/Constitutional and Legal Policy Institute and Oxford University: Centre for Socio-Legal Studies.

Galligan, Denis J. and Daniel M. Smilov. 1999. *Administrative Law in Central and Eastern Europe 1996–1998*. Budapest: Central European University Press.

Grzymała-Busse, Anna and Pauline Jones Luong. 2002. "Reconceptualizing the State: Lessons from Post-Communism." *Politics and Society* 30: 529–54.

Héthy, Lajos. 2000. *Interest Reconciliation and an Expanding World: A Decade of Interest Reconciliation in Hungary, 1988–1999*. Budapest: Friedrich Ebert Stiftung.

Howard, Mark Morjé. 2002. "The Weakness of Postcommunist Civil Society." *Journal of Democracy* 13: 157–69.

Hryniewicz, Janusz T. 2001. "Przekształcenia Instytucji Regionalnych (Transformation of Regional Institutions)." In G. Gorzelak, B. Jaùowiecki, and M. Stec (eds.), *Reforma Terytorialnej Administracji Kraju* (Reform of the State Territorial Organization), pp. 103–17. Warszawa: Wydawnictwo Naukowe "Scholar."

Jenkins, Robert M. 1999. "The Role of the Hungarian Nonprofit Sector in Postcommunist Social Policy." In L. J. Cook, M. A. Orenstein, and M. Rueschemeyer (eds.), *Left Parties and Social Policy in Postcommunist Europe*, pp. 175–206. Boulder CO: Westview Press.

Karatnycky, Adrian, Alexander Motyl, and Boris Shor. 1997. *Nations in Transit—1997: Civil Society, Democracy and Market in East Central Europe and the Newly Independent States*. New Brunswick NJ: Transaction Publishers.

Kornai, János. 1992. *The Socialist System: The Political Economy of Communism*. Princeton NJ: Princeton University Press.

Kuti, Éva. 2000. *1%: "Forint Votes" for Civil Society Organizations*. Budapest: Research Project on Nonprofit Organizations.

O'Donnell, Guillermo. 1994. "Delegative Democracy." *Journal of Democracy* 5: 55–69.

Pickvance, Katy. 1998. *Democracy and Environmental Movements in Eastern Europe: A Comparative Study of Hungary and Russia*. Boulder CO: Westview Press.

Rose-Ackerman, Susan. 1995. *Controlling Environmental Policy: The Limits of Public Law in Germany and the United States*. New Haven CT: Yale University Press.

Rose-Ackerman, Susan. 2001. "Trust and Honesty in Post-Socialist Societies." *Kyklos* 54: 415–43.
———. 2003. "Public Participation in Consolidating Democracies: Hungary and Poland." Draft. New Haven CT: Yale University.
———. 2005. *From Elections to Democracy: Building Accountable Government in Hungary and Poland.* New York: Cambridge University Press.
Rothstein, Bo. 1998. "The State, Associations and the Transition to Democracy in Sweden." In D. Rueschemeyer, M. Rueschemeyer, and B. Wittrock (eds.), *Participation and Democracy: An East–West Comparison*, pp. 132–56. Armonk NY: M. E. Sharpe.
Salamon, Lester M., Helmut K. Anheier, Regina List, Stefan Toepler, S. Wójciech Sokolowski, and Associates. 1999. *Global Civil Society: Dimensions of the Nonprofit Sector.* Baltimore MD: Johns Hopkins Center of Civil Society Studies.
Sólyom, László and Georg Brunner (eds.). 2000. *Constitutional Judiciary in a New Democracy: The Hungarian Constitutional Court.* Ann Arbor MI: University of Michigan Press.
Supreme Administrative Court (Naczelny Sąd Administracyjny). 2000. *XX lat Naczelnego Sądu Administracyjnego* (Twenty years of the Supreme Administrative Court). Warsaw: Supreme Administrative Court.
———. 2002. *Informacja o Dzialalności Naczelnego Sądu Administracyjnego w. Roku 2001* (Information on the Activities of the Supreme Administrative Court in 2001). Warsaw: Supreme Administrative Court.
Vachudova, Milada Anna. 2001. "The Czech Republic: The Unexpected Force of Institutional Constraints." In J. Zielonka (ed.), *Democratic Consolidation in Eastern Europe. Vol. 2: International and Transnational Factors*, pp. 325–62. Oxford: Oxford University Press.
Wieczorkowska, Grazyna and Eugene Burnstein. 2001. "Monitoring Adaptation to Social Change: Research at the Institute for Social Studies." In J. A. Bargh and D. K. Apsley (eds.), *Unraveling the Complexities of Social Life: A Festshrift in Honor of Robert B. Zajonc*, pp. 155–72. Washington DC: American Psychological Association.
World Bank. 2000. *Making Transition Work for Everyone: Poverty and Inequality in Europe and Central Asia.* Washington DC: World Bank.
Wygański, Jakub. 1998. Porozumienia, federacje, koalicje, bloki, fora ... (*Ententes*, Federations, Coalitions, Blocks, Forums ...). In A. Wojakowska (ed.), *Samoorganizacja Trzeciego Sektora* (Self-Organization of the Third Sector). Available at www.fip.ngo.pl/ze_starego/sts_body.html.

CHAPTER TWO

Neutral Institutions: Implications for Government Trustworthiness in East European Democracies

ANDRÁS SAJÓ

The creation of neutral institutions within the state is part of the attempt to create more trustworthy post-communist states. Yet some question whether it is possible for governments to remain neutral in matters that divide society. This specific concern brings up broader issues: What happens to trust when the state is increasingly identified with neutral institutions instead of democratically legitimized but partisan entities? Are neutral governmental and public institutions an answer to the legitimate distrust in the state that animates liberal constitutional institutional design? In seeking answers to these questions this chapter first analyzes the meaning of state neutralization and its implications for trust in government. The following section discusses independent agencies, primarily media regulatory authorities and central banks, and considers the level of independence and neutrality of prevailing post-communist institutions. Finally, some speculations are offered on the impact of neutral government institutions on public trust. Regulating public life by independent agencies differs considerably from the use of democratically legitimized power and authority. Hence new forms of trust in and loyalty to these institutions may emerge. Nevertheless, ostensibly neutral spheres of public life remain subject to governmental and partisan influence in Eastern Europe.

Neutralization of the State

The Emergence of Neutrality in the Public Space

Neutrality has become an important dimension of state activities, including civil service, government speech, science, arts funding, and so on. Nevertheless, the theory of state neutrality (including that of neutral institutions and neutralization) is underdeveloped, with somewhat troubling consequences (Schmitt 1996). Attempts to ensure government neutrality in crucial social areas have not yet led to the creation of systemic standards. This chapter argues that the modern state—as a network of organizations—pretends to be non-partisan or neutral in an increasing number of instances (Sajó 2001: 369–89). Institutional arrangements are developed to make that claim credible.

The meaning of "neutral" and "neutralization" in the context of the state and government is ambiguous. Historically, state neutrality referred to non-involvement in matters of religion. The neutral state *refuses to take a position* in matters of religion. A second idea of neutrality developed in the context of international law where neutrality referred to noninterference in the armed conflict of other states (Vagts 1998). A third tradition of neutrality refers to impartiality: Here, contrary to the other meanings, neutrality is safeguarded *notwithstanding* the involvement of the decision makers in public affairs.

This third type of neutrality is intuitively attractive. It seems to provide a minimal morality that is satisfied if "the rule serves no particular interest, expresses no particular culture, regulates everyone's behavior in a universally advantageous or clearly correct way. The rule carries no personal or social signature" (Walzer 1994: 7). This chapter discusses institutions that satisfy neutrality in the aforementioned sense, although in specific situations the noninterference aspect dominates.

The modern state is identified not only with representative institutions but also with administrative structures operated as public bureaucracies.[1] Public bureaucracies offer a degree of neutrality in the sense of not necessarily being politically partisan. However, the depoliticization of public administration remains incomplete. The social desire for a nonpartisan state machinery cannot be entirely satisfied through the establishment of a civil service. Rather, in order to further isolate some parts of the civil service from partisan politics, *neutral regulatory institutions* emerged in the late nineteenth century. (See, e.g., the creation of federal and state agencies to regulate railroads and public utilities in the United States.) In principle, these neutral institutions were to a great extent autonomous and independent of political bodies or democratic politics. The analysis of the actual institutions shows how limited such independence and autonomy actually was. Nevertheless, they often have enough autonomy to remain independent from the political branches if they really wish to do so. Autonomous bodies may be biased but, in principle, are beyond partisan politics and, therefore, their rule making and decisions are deemed to be neutral in the sense of nonpolitical. This trend is rooted in the growth of *independent expert bodies*. In complex societies, many traditional governmental functions were transferred to independent organizations, which were legitimated in terms of their professional expertise.

The transfer of decision making to neutral public institutions remains problematic. Policy-making institutions that are insulated from the democratic process are not necessarily fully neutralized in the sense of being exempt from political influence, but, at least, they are insulated vis à vis the democratic process. Of course, such insulation may also allow elected officials, government bureaucracies, and interest groups to exercise even more political influence than in a transparent democratic setting. Neutralization has very often been a way to protect particular groups by excluding contrary political influences. The design of insulated public institutions is, after all, left overwhelmingly to legislation that often follows a logic completely alien to institutional neutrality. The withdrawal of the state from certain public domains is often determined by major performance failures accompanied by successful resistance to government by the regulated. Quite often politicians seek to avoid responsibility and independent agencies allow them to do so. Note that most of the independent state agencies that were created to enhance credibility serve special interest groups and only indirectly the general public: It is the trust of these special interests that is at stake. (For instance, central banks directly serve the financial community, the media regulatory agency is catering to broadcasters, and so on.)

Implications for State Trustworthiness

The trend toward state neutrality is redrawing the modern state. Traditional grounds of trust in government have become obsolete. The shift resulted partly from a loss of legitimacy of participatory and bureaucratic forms of government. Once trust in—and loyalty to—institutions that offer participation diminished, a move toward some alternative nonparticipatory legitimacy became nearly inevitable. The switch is likely to have created new relations of state trustworthiness.

Trust here refers to trust in the state and its government (Levi and Braithwaite 1998). The individual trusts the state in a psychological sense, that is, the individual assumes fair treatment from the state and (in a welfare state) expects basic material support. Because of trust, the individual will be committed to the trusted institution (or person) even where and when alternative options may appear preferable (Levi 1998; Cook and Emerson 1978: 721–39). State neutrality and neutralization are situations where trust in and loyalty to state institutions and the state are not (or not primarily) based on democratic participation or democratic legitimacy (Carter 1998: 4; Fletcher 1993: 33). The institutional design of neutral institutions is intended to diminish partisan influence. It is exactly their isolation from the democratic process (in the sense of credibility and performance-based professionalism) that makes them trustworthy. Citizens expect a neutral institution to satisfy their "real" interest through professional considerations. The replacement of partisan (democratically responsive) organizations with neutral state institutions is an attempt to overcome the shortcomings of trust building in a democracy (Levi 1998: 96). Neutral institutions reflect public distrust in government and an attempt to overcome that distrust without creating better democratic institutions. They might even be considered more efficient than the distrusted democratic institutions.

Neutralization relies on a specific form of authority derived from the professionalism and expertise made possible by neutral institutional settings. Neutral institutions satisfy a normative expectation of trustworthiness as identified by Margaret Levi: "Institutional trustworthiness implies procedures for selecting and constraining the agents of institutions so that they are competent, credible, and likely to act in the interests of those being asked to trust the institution" (1998: 80). Neutral institutions are the ultimate attempt of state trust-building in an untrustworthy state.

Professionalism increases trust to the extent that people are conditioned to trust professional expertise. Professionalism promises efficient performance. A government (or its bodies) will be trusted on the basis of its past performance, especially where the continued existence of independent bodies seems to guarantee similar performance in the future. Furthermore, to the extent that neutrality implies impartiality, there is an additional element of trustworthiness, one that cannot develop in obviously partisan (interest) politics based on unprincipled logrolling. The shrinking of the state through various forms of decommissioning is a complementary means of solving the problem of diminishing trust. The insufficiencies of a privately provided service, even if it is state-sponsored, will not be attributed to the state, hence state credibility might improve.

Independent (Expert) Agencies in Eastern Europe

Neutrality of the state—and its partial failure—might be particularly important in the formation of trust in the state in post-communist Eastern Europe. The communist state was by definition partisan (a workers' state) where government privileges were granted on the basis of party loyalty. Post-communist constitutions were keen to establish that the state should not be ideologically committed and that its crucial public institutions should not be politicized. Partisanship, as created by representative governments, became (or was presented as) the source of dangerous social divisiveness. Although this might have been partly attenuated through the democratic system itself—namely by bringing in new governments at every election—neutral, nonpartisan bodies offered an alternative to partisan divisiveness. Furthermore, at the time the institutions were designed, the model of neutral institutions was fashionable in modern democracies. Of course, the way the East European countries have drawn lessons from other democracies makes all the difference. The institutional interests of the inherited agencies helped shape the reformed institutions such as judiciaries, state prosecution, state audit agencies, and central banks that survived the fall of communism. Finally, the shrinking of government activities and large-scale privatization increased the need for regulation, which was often delegated to new neutral institutions. It was the "independent agency" that was the favored institutional model.

It is likely that the large-scale privatization that occurred after 1989 had contradictory effects on the trustworthiness of the post-communist state.

Levi and Braithwaite (1998) indicate that the privatization of social services and the consequent nonuniversalism and nonstandardization in their provision (Smith and Lipsky 1993) are likely to increase distrust in government as an institution that enforces impartiality. Corruption permeating post-communist privatization also increased distrust in government (see Csepeli et al. 2004). The process itself increased the demand for neutrality both among the disenchanted general public and the political elites. As a result, they agreed to delegate some power to neutral institutions. This was face-saving for the political parties, and it also enabled them to continue to do "business as usual" behind less transparent institutions.

In what follows two important social spheres are considered: broadcasting and monetary (or price) stability. The choice is not accidental. From the point of view of regulating social signaling, both have a crucial part to play: The idea of specialized public neutral institutions goes hand–in–hand with the depoliticization of the political.

Regulatory Bodies in Broadcasting

Regulating broadcasting by independent agencies exemplifies a relatively recent worldwide attempt to neutralize oversight of the communications sphere. There are various institutional solutions to guarantee the independence of the regulated media and the neutral handling of broadcasting-related matters (Hoffmann-Riem 1996: 119).[2] This is done "officially" in order to avoid politicization or because the public interest cannot be served well in a partisan manner (Bell 1993: 346–7).

The contemporary solutions range from quasi–self-regulation, by non-governmental bodies to insulated independent governmental bodies. The preferred choice in the case of the Italian public television (RAI) was political partition, assigning a channel to each of the major political parties in parliament. Interestingly, this arrangement is currently advocated in Hungary by the opposition. In the United States, where private media were rather strong at the time when serious regulation was undertaken, the model of self-regulation of the industry prevailed.[3] In continental Europe broadcasting was for a long time a state monopoly and regulation formed part of the deetatization and privatization process. In both models the expectation is that the leadership of the regulatory authority, although it might be selected by the political branches, will not be subject to pressure from government. Members of the regulatory authority should not be politically committed to the government of the day, but they should rather follow strictly professional or broader ethical considerations.

In post-communist Eastern Europe the abolition of the state monopoly over broadcasting was understood as a fundamental requirement of pluralism. The matter was complicated because the role of the state was not clear in societies where every service had been provided by the state and the public expected the state to maintain television. The existing (former state) television stations fought for their interests. It was not clear to the political

elite how to depoliticize the media. Zdena Hulova, who headed the
Czechoslovak committee charged with drafting the act on broadcasting,
stated: "[Foreign consultants]...had to explain to us...even things that
were very basic, ... for example, that broadcasting should be separated from
the state."[4] Unfortunately, those who came to power in the first elections
had an immediate desire to control the existing state radio and television
stations.

Given the nature of broadcasting liberalization and the general influence
of West European models, most post-communist countries opted for independent regulatory agencies.[5] Such agencies are responsible for licensing and
general supervision of the broadcasting sector. Three different appointment
processes are used. First, following the structural arrangement that emerged
with the 1991 Broadcasting Act of Czechoslovakia[6] parliamentary appointment is used in many East European countries and in Turkey. Second, as of
1994, 14 out of 32 European countries including former communist countries had their agency's commissioners appointed/revoked by the executive
following the British model (Robillard 1995).[7] The British tradition requires
that the executive respect the independence of the authority. East European
countries insist on formal independence from government in the form of a
statutory prohibition on accepting instructions, and exclusive executive
appointment is nowhere accepted. Third, a stronger emphasis on formal legal
independence from the political branches is embodied in French law that
relies on mixed appointees (each political branch having its own appointees).
As of 1994, eight European countries followed that model. The French
model[8] prevails in Romania[9] and in Poland. In Hungary, the authorities'
powers and their independence resemble the French model, although the
method of appointment differs. In Hungary the governing and opposition
parties have equal representation in the regulatory body. The members are
elected technically by parliament, with the chairman being appointed by
the country's president upon nomination by the prime minister. In practice,
this means that the appointees will be loyal to the parliamentary majority and
personally to the prime minister in power at the time of the appointment.
The argument in favor of such an arrangement is that once the government
in power at the time of appointment is removed, the agency might act as a
check on the incoming government. In the Hungarian case each parliamentary faction has one representative on the board.

Notwithstanding the various guarantees of independence, no post-
communist country was spared major scandals regarding the activities of
independent regulatory bodies. Democratically elected politicians quickly
developed an appetite for unlimited access to television. When they met
resistance, they challenged the regulatory authorities and the directors of the
public channels. The standard form of open intervention was the recall of
members of the regulatory agency and/or the manager of the public broadcasting company. Provisions regarding recall were not clearly stipulated in
the early laws. Parliamentary majorities expressed a lack of confidence
resulting in the dissolution of the respective board.

The Czech story is quite telling. In 1993 the first new majority in the Czech House of Deputies amended the 1991 act under the pretext of problems created by the dissolution of Czechoslovakia. The amendment[10] empowered the parliamentary majority to recall the Czech Broadcasting Council (CBC) that was elected by a politically different majority (Pavlik and Shields 1999: 503). When the first national private license was awarded in 1993, the council became subject to political attacks from the parliamentary majority. Such attacks were justified by the fact that the nonwinning license applications had been made by financially much more sound, but foreign, companies. It was argued that the CBC opted for the unknown and financially not viable Central European Television for the 21st Century (CET-21) exactly because of the hope that this unknown and presumably week entity would accommodate the council and not vice versa (ibid.: 505). At the end of the parliamentary attack, three additional members were elected to the council, and the terms of reference of the license were amended. The attempt to recall the council failed by one vote, but in 1994 the parliamentary majority was more successful and appointed nine new members. "The signal sent from Parliament [to the CBC] was not 'behave according to your mandate' but rather 'show more obedience to us'" (Jakl 1994, quoted by Pavlik and Shields 1999: 505).

The vulnerability of the CBC might be due to institutional design (Sparks and Reading 1998: 158–9), but other models also had their problems. The Slovak council followed a model similar to the Czech one and was purged several times (ibid.). In Poland, the 1992 Act on Radio and Television created a French-type authority. Because the Act was silent regarding the dismissal of the chairman of the Committee for the Supervision over Radio and Television (CSRT),[11] President Walesa decided to dismiss the chairman of the CSRT, his own appointee. The decision was challenged by the ombudsman. The Constitutional Tribunal ruled that the president could not dismiss the chairman, except for a judicially established gross violation of the law.[12] President Walesa tried to avoid the ruling saying that it cannot apply retroactively, that is, for matters decided before the Tribunal developed its legal position. In 1995 the Tribunal ruled that its interpretations of laws are applicable from the date of enactment.

In Hungary a 1990 agreement between the government and the opposition provided that the appointment of public radio and public television Presidents be made jointly by the country's President (an opposition candidate) and the Prime Minister. In 1992 the President of Hungary refused to sign the dismissal of the President of the national television, initiated by the Prime Minister. Additional legal harassment by the executive followed, and the President resigned (Arato 1996). An independent regulatory agency was installed after the enactment of the 1996 Act on Broadcasting. As the act made it practically impossible to recall the members of the Radio and Television Authority (HRTA), the socialist–liberal majority refused to approve its budget in 2002. The Chairman resigned "to enable the smooth operation of the authority," though at the same time she admitted that she "felt obligations of loyalty" to the party that nominated her (the one that became the opposition in 2002).

In all these countries unhappy license applicants and scholarly evaluations highlight violations of conflict-of-interest rules, political rigging of licensing, and failure to intervene in the case of unfair political news reporting (bias in favor of the ruling government). Nontransparent political loyalties seem to determine licensing and other decisions. In Russia (at least in the electronic media) the political sphere continues to play a considerable role, and some argue that the media system (that includes its own regulatory agencies) will remain distinct from the Western model because of sociocultural differences (De Smaele 1999).

One can only agree with the remark that "Overall, then, it is obvious that the fine legal provisions about balance, impartiality, and so on were under siege, as indeed they have been in Western Europe, although at a rather lower intensity" (Sparks and Reading 1998: 154). They add that society was saturated with politics and, therefore, "the state broadcaster was seen by politicians as one of the spoils of office, and as a necessary means to winning the next election. On the other hand, the award of the potentially profitable private broadcasting franchises represented one of the pieces of patronage available to the government to reward its supporters" (ibid.). The politicization was probably inevitable because political parties were strong (and helped to stabilize the political system), and the relatively weak civil society and the media were forced to fit into the strongly politicized pattern. There was no time for a differentiation of the economic and even more of the cultural and social spheres: Policy matters remained political. Hence the policy-setting agencies cannot escape the pressure of the political, notwithstanding attempts to establish official impartiality and neutrality (Gross 2002).

The position of a regulatory agency depends not only on the politicians but also on the media industry, including owners and journalists. Media owners had little interest in a fully independent agency. Investors used political favors both to obtain licenses and to avoid the consequences of the application of the rule of law. In case of rule violations regarding, for example, content and advertisement, ownership broadcasters were often successful in "avoiding" sanctions. The pressure on the independent regulators comes not from political parties but more and more from businesses that find the original public service license conditions too onerous. The commercial media use political parties to exercise pressure on the authorities. In exchange, some broadcasters offer special access to politicians, self-censorship, and perhaps, campaign contributions. Nova, the Czech private broadcaster satisfied a number of requests of the then Prime Minister Klaus (originally a foe of Nova), and in exchange, notwithstanding the resistance of the regulatory agency, the license conditions imposing public service obligations on Nova were repealed via ex post legislation (Sparks and Reading 1998: 169).

The history of licensing and the amendment of license conditions suggest that the authorities are not neutral. Given the politicization of society and the enormous pressure at the time of privatization, independent broadcasting regulatory authorities were confronted with enormous tasks.The overburden and general politicization did not contribute to the genuine independence of the agencies that suffered because of failures in institutional design. Lack of transparency and accountability helps members' partisan orientations to prevail (though sometimes the councils were not biased in favor of the political majority but loyal to past majorities or private interests).Twisting the law has created dependency on the government, even in cases where the agencies were and remained independent enough to counter, at least, some government and party dictates (as is the case in Poland). However, commercial licenses were seldom revoked, notwithstanding political pressures to the contrary.

Nevertheless, the independent agencies did not fail completely, and their presence changed the rules of the game and triggered publicity for scandals that forced politicians to be less aggressive. Mass resistance to political intervention in public broadcasting in Prague in 2000 forced parliament to accept more neutral institutional arrangements. In some instances the independence of the regulatory agency shifted to noninterventionist neutrality (in the sense of nonintervention of nonbelligerents). Such nonintervention mostly, of course, favors the status quo.

The professionalism and transparency of the regulatory agencies have increased in the past decade. The institutional interest in autonomous power coupled with investors' and journalists' growing interest in a transparent and stable environment contributed to the more neutral, apolitical position of most agencies. Furthermore, the independent agencies rely upon a subgovernmental international network for legitimation. In the case of broadcasting regulatory agencies the European Platform of Regulatory Authorities (EPRA) plays that role.[13] This international networking results in an independent subgovernmental network policy that fits into the emerging international network governance (Slaughter 2003).

European integration developed new supranational dependencies that favored depoliticization through independent broadcasting regulatory agencies.[14] Business groups were quick to identify the European Union's (EU) position as means of putting pressure on the regulatory agency (Sparks and Reading 1998: 169).The national political elites had to take regulatory independence more seriously both in law and in action.The European "ideal," as expressed by the Council of Europe is an independent broadcasting agency that is *not responsible to any political branch* (Recommendation 2000). The European standard requires the regulatory authority to operate in an effective, independent, and transparent manner with *professional expertise*.The Council of Europe believes that "specially appointed independent regulatory authorities for the broadcasting sector, with expert knowledge in the area, have an important role to play within the framework of the law." Neutralization requires the guarantee not only of the financial independence of the organization but also the personal independence of the members of the authority "so as to protect them against any interference, in particular by political forces or economic interests" (ibid.). Dismissal is practically prohibited. Accountability is granted through transparency, which is provided by regular reports and duly reasoned decisions open to review by the competent jurisdictions and made available to the public (ibid.: par. 26).

Notwithstanding the level of political intervention and partisan loyalty within the independent regulatory agency, most countries in the region have followed the same pattern as Hungary where "there was a significant move from the overwhelming presence of the state in the media to more limited state interventions" (Gulyás 2002). Others saw it differently (Gálik 1999). As European integration proceeds, more and more formal guarantees of independence are granted.[15] However, isolation from the political branches will generate its own problems of partisanship. In a politicized society lack of accountability may enable political loyalty and personal bias to prevail, resulting in additional conflicts between independent regulators loyal to past power holders and the political powers of the day.

Central Banks

An efficient market economy presupposes the isolation of the market from politics. Political needs and market imperfections, however, open up the economy to intervention.

The analysis of the independence of central banks helps illustrate the state's efforts to satisfy the neutrality requirement in cases of economic intervention.[16] Central bank independence is intended to serve monetary stability and, therefore, it applies to an area of economic activity where distrust in politics is particularly proper (Hardin 2002: 84).

Geoffrey P. Miller points out that the constitutionalization of central bank independence is a necessary precommitment in a democratic (vote-maximizing) system because otherwise "the incumbent party may engage in stimulative monetary policy in the period immediately before an election, in order to increase economic activity, raise employment, and create a strong, if temporary, sense of well-being among the voters" (1998: 436–7). Nevertheless, the independence and neutrality of the central bank is not required by any traditional separation of powers doctrine of liberal constitutionalism. It is not fully constitutionalized even in the former socialist countries where the formalization of such independence went perhaps further than elsewhere (Giordani and Spagnolo 2001).

Given the domestic and international importance of credible monetary policies, it is not surprising that the concept of central banks as independent agencies is spreading around the world (Posen 1995: 260). There seems to be some basic consensus in the economics literature (and in comparative legislation) regarding the essential features of central bank independence. These features generally include independence in personal matters, financial autonomy, and policy (Haan and Eijffinger 2000). The similarities with broadcasting regulatory agencies are remarkable. Formal guarantees of independence are not always necessary for independent and transparent operation nor are such guarantees sufficient to obtain independence.

The creation of independent central banks in Eastern Europe occurred at a moment of institutional design when the influence of foreign models and pressures was overwhelming. Communist countries had weak financial institutions. After the collapse of communism, at the time of designing financial institutions these countries were very dependent on foreign financial institutions, which had a clear interest in creating a banking system that would be familiar to them. In the region and elsewhere in the developing world an independent bank was considered a safeguard of monetary policies that would facilitate the repayment of loans and the smooth operation of international financial operations (Maxfield 1997: 36). In Eastern Europe, international "expectations" were consolidated by the EU's legal expectations in the case of the accession countries. Politicians were rather slow in realizing the political costs of monetary stability; particularly because many early reformers were trained economists who were committed to nonpopulist economic policies—at least before they had to stand for new elections. In East Central Europe the political (electoral) pressures to increase welfare spending increased only after the first institutional arrangements establishing independent central banking were already in place.

Given the aforementioned considerations, most East European countries have accepted without much political deliberation or debate the design or, at least, the idea of an independent central bank. Preexisting arrangements were to some extent statutorily consolidated, with additional advantages given to the institution. For example, Hungarian laws on the central bank were written to protect the personal privileges of the bank's president.

Central bank independence did not generally form part of the East European constitutional precommitment. The standard constitutional formulation only prescribes the bank's role as a guarantor of monetary stability. Only the Russian Constitution and the Slovenian Constitution declare the independence of the central bank (Article 75 and Article 151, respectively). At the other end of the spectrum, intervention into the affairs of the central bank is constitutionally permitted on statutory grounds (Czech Constitution Article 98). Article 53 of the Croatian Constitution states that the central bank is accountable to parliament. The Romanian, Slovak, and Bulgarian constitutions do not specifically discuss the position of the central bank. The Central Asian countries allow the head of the executive branch to fill the central bank with political appointees; guarantees against dismissal are missing.

The Lithuanian and the Polish constitutions have provisions covering the central bank. Both these post-communist central banks have constitutionally mandated boards of directors. Article 227 of the Polish Constitution provides that the Council for Monetary Policy shall formulate the annual monetary policy that is to be submitted (as a source of information) to the Sejm (House of Representatives) at the same time the draft budget is submitted. The Polish desire for precommitment was so strong that it was written into the 1997 Constitution. The composition of the Council for Monetary Policy follows a model of branch representation similar to the French and Polish broadcasting regulatory agencies with members appointed in equal numbers by the Senate, Sejm, and the President. Professional expertise and political nonpartisanship (with regard to the bank's president) are also constitutionally mandated.

In most other East European countries bank presidents are elected by parliament, although in some cases it is the president of the country who has appointment or recommendation powers that may temper parliamentary majoritarianism. The Czech Constitution provides that the president of the republic should appoint the members of the Monetary Council. When in 2000 President Havel appointed the vice president to become governor of the central bank without countersignature, the prime minister brought a petition to the Constitutional Court against the measure. The countersignature was not found to be a constitutional condition, notwithstanding the lack of political responsibility of the president because "one component of the guarantee of the CNB's [Czech National Bank] independence is that the power of appointment is in the hands of a nonpartisan president."[17] In Hungary the bank's president is appointed by the president of the country upon the proposal of the prime minister.[18]

One could argue that the independence guaranteed at the statutory level is not a very serious legal precommitment. The legislative majority may alter it, reshaping decision-making bodies or altering the terms of the president of the bank. Appointment of independent-minded bank presidents is always questionable (Maxfield 1997: 57).[19] Recent attempts to redraw the powers of central bank presidents and attempts to increase the government's power (e.g., through various hidden forms of overdraft) were met with resistance, especially if the president of the bank happened to be the choice of a previous government. This was the case in Poland in 2001 and in Hungary in 1991, 1998, and 2002. The resistance of bank presidents was successful, among other reasons, because of the political support coming from the European Central Bank (ECB). Brussels argued that such attempts run against the obligations of the accession countries.[20]

Statutory or formal personal independence of central bank leaders is not a guarantee per se of independence and professionalism. This is true not only in the case of Belarus where the independence of the president of the central bank is well protected in principle, but where the bank's president is a handpicked appointee of the country's president. Board members generally have a limited role in most East European central banks; in some of the cases they are, at least in part, political appointees or handpicked by the bank president.

The formal independence of central banks does not necessarily result in nonpartisanship. In Poland and Hungary, whenever the president of the National Bank was an appointee of the previous government, the government of the day criticized him for being loyal to the government that appointed him and for following a policy that deliberately hampered the economic policies of the government. After the Hungarian socialists came to power in 2002 and started a spending spree, the National Bank's president accused the government of impermissible budget deficits that necessitated tight monetary policies. Arguably the speculation in favor of the Hungarian forint in early 2003 was made possible by a politically motivated conflict between the National Bank of Hungary (NBH) and the government. The bank refused to diminish the prime rate arguing that this was the only way to guarantee price stability against the government's excessive deficit. The high interest rates attracted massive purchases of the national currency pushing the exchange rate below the band. In two days the NBH bought several billion euros to keep the forint within the band, then cut the prime interest rate by 2 percent at the end of the second day. The actual interest rates of the commercial banks dropped below the inflation rate. The governing parties and many economic actors and analysts claim that the bank damaged first exporters, then depositors, and, in particular, did not provide predictability,[21] preventing financial and other actors from building trust and confidence in the bank's policy. All these claims and counterclaims of lack of professionalism (and professional dictates) are only part of the ongoing professional debate regarding the single or dual function of the central bank. The "euro zone" opted for the absolute priority of monetary stability against development goals, but the increasing difficulties of the national economies indicate that the euro arrangement, although institutionally nearly impossible to review, is quite problematic.

It is impossible to reach a conclusive position regarding central bank independence and neutrality, an issue that is much more local than textbook economics would suggest. Some economists argue that in the less developed accession countries looser monetary policies and therefore less bank independence are needed (as least where the central bank is not a partner in a "modest inflation in favor of growth" fiscal policy). However, a reasonable monetary policy can be applied without giving up bank independence. There can be reasonable coordination between fiscal, income, and monetary policy with an independent bank. Perhaps the real issue is not bank independence but goal setting. In the prevailing independent bank model, the central bank follows a statutorily imposed single goal, namely price stability. A narrow-minded bank policy will not consider other legitimate economic goals like growth. The defense of a stable currency remains a neutral goal, but its effects may not be neutral. It remains to be seen how successful the monetary stability ideal of the ECB will be in times of high unemployment and low growth. It is at this European level that the neutrality/loyalty game of the accession countries will be decided.

Assessing East European Independent Agencies

In established democracies, central banks and independent media authorities are often successful in avoiding direct partisan political influence and are capable of creating a temporary public image of nonpartisanship. Nevertheless, these institutions are not exempt from political bias, and the personal political loyalties of the members of independent agencies may play a role in policy decisions. Perhaps the regulated private interests (e.g., private and public broadcasting, or private banks) are less independent from the political sphere in the transition countries. Private economic activities often depend on the state in the prevailing clientelistic structures (Sajó 1998, 2002). Civil society is quite politicized and weak, and its weakness increases state dependency.

Given the economic vulnerability and dependency of the emerging East European democracies and the desire to "imitate Western solutions", international organizations were in the position to influence and define domestic institutional arrangements. Institutional neutrality was "imposed" from outside. The domestic players often were not fully aware of the consequences of adopting such models. Quite frequently, neutral designs were accepted where domestic political actors could not agree and instead attempted to save face by "delegating" the substantive decision to an international expert body not subject to domestic interests. Though such neutralization is present in many areas of life and increasingly crucial in globalization, it is of particular relevance for the EU accession countries. The accession imposes a kind of neutrality on these countries. The rules of the legal system are not presented as the result of domestic (democratic) politics. These rules are neither rational policy answers to locally articulated concerns nor hard-to-reach compromises that have been worked out among interest groups. The imposed rules appear to be neutral in the sense of a natural disaster or God's noncapricious punishment. The rules are above political debate; the political opposition in parliament and the politicians, in general, are voiceless if confronted with rules that are presented as part of the EU *acquis*. As indicated by Stephen Holmes:

> Accession means that Western Europe is exporting its own health and safety standards, product quality standards, environmental standards, and auditing standards to Eastern Europe. All of these may look neutral on their face, but in fact work prejudicially to favor West European producers, who not only have greater access to the kind of credit needed to make the necessary investments, but who are already substantially in compliance. (2003: 112)

The neutral institutions operate in an international setting that is becoming decisive for these transition countries. Even where the neutral design does not fit well into the local environment, it serves an international network well. The need to imitate institutional models is imperative in the accession process, but it is also pressing in the context of international economic dependencies, as is the case with international lending and financial institutions. It should be added, however, that the acceptance of neutral institutions cannot be explained by external dependence only. The building of neutral institutions (with all the hidden and built-in partisanship) had a genuine local component, even where the original design was adopted without much reflection. The independent media regulatory agencies and public broadcasting boards were intended to placate the bitter war among the ruling political elites. The neutral regulatory and adjudicative agencies were redesigned time and again to accommodate the inter-elite truce of the day. What is more important, even if the original external institutional design defined a certain path, the local elite accepted the emerging institution because institutions of naked partisanship would have undermined the possibility of public trust in a neutral state. The elite learned how to use the design to its advantage and to accommodate the emerging new economic deals within the neutral institution (e.g., the readiness of the broadcasting authorities to redraw license conditions).

Although the imposition of neutral institutional designs was rather successful, hidden political loyalties continue to endanger neutrality. This is partly a problem of the specific institutional designs that emerged in the "domestication" of the imposed models: Neutralization through nonpartisan independent agencies is perhaps less conducive to nonpartisanship than it is believed. Cass Sunstein has pointed out that the clearly political, though *bipartisan* composition of U.S. agencies may contribute to *less* partisanship than facially nonpartisan professional appointment (as is the case, in theory, with federal judicial appointments in the United States). U.S. independent agencies cannot be monopolized as "the law requires that no more than a bare majority of agency members may be from a single party" (2002: 69). If appointments are openly partisan and there is a built-in need for compromise, the agency's performance might be closer to neutrality even where the majority of the agency is close to the government of the day. The HRTA serves as an example. Alternatively, in the case of the president of the NBH partisan bias is easier to establish. Here a single political appointee has the lion's share of decision-making power. The NBH with a quasi one-person leadership, supported by his handpicked council, can act in a partisan way. The result is conflict with the political branches.

Because of bitter partisanship in Eastern Europe, politically mixed bodies may not act in the same way as mixed composition bodies do in the United States. In some East European independent agencies, notwithstanding legal requirements of impartiality, agency members perceive their role as that of a party representative (e.g., the board of the Hungarian Public Television). Nevertheless, in line with Sunstein's prediction, members of the HRTA tried to minimize their internal disagreements, although in the fundamental private television licensing cases the voting was not only divided along party lines but the differences were publicly voiced.

Officially even partisan appointees are required to be neutral professionals, legally obliged to act impartially. However, most East European neutral institutions were designed under the assumption that the same government that is designing the new institutions will have a free hand in picking the people who will run them. As long as the government could take it for granted that it could place its *cadres* into all key positions, it was not concerned about rules that mandated independence.

Neutralization of government through the building of autonomous, professionally motivated institutions is clearly preferable to ordinary politics as it exists in Eastern Europe. This neutralization comes with a price: *non-accountability*. The institutional arrangements still require external government supervision that is independent from goal setting. Neutrality might be in jeopardy because of lack of accountability. This is clearly evidenced in the cases of media regulatory agencies and central banks. Institutional neutralization can result in low levels of accountability and minimal political responsibility. The standard reason for nonaccountability is that external independent supervision may undermine the autonomy of the institution. Such danger can be limited if monitoring occurs ex post and is carried out by a body that does not necessarily share the interests of the goal-setting (political) body.

Some level of substantive judicial review is desirable regarding allegedly neutral institutions, especially if the decisions affect fundamental rights. Judicial supervision exists in many countries. This solution is advocated by the Council of Europe in the case of broadcasting authorities as a substitute for personal accountability; many countries, including Hungary allow judicial review of specific regulatory decisions including licensing, but have little review of general rule making.

Judicial review is, anyway, slow, costly, and limited. Courts are not willing to undertake substantive review because the substantive departure from neutral categories is not visible or cannot be successfully argued. This is certainly the case with central bank policies and their implementation. It may seem that a given decision satisfies fairness and is determined by expertise and scientific wisdom. To challenge these visible features on the basis of substantive analysis is difficult. Sometimes there is simply no forum granted, as is the case with the secretive ECB that increasingly serves (imposes itself) as a model.

Trust and Neutral Institutions

Neutrality, together with other fuzzy concepts (impartiality, integrity, autonomy, etc.), plays a considerable legitimating role in liberal democracies. It promises that public and private spheres of life will avoid the totalitarianism of the "political." In principle, the neutralization of public institutions will enhance their trustworthiness. One may assume that the existence of trustworthy institutions may have a positive impact on the political trustworthiness of the whole political regime. This is, however, hard to corroborate. The actual institutional designs and political realities offer limited possibilities for nonpartisan neutral professionalism to prevail.

Even where professionalism prevails, neutrality may suffer from insularity. If insularity means noninterference it may result in a lack of social responsiveness. If the performance of the neutral institution follows the dictates of the internal self-interest of the organization (becoming a hotbed of corruption), it will undermine trust in the institution, notwithstanding the formal fairness of its procedures. Moreover, these institutions, at least in Europe, tend to keep their decision-making process nontransparent.

The examples of central banks and broadcasting regulators show that institutional neutrality might be limited and may disguise partisan political loyalties and bonds. The East European record (so far) indicates that in some instances seemingly neutral institutions are designed to operate as partisan bodies. Independence is needed for future partisanship. Independence enables the institution to work against the majority of the day. The conflicts might undermine trust based on professional neutrality. Such conflicts between political and neutral institutions may, however, also increase the trustworthiness of the state. The conflict will demonstrate that there are, indeed, credible limits to the use and abuse of political power. It may also increase trust in the political system in the sense of improved performance. If the independent state prosecutor is more loyal to the previous government, he will be reluctant to prosecute the economic crimes of politicians of the previous government. At the same time, the office cannot be abused to administer the victors' political justice. It is likely that in the long run democratically elected politicians and independent agencies will seek a compromise. Established democracies seem to be more "respectable" than their more recent counterparts only because a long-term compromise has been agreed upon and normalized. However, at present in Eastern Europe "consensus building" or compromise may be seen as a betrayal of justice (illegalities are not wiped out, certain promised policies are not carried out).

One reason to trust neutral institutions is that these institutions and agencies are designed (using special guarantees of independence and professionalism) to serve the public interest. Neutral institutions are designed to be able to maintain their (generally loose) public commitments. The political branches, political parties, or special interest representation are easily sidetracked as far as their public commitments are concerned. Neutral institutions have a better chance to develop a good track record of "delivering" on their promises. Therefore, citizens and clients might see the neutral institution as deserving trust (Levi 1998: 93). However, the design might fail because of the lack of accountability of the independent agency.

Independent regulatory agencies and neutral social institutions emerged where the credibility of information is crucial (science, accuracy of government and other spending data, information about assets with regard to publicly traded companies, signaling about prices, etc.). Neutrality might be relevant in the context of information trustworthiness and also regarding information *about* trustworthiness. Moreover, acceptance into the neutral professional community has informational value to the extent that it guarantees some trustworthiness or lack of bias (partly because of the selection criteria and partly because of the nature of the control exercised by the neutral institution).

Trustworthiness flows from the design of the institution not from a sense of past obligation-performance, though institutions themselves may have a record of obligation-performance that might increase trust. Here, the institution's obligation is that of performing a public duty; hence we face certain difficulties with the traditional personal models of trust where the obligation is toward the interested person (see Hardin 2002). A person who utilizes a neutral institution often has only secondhand information about its reputation. This serves to build confidence in the institution but not trust in the official who is supposed to perform, though the two are related.

The prevailing view is that, notwithstanding the shortcomings of democracy, the fundamental features that are generative of trust are in place in a democracy (Levi 1998: 91). The lessons of neutralization point to a different reading. Evidence suggests that state neutrality emerged as an alternative (or addition) to democratic/participatory legitimization and trust building, after the failure of democracy that turned into spoils-oriented interest politics. Neutralization is partly related to the state's (or governing elites) agnostic attitude to complex social phenomena and partly to the legitimacy crisis of the democratic spoils system of interest politics. "Scientific detachment" and professionalism, hence impersonal predictability, are the source of trust as credibility.

The "continued rehearsal" of competitive elections and the reopening of issues contributes in Eastern Europe to the sense of division, heterogeneity, and conflict. The experience of never-ending conflicts and infighting increases the feeling that matters are handled unprofessionally and the alternative should be a professionally determined "ultimate solution." The unfinished business of interest politics, it is believed, can be countered by neutrality arising from professionalism. The trust in the state that was based on elections might be replaced or complemented with independent neutral institutions to the extent neutral institutions resist the political branches of power. However, such involvement in the political sphere will also undermine the trustworthiness of neutral institutions that were created with the promise of professional insularity. Once the neutral institution has to defend its professionalism in the political sphere, it might be seen as just another, partisan, political institution, which undermines the belief in its independent impartiality.

A neutral institution tries to keep its distance from political life. Professionalism—because of the "technical" language used in communication and institutionally designed, professionally sanctioned insulation—keeps the public at a distance. Obviously, the source of public trust in such context shifts to efficiency. As such, the source of trust is not fundamentally different from trust in democratic government in general. Hardin (2002) argues that it is the *effective performance* of certain political institutions that creates public trust in government. Neutral institutions are different in one respect, namely, that some kind of ex ante trust exists in institutional performance. Insulated professionalism is seen as the safeguard and source of efficiency.

Of course, to the extent that promises of professional neutrality are not met, the neutral institution may loose all its trustworthiness. Such a loss is likely, given the imperfection of neutralization and built-in political and other biases and influences. However, because these expert systems are designed not to react to external criticism, the loss of trust may not influence the neutralized system.

Neutralization, even if it is successful, may impoverish the public sphere. Where neutral policy is opposed to interest politics, politics will become by definition the area that does not require professional knowledge. The neutralized aspects of the state will be subject to efficiency considerations and distant or sheltered from public criticism. The general public will be considered incompetent. Neutralized spheres of the state are presented as entities that follow professional, scientific considerations. Moral criticism coming from citizens, allegedly the only acceptable critical capacity of the layperson, is therefore seen as inappropriate. The neutralized sphere is not simply not morally oriented, but is above moral evaluation or criticism. Secret services are the utmost example of this development. Lack of the moral dimension and moral sentiments, however, may undermine political loyalty.

It is hard to evaluate the impact on state trustworthiness of neutral state institutions in East European transition countries given the short history of such institutions. They have had little time to develop reputations. However, neutral institutions were rather attractive at the early stages of institutional design, partly because of the distrust in government that prevailed at the moment of transition as a result of the historical distrust toward the communist governments. Neutral professionalism looked attractive also because in the inherited communist (and other) ideologies distrust of representative democracy was strong. It was expected that a neutral state would act in everybody's interest, while partisanship was understood as betrayal of general trust. "Partisanship is divisive" is a common sentiment expressed in Hungary.[22] The assumption is perhaps understandable in countries where communists expressly stood up for partisan bias like class justice. Products of art and the press were expected to take sides in favor of the communist state. The new representative governments were seen as inefficient, corrupt, and divisive. Hence neutrality seemed attractive, even without a strong performance record. In some countries constitutional courts (basically neutral institutions) are the most popular public institutions. This, however, is partly due to the somewhat populist politics of these courts in Poland and in Hungary where they, at least occasionally, protected pensioners' entitlements and other welfare interests. In addition, political parties have a vested interest in accepting court rulings.[23]

The hidden partisanship in East European neutral institutions combined with a lack of accountability seems to have negative effects on institutional credibility. The institutional guarantees that provide for the self-enforcement mechanisms necessary for trust (Levi 1998: 86) are not well developed, precisely because of institutional insulation (i.e., lack of accountability).

Neutral government institutions seldom have a direct influence on the general public, at least not in an easily attributable way. Inflation or deflation has a direct impact on citizens' lives and their trust in the political system, but in the public mind this is hardly attributed to the central bank. Most of those who are directly affected by neutral governmental institutions belong to the elite, and it is their trust that is at stake. It is above all the trust developed by these actors toward these institutions that will matter. Trust—especially in the case of central banks—is generated by predictability and (alleged) rationality. Of course, the more the elites trust neutral institutions the more the general trust of the public might increase in a spillover effect.

Notes

1. Impartial institutions (like courts and constitutional courts, in particular) also contribute to the neutralization of the state. Contrary to institutions like independent agencies, courts stand *above* identifiable contests. They are impartial in the sense that they do not follow independent professional policy goals other than that related to self-preservation. See Sajó (2004).

   U.S. independent agencies, such as the Federal Trade Commission (established in 1914), were originally designed to be exempt from *executive* control; see *Humphrey's Executor v. U.S.* 295 U.S. 602 (1935). This understanding differs markedly from the one voiced by the Council of Europe, which denies *legislative* oversight. Note, further, that the characterization of agencies as "executive" or "independent" is the result of ad hoc political decisions (Strauss 1984).

2. A slightly different arrangement applies to the director and board of public radio and television.

3. *CBS Inc. v. Democratic Nat. Committee*, 412 U.S. 94 (1973), Burger CJ.

4. Quoted by Pavlik and Shields (1999: 497). See also Sparks and Reading (1998).

5. The problem of political neutrality is also a key issue in the context of the governing boards of public broadcasting companies. In Poland the president of the public television is appointed by the Broadcasting Authority. Other CEE countries adopted elements of the German model, though the board members are elected by parliament. Following the public demonstrations in December 2000, the Czech law was changed in this regard, and the director of the public broadcaster is appointed by representatives of the public instead of the House of Deputies.

6. The Slovak and the Czech councils kept to this model even after new laws were enacted in 2000 in order to comply with the EU requirements. Professional and civil society organizations may present candidates to parliament.

7. In some countries certain NGOs have the power to nominate regulatory board members.

8. As the German model presupposes a federal and strongly neocorporatitist structure, it was the French model that became prevalent. The *Conseil supérieur de l'audiovisuel* (CSA) has nine members appointed for one six-year nonrenewable term and one-third of the members are renewed every three years. Three of the members are appointed by the president, three by the president of the senate, and three by the president of the national assembly. The political influence in appointments is clear, though cohabitation and staggering renewals may render the political orientations in the council more balanced. Members are subject to strict conflict-of-interest rules, including all elected positions. The system goes back to *loi du 30 septembre 1986*.

9. Romanian Law on Radio and Television Broadcasting [Act 48, May 21, 1992, Article 25 (2)]. It is supposed to be replaced in the process of the EU accession.

10. The 2001 Czech Broadcasting Act still does not require specific professional qualifications (other than financial) of the council members. They cannot follow instructions and accept functions in a political party or act on its behalf. The council can be dissolved by the House of Deputies, and individual members can be recalled by the prime minister upon the initiative of the House. Members are elected by simple majority, and therefore represent the majority of the day for six years (with the possibility of later conflict). The council reports to the House of Deputies and the minutes of the meetings are public.

11. The CSRT is an independent body overseeing the activities of broadcasters. The members are appointed by the various branches of power. It is expected to safeguard media independence.

12. The decision of the tribunal was based on its doctrine of "the state governed by law" (rule of law), which dictates that a state body's powers must be expressly conferred by law. Decision of May 10, 1994 W 7/94.

13. An EPRA representative claimed that "some of the Central and Eastern European countries have found it quite helpful to be able to rely on such a structure. Last time, a delegation said, 'It helped us overcome our isolation. The opportunity to become part of this forum of broadcasting regulators in Europe was of great assistance to us'" (statement by Mr Greger Lindberg at the expert seminar "Audiovisual Media and Authorities" Federal Chancellery jointly organized with

Directorate-General X of the European Commission, Vienna Hofburg, November 26–27, 1998, http://europa.eu.int/comm/avpolicy/legis/key_doc/austria_en).

14. Supranational dependency went further in the banking sector (Havrileski 1993).

15. In Poland, reflecting domestic struggles and scandals, the Broadcasting Authority's independence and its structural requirements have been consolidated in the 1997 Constitution (Articles 213–15).

16. The U.S. Federal Reserve, established in 1913, in the formal sense has little guaranteed independence, and contrary to the continental central bank model, it has dual purposes: monetary stability and employment (Meyer 2001).

17. Pl. U.S. 14/01, Czech Constitutional Court. Members of the court were all appointed by President Havel, one of them being his former legal advisor. Five justices dissented. The Czech Parliament amended the National Bank Act during the process, requiring that in the future the government should propose the candidates to the president.

18. The 2001 Act on the National Bank of Hungary gives considerable power to the president of the bank. The Monetary Council makes only general policy decisions, like the exchange rate regime including the width of the fluctuation band. Members are handpicked by the bank's president and only he may initiate dismissal. The grounds for dismissal are obscure. The president's position is protected against the political branches: Parliament only receives a report that is not subject to review. Appointment and dismissal initiative regarding the president (in case of "violation of obligations") rest with the prime minister and is decided by the country's president. A precondition for dismissal is a court finding of serious violation of professional duty. In the first 13 years of post-communist Hungary, half the time the country's president and the prime minister were of a different political orientation, making dismissal highly unlikely.

19. The Russian Duma was notoriously adamant for easing credit and refused in 1995 to accept the appointment of Tatiana Paramonova who had a record of independence and commitment to price stability as acting governor of the bank.

20. For a warning addressed by the ECB to Poland in 2002 see http://www.eubusiness.com/news/stories/760/75912.html.

21. The minutes of the Hungarian Monetary Council are not published, and the bank does not always specify the time horizon of its forecasts. This lack of transparency is, however, encouraged by the ECB. ECB Council deliberations remain confidential and not even subject to study for a period of 16 years.

22. This desire for neutrality has ironic consequences. At least in Hungary, even partisan bias has to be presented and often understood as being fair because it is neutral. For example, the government subsidy to churches is understood to satisfy a concept of benevolent state neutrality in line with the constitutional requirement that the "state is separate from the church."

23. Constitutional court rulings seldom affect power politics directly for various reasons: Specific decisions are still to be taken in the ordinary political process, the juridicization makes the loss less painful or visible, and courts are generally careful not to embarrass the political elites too much.

References

Arato, Andrew. 1996. "The Hungarian Constitutional Court in the Media War: Interpretations of Separation of Powers and Models of Democracy." In A. Sajó and M. Price (eds.), *Rights of Access to the Media*, pp. 225–41. The Hague, London, New York: Kluwer Law International.

Bell, Desmond. 1993. "The Corporate State and Broadcasting in Ireland: A National-Popular Program." *Cardozo Arts and Entertainment Law Journal* 11: 337–59.

Carter, Stephen L. 1998. *The Dissent of the Governed: A Meditation on Law, Religion, and Loyalty.* Cambridge MA, London: Harvard University Press.

Cook, Karen S. and Richard M. Emerson. 1978. "Power, Equity, and Commitment in Exchange Networks." *American Sociological Review* 43: 721–39.

Csepeli, György, Antal Örkény, Mária Székelyi, and Ildikó Barna. 2004. "Blindness to Success: Social Psychological Objectives Along the Way to a Market Economy in Eastern Europe." In J. Kornai, B. Rothstein, S. Rose-Ackerman (eds.), *Creating Social Trust in Post-Socialist Transition*, pp. 213–40 New York: Palgrave Macmillan.

De Smaele, Hedwig. 1999. "The Applicability of Western Media Models on the Russian Media System." *European Journal of Communication* 14: 173–89.

Fletcher, George P. 1993. *Loyalty: An Essay on the Morality of Relationships*. New York: Oxford University Press.

Gálik, Mihály. 1999. "Media Concentration and Control in Hungary." Paper presented at the Media Ownership and Control in East-Central Europe Colloquium organized by the European Institute for Communication and Culture and the University of Ljubljana. Piran, April 8–10.

Giordani, Paolo and Giancarlo Spagnolo. 2001. *Constitutions and Central Bank Independence: An Objection to McCallum's Second Fallacy*. SSE/EFI Working Paper Series No. 426 in Economics and Finance. http://swopec.hhs.se/hastef/papers/hastef0426.pdf.

Gross, Peter. 2002. "Media and Political Society in Eastern Europe." *Media Development* 1. http://www.wacc.org.uk/publications/md/md2002-1/gross.html.

Gulyás, Ágnes. 2002. "Democratisation and the Mass Media in Post-Communist Hungary." *Media Development* 1. http://www.wacc.org.uk/publications/md/md2002-1/gulyas.html.

Haan, Jakob de and Sylvester C. W. Eijffinger. 2000. "The Democratic Accountability of the European Central Bank: A Comment on Two Fairytales." *Journal of Common Market Studies* 38: 393–407.

Hardin, Russell. 2002. "Liberal Distrust." *European Review* 10: 73–89.

Havrilesky, Thomas M. 1993. *The Pressures on Monetary Policy*. Boston MA: Kluwer Academic Publishers.

Hoffmann-Riem, Wolfgang. 1996. *Regulating Media: The Licensing and Supervision of Broadcasting in Six Countries*. New York: Guilford Press.

Holmes, Stephen. 2003. "A European *Doppelstaat?*" *East European Politics and Society* 17: 107–18.

Levi, Margaret. 1998. "A State of Trust." In M. Levi and V. A. Braithwaite (eds.), *Trust and Governance*, pp. 77–101.

Levi, Margaret and Valerie A. Braithwaite (eds.). 1998. *Trust and Governance*. New York: Russell Sage Foundation.

Maxfield, Sylvia. 1997. *Gatekeepers of Growth: The International Political Economy of Central Banking in Developing Countries*. Princeton NJ: Princeton University Press.

Meyer, Laurence H. 2001. "Comparative Central Banking and the Politics of Monetary Policy." Remarks by Governor Laurence H. Meyer at the National Association for Business Economics at the Seminar on Monetary Policy and the Markets. Washington DC, May 21. http://www.federal reserve.gov/boarddocs/speeches/2001/200105212/default.htm.

Miller, Geoffrey P. 1998. "An Interest-Group Theory of Central Bank Independence." *Journal of Legal Studies* 27: 433–53.

Pavlik, Petr and Peter Shields. 1999. "Toward an Explanation of Television Broadcast Restructuring in the Czech Republic." *European Journal of Communication* 14: 487–524.

Posen, Adam. 1995. "Declarations are not Enough: Financial Sector Sources of Central Bank Independence." *NBER Macroeconomics Annual—1995*, pp. 253–74.

Recommendation. 2000. "Rec (2000) 23 of the Committee of Ministers (Council of Europe) to Member States on the Independence and Functions of Regulatory Authorities for the Broadcasting Sector." http://cm.coe.int/ta/rec/2000/2000r23.htm.

Robillard, Serge. 1995. *Television in Europe: Regulatory Bodies*. London: John Libbey.

Sajó, András. 1998. "Corruption, Clientelism, and the Future of the Constitutional State in Eastern Europe." *East European Constitutional Review* 7: 37–46.

———. 2001. "Government Speech in a Neutral State." In N. Dorsen and P. Gifford (eds.), *Democracy and the Rule of Law*, pp. 369–89. Budapest, New York: Central European University Press.

———. 2002. "Clientelism and Extortion: Corruption in Transition." In S. Kotkin and A. Sajó (eds.), *Political Corruption in Transition*, pp. 1–21. Budapest, New York: Central European University Press.

——— (ed.). 2004. *Judicial Integrity*. The Hague, London, New York: Kluwer Law International.

Schmitt, Carl. 1996 [1934]. "Das Zeitalter der Neutralisierungen und Entpolitisierungen." In C. Schmitt, *Der Begriff des Politischen*, pp. 79–96. Berlin: Duncker & Humblot.

Slaughter, Anne-Marie. 2003. "Global Government Networks, Global Information Agencies, and Disaggregated Democracy." *Michigan Journal of International Law* 24: 1041–75.

Smith, Steven Rathgeb and Michael Lipsky. 1993. *Nonprofits for Hire: The Welfare State in the Age of Contracting*. Cambridge MA: Harvard University Press.

Sparks, Colin and Anna Reading. 1998. *Communism, Capitalism and the Mass Media*. London: Sage Publications.

Strauss, Peter L. 1984. "The Place of Agencies in Government: Separation of Powers and the Fourth Branch." *Columbia Law Review* 84: 573–633.

Sunstein, Cass. 2002. *Conformity and Dissent*. John M. Olin Law and Economics Working Paper No. 164 (2nd series), Chicago IL: University of Chicago Law School.

Vagts, Detlev F. 1998. "The Traditional Legal Concept of Neutrality in a Changing Environment." *American University International Law Review* 14: 83–102.

Walzer, Michael. 1994. *Thick and Thin: Moral Argument at Home and Abroad*. Notre Dame IN: University of Notre Dame Press.

CHAPTER THREE

Does Lustration Promote Trustworthy Governance? An Exploration of the Experience of Central and Eastern Europe

CYNTHIA M. HORNE AND MARGARET LEVI[*]

Introduction

Post-Soviet governments in Central and Eastern Europe (CEE) face a double bind in their transition to democracy. They aspire to create responsive and trustworthy governments operating within the rule of law. Simultaneously, they want to meet the demands of citizens and politicians to hold accountable those who maintained the discredited regime and especially those who participated actively in the reign of terror. Trustworthy government rests on due process and equity; revenge and punishment often entail violation of these principles. The trade-off between respect for individual rights and the implementation of transitional justice is a dilemma for many societies with a legacy of dictatorship and repression (Barahona de Brito et al. 2001).

Lustration represents the regional solution of CEE countries to problems of transitional justice. It is a legal process for obtaining knowledge about key collaborators with the past regime and, when deemed appropriate, inhibiting their involvement in the present one. Lustration laws authorize governments to engage in the mass screening of candidates for positions in the new government and/or to instigate legal proceedings against elites, state bureaucrats, and other authorities in the former regime (Letki 2002: 530). However, punitive actions do not, as a rule, involve criminal penalties.

The term lustration derives from the Latin word *lustratio* meaning "the performance of an expiatory sacrifice or a purificatory rite."[1] Within CEE it has come to imply "the purification of state organizations from their sins under the communist regimes" (Boed 1999: 358). Lustration varies considerably across countries and time, but at its broadest it covers a wide range of individuals and offices. For some authors, its breadth distinguishes lustration from "decommunization," the purging and vetting of only former communist nomenklatura (Los 1995: 121), but for most authors the concepts are used interchangeably within the CEE context (Gonzalez-Enriquez 2001; Darski 1993; Gibney 1997).

Lustration laws are legislative acts, implemented through judicial proceedings and susceptible to review by constitutional courts. They all involve processes for revealing collaboration with the past regime, especially its secret police. The laws differ, however, in terms of who initiates the process of lustration—it can be the individual in question or a public institution. The laws do not criminalize past behavior even when they authorize punishments, but they do vary in the treatment of the lustrated individual. Some laws require only self-explanation of collaboration, others public exposure of collaborators, and still others the removal and barring of former "collaborators" from public office or other positions.

The meaning of actionable collaboration also varies. All the laws cover collaboration with the secret police. In Hungary and Poland, secret police collaborators are the sole focus of lustration. In Albania, Romania, and the Czech Republic, the definition of targets is wider. Simply being a member of the Communist Party and holding certain positions can be grounds for lustration. Some laws define as collaborators those who unknowingly talked to the secret police, taught communist theory in universities, were active members of the Communist Party, or simply were named in the secret police files.

All of the lustration processes rely on information in the secret police files of the former regime to assess the past regime involvement of individuals. The laws vary, however, in terms of public access to and publication of the information from the files. Some lustration laws permit citizens to have access to the secret police files on themselves. For example, the Czech Republic requires publication of lists of individuals holding public office whose names appeared in secret police files. Poland keeps the information in the files confidential as long as an individual accurately admits past regime collaboration, publishing the secret files only if an official is caught in a "lustration lie." Hungary created commissions to review the files; former collaborators are then subject to pressure to leave certain positions, pressure that can include publication of their names.[2]

This essay takes up several interrelated questions. One is the effect of the lustration process on the establishment of trustworthy government. We are interested in how lustration affects citizen perceptions of both politicians and the institutions of government, but we are also concerned about the extent to which lustration undermines due process and other characteristics of an objectively trustworthy government. Our driving interest in the effects of lustration laws on the establishment of trustworthy government has made us aware that the laws and implementation of lustration vary considerably among countries.

Moreover, lustration is now in a second phase. Lustration in CEE was designed to facilitate the transition from the pre-1989 past to the future. Yet, well over a decade later, a number of countries have extended the duration and scope of lustration laws or even introduced them for the first time. Are these changes in response to concerns by citizens about the trust-worthiness of politicians and governments, or are they, as we shall argue, the consequence of a particular cycle of political competition? Do these newer lustration laws help build citizen perception of the trustworthiness of government, or do they fuel distrust of politicians? In sum, under what conditions do lustration laws promote trustworthy government, and under what conditions do they undermine public confidence in government institutions and personnel? And what accounts for the cross-national variation in their duration, scope, and timing?

The current literature on lustration only provides hints of answers to our questions. There are relatively abstract and general assessments of transitional justice and country-specific studies.[3] Although in no way minimizing the importance of this research, our aim is somewhat different. We attempt to identify and then understand factors affecting commonalities and differences in lustration in CEE. A comparative approach allows us to construct a model of the lustration process. This gives us sufficient theoretical distance from a historically charged issue to conjecture about how this act of symbolic politics may affect the potential for democratic consolidation in CEE.

After considering lustration as one of the possible choices available to countries in transition, we discuss how lustration might affect the trust-worthiness of politicians and governance institutions. We then develop a first cut of a model about the variation in lustration practices and the relationship between lustration and trustworthy government. Our model derives from a first reading of the laws and experiences of the CEE countries. After deriving testable implications, we use the model to organize our initial review of lustration in CEE. Our approach is that of an analytic narrative (Bates et al. 1998), but the full development of both the analytic and the narrative must await future research.

Lustration as a Form of Transitional Justice

All governments that break from a nondemocratic and repressive past have a daunting task in front of them, especially if their aim is to create a democratic and just society. How to resolve the "torturer problem" in a way that promotes and nurtures strong, fair democratic regimes (Huntington 1991: 211–31; Moran 1994; Barahona de Brito et al. 2001: 25–39) is often an issue for transitional governments. Many transitional societies therefore face the problem of "corrective" (Ackerman 1992) or "transitional" (Elster 1999) justice. Stanley Cohen (1995: 11–12 and passim) outlines various phases through which transitional societies generally absolve themselves of the past by (1) establishing truth about the past regime, (2) rendering justice for past abuses, (3) determining who gets impunity, (4) granting expiation, and (5) reconciling and reconstructing. However, societies differ in the policies they adopt to navigate these phases. Lustration is only one possible policy option to the problem of rendering transitional justice.

According to Luc Huyse (1995: 51–3), there are three major alternatives to lustration: outright criminal prosecution, unconditional amnesty, and amnesty in the form of truth and reconciliation. The French Revolution's Terror exemplifies the outright criminal prosecution of individuals associated with the former regime. Milder forms of criminalization include European justice in post–World War II Netherlands, Belgium, and France (ibid.: 66–7), and Latin American investigatory commissions (Popkin and Roht-Arriaza 1995; Barahona de Brito 2001; Sieder 2001). Unconditional amnesty—or close to it—characterized the post–Civil War United States. A more recent example is post-Franco Spain (Huyse 1995: 52; Aguilar 2002); however, there is now some resurgence of interest in truth and reconciliation because the forms of Spanish amnesty have not "put the past to rest" for some people (Sciolino and Daly 2002: 3). South African "truth and reconciliation" commissions (Berat and Shain 1995; Goldstone 2000; Wilson 2001) represent the last type. Each of these categories actually encompasses a continuum, both within and between categories. Lustration lies somewhere between outright criminal prosecution and unconditional amnesty, according to Huyse's taxonomy.

There is an imperfect correlation between the kind of transition and the form of transitional justice. Forgiveness seems more likely where there is no regime change, as in the United States after the Civil War. Punitive action seems more likely where there is a radical break from the past, as in revolutionary France. However, counterexamples, such as post-Franco Spain and South Africa, suggest that other factors, such as negotiated pacts, can affect the form transitional justice takes.

Across the board, the countries of CEE gravitated toward lustration as a way to address problems of transitional justice. Historical, cultural, and institutional factors distinguish the CEE transitions from other transitions and affect policy choices about the best means to deal with the past. Crucial differences in the scope of citizen collusion, the nature of the offenses committed, and the nature of the break with the past (Huyse 1995: 71–6; Barahona de Brito et al. 2001) help explain why CEE countries turned to lustration, instead of the other possible information and reconciliation options. Popular opinion early in the transition process also contributed to the sentiment that lustration was an appropriate regional choice for transitional justice. There were feelings that punishment should go beyond outright collaborators to include individuals who disproportionately benefited from the former regime, who took part in decisions that indebted the regime, or who persecuted individuals with other political beliefs.[4]

The scope of citizen collusion in CEE makes it difficult to assess blame. In Latin America or South Africa, for example, there was a clearer division between oppressors and oppressed. The military was primarily, although far from exclusively, responsible for gross human rights violations in Latin America. Racial differences largely marked oppressed and oppressors in South Africa. For CEE, as Adam Michnik and Vaclav Havel said, "we are all in this together—those who directly, to a greater or lesser degree, created this regime, those who accepted it in silence, and also all of us who subconsciously became accustomed to it" (1993: 21). If most of society was complicit with the former regime, how is one to determine gradations of guilt? Who should be punished? How to determine what constitutes "active" as opposed to "passive" collaboration, and are there circumstances that legitimate "quasi-active" compliance?

The fact that "crimes" in CEE were more psychological than physical (Huyse 1995: 72–3) further complicates the estimation of blame. Torture and murder characterized Latin America military dictatorships, but in the post-Stalinist era there was relatively little physical abuse in CEE. The emphasis instead was on creating widespread mistrust in which individuals were encouraged to feel suspicious of their fellow citizen, neighbor, or even family member.

Regime changes in CEE involved mostly peaceful transitions and often the retention of former communist officials in public office. In Bulgaria and Romania, many former communist officials never left office. In Poland, Hungary, and the Czech Republic, communist officials have gradually been elected to positions of power, sometimes even constituting a parliamentary majority.[5] Not only are high-ranking officials from the former regime able to participate in the new system, but lower-ranking bureaucrats have largely remained in their positions or advanced. Some have labeled this "the revolution of the deputy section leaders."[6] East Germany and the Czech Republic may be the two exceptions (Gibney 1997: 99). By contrast, Latin America, postwar Europe, and South Africa all experienced substantial personnel alteration.

Lustration quickly emerged as a focal point for political leaders and citizens and became the primary regional solution to the problem of transitional justice. There were both historical and institutional precedents for lustration as a way to solve problems of government legitimacy and trustworthiness. To the extent lustration is a form of purge, its practice resonates with the communist past. In 1991, the Czechoslovakian government adopted the language of the country's own former secret police (StB) for its legal process of decommunization (Bertschi 1995: 436). The StB used the Czech word *lustrace* to describe checks conducted on citizens' loyalty to the Communist Party (Cohen 1995: 27).

The Czech adoption of lustration further authorized it throughout the region. The Czechs had a history of dissident activity and resistance to the Soviet system, and because Havel was so closely identified with that resistance, his country and policies possessed a moral force that only Hungary and Poland could also claim. We suspect that if lustration had first occurred in Romania, for example, it would have been far less likely to have been emulated. The initiation of lustration was a contingent event perhaps, but it nonetheless started a process that can be modeled in a way to produce testable hypotheses.

Lustration and Trustworthy Government

Politicians of the new regime claim and often believe that for citizens to view government as trustworthy, government must distance itself from the people and practices of the delegitimized past. However, governments must prove themselves both just and competent in this process. This implies a fair process for sorting those whose actions were inexcusable from those who should be given a second chance. If the officials' motives seem to be personal ambition or vengeance, they will hardly appear just. If the process removes from office too many of those trained and skilled in essential bureaucratic and governmental tasks or if they demonstrate an incapacity to identify correctly those who should be punished, government will appear incompetent.

A trustworthy democratic government possesses a combination of such attributes as competence, fairness, honesty, the capacity to make credible commitments, accountability, dedication to the public interest, and a willingness to protect private rights.[7] These attributes are not always compatible even in long-standing, highly democratic polities. Competence in such matters as policing, domestic security, and espionage can often lead to discriminatory behavior and violations of civil liberties and private rights. Competence in dealing with economic crises can undermine promises made during elections or under different economic circumstances. This has been the experience of both long-established and transitional democracies as they adopt neoliberal policies (Stokes 2001a,b).

Competence and fairness are at the heart of a trustworthy democratic government. The first can be hard to measure and difficult to assess; moreover, a government competent at one task, such as running the economy, may be incompetent at another, such as running a war. Fairness refers to democratic and representative policy making as well as to nondiscriminatory implementation of the policy (see also Rose-Ackerman, this volume). Fairness is generally a contested standard, especially in transitional periods and certainly in the societies under consideration here. For some it implies retribution; for others it entails forgiveness or rehabilitation. Although the grounds of assessment may differ among the citizens of the polity, all must have confidence that the processes of government are fair according to prevailing standards within their group. For important policies that affect them directly, they must also feel that their preferences are heard and taken into account in policy making.[8]

The trustworthiness of government, as defined here, can be objectively determined by assessing the extent to which government or its relevant agencies possess these critical attributes. The perception of government trustworthiness and its actual trustworthiness are analytically separable, however. In principle, so are public perceptions of the trustworthiness of government versus the trustworthiness of politicians, but American survey researchers (Levi and Stoker 2000; Burns and Kinder 2000; Rahn and Rudolph 2000) are only just beginning to find ways to get at this distinction. Moreover, citizen perceptions of trustworthiness may vary with policy arena and agency (also see Rothstein 2000, 2004).

Our concern here is less with how trustworthy government and its agents really are, and more with the subjective perceptions of citizens.

Citizens, sometimes the majority, conflate their attitudes toward and judgments about politicians with those about government itself, leading to a widespread distrust of government. They can be wrong or biased, and they can also get it right. Whether right or wrong, perceptions are often what motivate citizen behavior. The degree to which citizens perceive government as trustworthy affects their willingness to obey the laws (Tyler 1990) and to contingently consent and thus comply with government prescriptions (Levi 1997). The extent to which they judge politicians to be trustworthy may influence support of policies advocated by those politicians and support of the politicians themselves (Levi and Stoker 2000).

Transitional governments, which are simultaneously creating a democratic constitution and cleansing themselves of the residue of a tainted past, may find themselves compelled to make trade-offs among the dimensions of trustworthiness. Responsiveness to citizen demands for vengeance may conflict with upholding due process and individual rights. Efforts by government to demonstrate its competence may further undermine fairness. To establish transparency, governments may make files available to all, thus facilitating accusations and recrimination based on tainted records. To expedite the process and display efficiency, governments may rely on guilt by association or circumstantial evidence. Too often individual rights are trampled in the name of the collective interest in exposing collaborators.

As Claus Offe has remarked, there is a tension between "backward looking justice" and "forward looking justification" (Offe 1992, 1996). The public and/or politicians might understand lustration as a solution to problems of government trustworthiness, but it is at best a short-term and backward-looking solution that could actually undermine the long-run credibility and legitimacy of democratic institutions and officials.

Developing a Model of Lustration

In this section, we provide a first-cut at a model to account for variation in lustration processes and citizen perceptions of the trustworthiness of government. Our purpose here is to begin to develop the comparative statics and to derive several testable implications in order to produce an analytic narrative (Bates et al. 1998). We draw from an initial reading of the historical record to develop our argument and consider the plausibility of our claims. The in-depth and detailed case research necessary to elaborate and test the model awaits further research.

Key Actors

The key actors in the lustration process are politicians and political elites, citizens, the media, constitutional courts, and international institutions. Throughout we assume that the key actors are politicians (legislators and executives) desiring reelection. Driving their behavior is interparty competition, the causal mechanism in our model. They operate strategically with other players: justices who are sometimes independent and sometimes party hacks, bureaucrats keen to keep their jobs, and citizens whose perceptions of the trustworthiness of government and of politicians affect their electoral behavior, their cooperation with government demands, and their interactions with each other. Politicians are constrained somewhat by the existing laws and norms although, given the nature of the transition, they sometimes have the capacity to change those constraints, particularly the rules. They are also in strategic interaction with international actors who are assessing the government they create; this has implications for membership in the European Union (EU), something CEE countries universally seek.

Lustration laws are routinely justified by politicians as a function of popular demands. Although there is certainly an incentive for politicians to manipulate popular sentiment to achieve their own political ends, voter support for and opposition to such policies influence the politician's calculus. The media's representation of issues of transitional justice affects the salience of the issue for the public. The media helps shape public perceptions about the importance or necessity of transitional justice, government fairness, and efficiency in administering lustration laws, and the overall efficacy of the laws in effecting democratic transitions. Theorizing the role of the media will await future research. At this point we wish only to point out the important role of this quasi-captured, quasi-independent actor in shaping public perceptions about the relationship between lustration and trustworthy government.

Constitutional courts are potentially independent actors in the lustration model, moderating the self-serving interests of politicians. The degree of constitutional court autonomy affects its ability to render unbiased decisions. The greater its autonomy from the influence of politicians and powerful citizen groups, the more closely we might expect the implementation of lustration laws to reflect the actual letter and spirit of the laws. As such, constitutional courts have a potential moderating influence on the use or misuse of lustration over time.

Finally, international institutions and international actors affect the nature of the lustration process in CEE. In general, international institutions and extra-regional countries have been summarily opposed to lustration. International institutions such as the International Labor Organization (ILO), the Council of Europe, Helsinki Watch, and the International Helsinki Federation for Human Rights have publicized how CEE domestic laws conflict with international treaty obligations in an effort to persuade countries in the region to change their lustration laws (Cohen 1995: 27). For example, these international institutions have publicly questioned the constitutionality of the Czech Republic's lustration law, showing how the law violated its obligations under various international agreements (Kritz 1995: 335). European governments have generally been unfavorable toward CEE lustration policies, and have exerted subtle pressure to dissuade politicians from pursuing widespread screening or political retribution (Letki 2002: 539).

The Lustration Cycle

In the abstract, once lustration is in place, it becomes an equilibrium from which politicians find exit difficult, as Bruce Ackerman recognized in the early 1990s: "If the files remain, members of the new government will be tempted to use them to blackmail the opposition. This will create precedents for later abuses when ministries change hands. The resulting dynamic will be a spiral of incivility, which will poison the political atmosphere by leading to charges and countercharges, public and private, over past collaboration" (1992: 81).

We build upon Ackerman's insight as well as the subsequent events that seem to support his claim. We argue that politicians have an incentive to use lustration against their opposition as a means of discrediting their competitors with the electorate. Once this is done, the opposition, when it obtains power, retaliates. Under certain conditions, this leads to a cycle of escalation in which laws are extended in time and scope, and the initial impulse to limit lustration loses force. This kind of cycle is similar to those that occur among firms, who match each other's price-cuts, in order to obtain more of the market; with the result that all firms are worse off.

There are several ways out of such vicious cycles. Political parties themselves can break the cycle of escalation. For example, cartels or, in politics, cross-party coalitions might occur if sufficient popular antipathy to the process develops. Or, lustration processes can be slowed or stopped by the reemergence of socialist parties whose members will be disproportionately and negatively affected by lustration. A second option is the existence of a superordinate power able to impose cooperation. In the case of competitive firms, this means government regulation, but only constitutional courts, if they are deemed legitimate, are likely to have this kind of authority over governments themselves. A third possibility is that influence from international bodies, including the EU, could pressure CEE countries to end the lustration cycle. Which, if any, is most likely to occur and what are the necessary conditions for success are questions we shall take up at the end of this essay, after considering some of the empirical material.

From this overly stylized account, we can lay out the comparative statics of lustration:

1. As interparty competition increases in intensity, legislators will attempt to expand the scope and duration of lustration laws (a) unless socialist parties or certain kinds of ideological parties come to power, (b) unless there is evidence of popular voter rebellion toward the continuation of lustration laws.
2. The greater the insulation of constitutional courts from politics (a) the less likely it is that lustration laws will be extended, and (b) the more likely that these laws will be declared unconstitutional or otherwise limited in scope.
3. The greater the pressure from important international bodies, the more likely it is that a cross-party coalition will form to end lustration.

This suggests that a vicious cycle of lustration will commence only in the specific condition of intense interparty competition and will end only if certain institutions are in place and effective and/or if certain pressure groups have sufficient clout with politicians. However, there is also reason to believe that time should moderate the political salience of lustration for all political parties, as well as citizens.[9] The problem remains, however, of how to end the vicious political cycle once started.

Effects on the Trustworthiness of Government

We suspect that lustration, over time, adversely affects citizen confidence in politicians. First, the public cares less than the politicians themselves do about the competition among parties, especially if their policy differences are small. Second, there is historical and cross-national evidence that the public fatigues of political infighting over time. We suspect this is also the case in CEE. Third, there is huge diversity among the population. The transition is now more than a decade old; younger voters have little memory of the past regime while for some older voters the memory may be fading. Other voters are nostalgic for or romanticize the past, making them more forgiving of those whose "crimes" did not involve torture or other forms of direct harm of others—if they even perceive such behavior as problematic. Still others may fear being implicated.

In our understanding of lustration, time is very important. Lustration is a very real political concern early in the transition process. Government institutions lack credibility. Citizens largely perceive all government bureaucrats and apparatchiks as corrupt. There is a general popular belief in the need to cleanse the existing institutional problems in order to forge ahead with democratic consolidation. So the salience of lustration among citizens and politicians is particularly high early in the transition during the initial drafting and implementation of the laws. As the transition continues, and citizens perceive that democracy is here to stay, lustration becomes less salient. Citizens gradually turn their attention to other matters, such as bureaucratic competence and the government's ability to meet citizen demands. As time goes on, citizens are likely to become fatigued with lustration and the process of purging.

Perceptions of the trustworthiness of politicians can affect perceptions of the trustworthiness of government. This is for at least two reasons. First, citizens often feel more antipathetic to and critical of government institutions when they are displeased with politicians. Second, many people believe that the institutions are only as trustworthy as those who people them. However, perceptions and beliefs vary among the population, sometimes for quite personal reasons but often on more structural grounds, such as income, education, or ethnicity.

The objective trustworthiness of government depends on which services it is providing, how it determines what policies to enact, and how it implements those policies. It also depends, of course, on the extent to which it has in place devices for monitoring and constraining those who carry out policies. Even if the elected politicians are untrustworthy, even if they are venal, corrupt, and narrowly self-serving, government itself could be trust-worthy if the laws are fair and the bureaucrats carry them out impartially and competently.

The comparative statics of the argument are that the longer lustration continues, (1) the less popular support there will be for government policies, particularly lustration policies; (2) the more there are likely to be negative ratings of "trust in government" on surveys; and (3) the more noncompli-ance with government policies will occur unless government itself can effectively demonstrate its objective trustworthiness by delivering popular policies fairly and competently.

We shall not be able to consider the third hypothesis in what follows, but we shall offer some preliminary evidence on the first two.

Lustration in Practice: Political Cycling

We hypothesize that given the desire of politicians to maximize voter sup-port, under certain conditions, lustration laws will be caught in a cycle of political escalation. As competition for voter support between political par-ties increases, there will be an increase in proposed lustration amendments. These amendments will reflect attempts by political parties to restructure the rules of the game to advantage themselves over other parties. There are at least two distinct amendments to lustration laws that have been proposed by CEE political parties: extending the scope of those covered by lustration laws and extending the time period for lustration. There is substantial variation in terms of countries that extended the scope or time-frame of lustration. These differences will be explored in the following sections.

Extending the Scope of the Lustration Laws

In many CEE countries there was cross-party support for the initiation of lustration laws. Only the remnants of the former Communist Party (often with new names and new agendas) have consistently opposed lustration policies, because such policies might negatively affect their ability to par-ticipate in the new democratic system. In Hungary, the Hungarian Socialist Party (HSP) was the only parliamentary party to vote against the adoption of a lustration law (Kritz 1995: 666). In Czechoslovakia, all political parties competing in the first parliamentary elections in June 1990, except the communists, asked the Ministry of Interior to screen candidates for possi-ble secret police connections (Boed 1999: 367). In the Slovak Republic the parliament overwhelmingly overrode the presidential veto and approved a lustration law to open the files of the communist secret police (RFE/RL, August 21, 2002, Vol. 6, No. 157, Part II). In Poland, the original lustration law was proposed by the former Solidarity-dominated coalition in the

Sejm, and was approved with widespread multiparty support (RFE/RL, February 26, 2002, Vol. 4, No. 8, Part II).

The political orientation of the dominant party affects the initiation and content of the lustration laws. Countries in which the Communist Party has retained the majority in parliament have been hesitant to enact broad lustration laws. In Bulgaria, the communist-dominated parliament has prevailed in sealing the files of secret collaborators for 30 years. Despite the election victory of the opposition coalition, the Union of Democratic Forces (SDS), in October 1991, and various lustration law proposals, the Bulgarian Constitutional Court has revoked the lustration law as unconstitutional and only approved a vetting law related to academics (Ellis 1997: 188).

Hungary has been particularly susceptible to cycles of political escalation. There have been four phases in the lustration discussion, according to Péter Hack, former chair of the Hungarian Parliament's Constitutional Affairs Committee.[10] These include three major proposals to revise the original scope and duration of lustration laws. First, in 1995 a major revision in the scope of the lustration law provided for citizen access to their secret police files, something not permitted in the original 1990 draft law.[11] Second, in 2002 proposals were made to change the 1990 draft "Law on Background Checks to be Conducted on Individuals Holding Certain Important Positions" that allowed access to information only from Department 3/3 (domestic political repression) of the Interior Ministry. The proposed changes would access archives from all the other departments, including Department 3/1 (foreign intelligence) and 3/2 (counterintelligence) (RFE/RL, July 11, 2002, Vol. 6, No. 128, Part II). These amendments were separately proposed by the governing Socialist–Free Democrat coalition and the opposition parties, FIDESZ and the Hungarian Democratic Forum (MDF) (RFE/RL, June 25, 2002, Vol. 3, No. 25, Part II). Third, the 2002 draft law also proposed changes to citizen access to the files. The amendments under review in 2002 would allow people to know the names of police informers, whose identities are currently protected under the original legislation (RFE/RL, September 12, 2002, Vol. 6, No. 172, Part II). In sum, the Hungarian lustration law has expanded in terms of both the scope of positions to be lustrated and the type of information deemed public at least three times since its inception.

Hungarian political parties have proposed many amendments that have failed to gain parliamentary approval. In 1994, parliament rejected an MDF proposed amendment to include local government deputies in the lustration process. This proposed change would have increased the number screened from 10,000 to 28,000. The parliament also rejected an amendment proposed by two members of the radical populist Hungarian Justice and Life Party (MIÉP), whereby church leaders could have been screened if 20 percent of all active priests voted in favor of such action (Kritz 1995: 665).

The Czech Republic has also seen waves of political escalation. A new lustration bill approved by the Senate in 2001 to declassify the files of the communist secret police, substantially changed access to the files.

The original law did not allow the data gathered by the StB to be disclosed without the consent of the individual. The new bill allowed public access to all materials in the files (RFE/RL Newsline-Central and Eastern Europe, August 20, 2001, Vol. 5).

In the case of both Hungary and the Czech Republic there is some evidence that political parties attempt to restructure the scope of the original lustration laws to strengthen their political power vis à vis other political parties (Gonzales-Enriquez 2001: 241–3; Tworzecki 2003: 67, 89–90). As the intensity of the political competition between parties increases, one would expect to see commensurate changes proposed to the scope of the lustration legislation. Under certain conditions, one might expect the scope to be expanded, especially if such an expansion in the scope of the laws might permit their more intensive use against political rivals. In the cases of Hungary and the Czech Republic, as socialist parties have increased their political power, center-and right-wing political parties have attempted to increase the scope of the laws so as to counter the growing political competition posed by those political candidates.

Under other conditions, one might expect proposed reductions in the scope of the lustration laws as a way to fortify political power, such as when socialist parties are reelected into power or become members of the dominant coalition. In the Czech Republic, the recent election of the Communist Party of Bohemia and Moravia has resulted in a proposal by that party for the repeal of the lustration law (RFE/RL, July 1, 2002, Vol. 6, No. 119, Part II). In Poland in 2002, the leftist-dominated Senate proposed amendments to the 1997 lustration law, removing intelligence, counterintelligence, and border-protection services from the list of positions subjected to lustration (RFE/RL, February 26, 2002, Vol. 4, No. 8, Part II; June 26, 2002, Vol. 3, No. 26, Part II). After winning national elections in September 2001, these amendments were supported by the governing Democratic Left Alliance (SLD)–Labor Union (UP) bloc and a majority of lawmakers from the Self-Defense Party (RFE/RL, February 26, 2002, Vol. 4, No. 8, Part II). These amendments narrowed the scope of the officials who could be lustrated (changing the definition of collaboration and excluding certain positions), substantially diluting the laws. However, in the end the changes were ruled unconstitutional by the Polish Constitutional Tribunal and rescinded.

In sum, the scope of the lustration laws is subject to political manipulation by political parties. As party competition increases, we find, as we expected, an increase in proposed amendments to the scope and intensity of the lustration laws, *ceteris paribus*. We also have been able to begin to specify the conditions that result in the intensification or dilution of lustration.

Extending the Time Frame for Lustration

Lustration laws, in their original incarnations, were designed to expire after a certain period of time. However, once they get caught in political cycles, the time periods might be extended by political parties who find them a useful means for smearing the opposition. The extension of the time period for the laws often contravenes expressed popular sentiment.

In the Czech Republic, the lustration bill was originally drafted to last for five years (Ellis 1997: 182). It was first extended to 2000 by parliament and later indefinitely, overriding the objections of President Havel (RFE/RL, September 22, 2000, Vol. 2, No. 25, Part II; December 13, 2001, Vol. 2, No. 49, Part II). In Hungary the laws were designed to take effect on July 1, 1994 and to expire on June 30, 2000. They have continued to be extended, and in 2002 enjoyed an unusually active period of parliamentary activity and revision corresponding with particularly heated rounds of national elections (Tomiuc 2002). Yet, public opinion largely opposed continued lustration policies. Opinion polls in 2002 showed that 75 percent of Hungarians thought the investigation of the communist era secret service should end, and 49 percent of citizens were not interested in finding out which politicians collaborated with the communist era secret service (RFE/RL, September 24, 2002, Vol. 6, No. 180, Part II).[12]

Lustration in Practice: Trustworthiness of Government and Politicians

Although there are theoretical reasons to believe that lustration might be constructive in supporting the development of trustworthy government, in practice, lustration laws are susceptible to political manipulation and abuse as political entrepreneurs vie for power. The results, we hypothesize are: negative effects on perceptions of the trustworthiness of government, or at least particular government agencies; and a decrease in citizen support for lustration over time and in citizen confidence in politicians.

"Velvet Revolutions" involved roundtable negotiations with members of the communist regime.[13] The negotiated regime change was relatively peaceful and ensured that former politicians and apparatchiks retained the perks and benefits they received under the former system or were able to continue to hold office and participate in the new political system (Sustrova 1992). There was no credible break with the past political system to demonstrate to the population, no definitive ending of the former system. This fact fueled the skepticism of some citizens about the substance of governmental change and created a demand for some form of purge or cleansing. Early in the transition citizens wanted not only former regime leaders and collaborators, but also people who disproportionately benefited from the former regime or who contributed to the ideological oppression to be punished.[14] The early lustration laws were based on the assumption that officials and collaborators of the former regime would undermine the new democratic system (Boed 1999: 359). This assumption might or might not be true.

The Czech case is illustrative of why some perceived lustration was necessary early in the transition process. Following the November 1989 Velvet Revolution and the removal of the communist government, the new parliament suffered a crisis of legitimacy. Rumors abounded that the parliament was filled with former secret police agents and informers, that there had been no revolution in governance. To alleviate public anxiety, the new parliament passed a resolution to vet the entire body of officials. This allowed for the opening of all sealed secret police files on parliamentary members and the removal of individuals found to have collaborated with the secret police of the former regime (Weschler 1992: 68).

Lustration laws have not proven to be a magic panacea. There is not even consensus about the need for lustration. There is disagreement over the importance of instituting a radical break with the past given competing pressures for continuity and change in the new system. Discord over lustration also reflects the complexity of separating the innocent from the guilty in societies where so many were both. As János Kornai argues, "In a totalitarian system, everyone is to some extent a victim and to some extent a collaborator."[15] He suggests three categories of people with different relationships toward communism: (1) people who evolved from procommunist to anticommunist, (2) officials in the communist regime who did both good and bad through their positions, and (3) dissidents or members of the resistance who might have been forced to comply with the communist regime as a result of blackmail or coercion. In all three cases the individuals abetted the communist system, yet the degree of complicity and the relative harm done to others as a result of this "collaboration" differ widely. Gonzalez-Enriquez argues that the primary political effect of the Czech lustration law "was to delegitimate left-wing Marxists and the heirs of the liberalizing socialist movement of 1968," those very dissidents who fought for change and suffered most from the repression of the past (2001: 227).

Vaclav Havel, the former president of the Czech Republic, expressed the sentiments of many when he argued, "our society has a great need to face that past, to get rid of the people who have terrorized the nation and conspicuously violated human rights, to remove them from the positions that they are still holding" (Michnik and Havel 1993: 25). Arguments before the Polish Senate echoed this opinion: "The removal of former agents and collaborators of the security services from important state functions, together with the enactment of legal measures to prevent them from assuming such functions in the future, is a basic requirement of justice and an essential condition for the safe development of democracy in Poland" (Bertschi 1995: 446).

Others advocated a "thick-line" philosophy, meaning that a thick line should be drawn between the past and the present; in order to have reconciliation one cannot dig up the past or enact a wholesale purge of the state (ibid.: 444).[16] Lech Walesa, Solidarity leader and then President of Poland, has said repeatedly that the best way to allow former regime collaborators to make amends is to have them maintain their positions and use their bureaucratic expertise to build the new democratic state (Huyse 1995: 63). Jorge Semprun, a prominent Spanish writer, eloquently described the need for forgiveness and putting the past to rest in post-Franco Spain when he said "If you want to live a normal life, you must forget. Otherwise those wild snakes freed from their box will poison public life for years to come" (Michnik and Havel 1993: 24). One of the primary arguments against lustration as a tool for building a strong democratic, rule-of-law state, is its assignment of collective guilt without determining individual responsibility for actions or harm (Ellis 1997: 182). As a result, lustration may unjustly punish individuals on the basis of association rather than actual guilt, and, as such, undermine the fundamental right to due process and individual liberties inherent in a rule-of-law state. The international human rights community has spoken out strongly against lustration laws for their violation of individual liberties, such as freedom of expression, right to privacy, and due process (Cohen 1995: 27; Ellis 1997: 186).

Additionally, lustration laws may violate fair employment laws, especially if the individual is not afforded the right of appeal before removal from his position. On such a basis, the ILO has therefore spoken out against the laws in both theory and practice (Weschler 1992: 80). If the stated objective of lustration is to build trustworthy government, then unjustly accusing and punishing "innocents" will not further this cause. In fact, lustration might have the counterproductive effect of undermining individual confidence in government.

The veracity and comprehensiveness of the files themselves is cause for concern (ibid.: 69). Given the need of the secret police to disseminate false or misleading information under the former regime, the perverse incentive to enlist "dead souls" or false names, and the tendency to fabricate confessions and half-truths, it is questionable whether guilt or innocence could be accurately judged on the basis of the contents of secret police files (Los 1995: 132). In many cases, all or parts of the files have been selectively destroyed or published, leaving one to question the degree to which the files can accurately represent all or even most former collaborators. In the Czech case, prior to the parliamentary investigation of StB files, all the active files had been destroyed, leaving only the inactive oves that had already been archived for investigation (Boed 1999: 367–8). It is estimated that 90 percent of the Czech files had been destroyed or stolen before lustration even started (Kritz 1995: 350).

Adam Michnik, one of the leaders of the Polish opposition to communist rule, summarized the problems adroitly when he said, "it is absurd that the absolute and ultimate criterion for a person's suitability for performing certain functions in a democratic state should come from the internal files of the secret police" (Michnik and Havel 1993: 23). Not only are the files themselves dubious, but the handling of this information by the new "democratic" regimes has also been questionable, especially as the information has been manipulated by political parties vying for popular votes in national and local elections. Relying on these inadequate and incomplete files in order to build a foundation of trustworthy governance provides a weak foundation for any government.

Politicians and political theorists, such as Vaclav Havel, have asserted, "a severe law is better than no law at all" (ibid.: 24). Andrzej Gwiazda, one of the principal leaders of Solidarity in Poland, has a more extreme position; he contends that worrying about unjustly accusing innocents through a flawed lustration process is unnecessary. The need for purging the past by any means necessary is so great that, "it is best not to worry about moral considerations because they simply do not exist" (Gwiazda 1991: 81). A top-ranking official in the Czech Interior Ministry explained how his office viewed lustration. "I believe that those who knowingly collaborated, even if they did nothing harmful, even if they were just playing games, should be lustrated. . . . We are attempting some kind of moral cleanup here, to clean the society of those who morally compromised themselves. And one of the criteria we're using is that people not have knowingly collaborated with the StB—it's as simple as that" (Weschler 1992: 93).

Supporters of lustration argue that the government must not turn a blind eye to former regime abuses. Allowing former regime collaborators, or Communist Party officials, or members of the nomenklatura to enjoy their spoils in the new democratic system might dismay citizens who have been economically or socially disadvantaged by the dislocating reform process, and contribute to lack of public trust in the egalitarianism of the new government. To supporters of lustration, the perceived danger is twofold. First, former regime collaborators are assumed to have a broken moral compass making them a potential danger to the establishment of trustworthy, honest government. This rationale explains why both people who collaborated with the secret police as well as important communist officials or members of the nomenklatura are included in the lustration process in some countries. Second, even if former regime collaborators wanted to help develop a strong democratic order, they would always be in danger of being blackmailed because of their past. Therefore they would be ripe for corruption in the future. This rationale applies mostly to individuals who covertly collaborated with the secret police. In sum, for those who favor lustration, former collaborators as well as communist officials are perceived to be a latent danger to the creation of a new democratic system.

How do governments establish they are trustworthy? How do they demonstrate to skeptical constituents that a new moral order is being established? How do they put aside the past and construct a future that is democratic and under the rule of law? To change deeply held beliefs and norms of behavior, to correct the perception that the government is corrupt and the rulers are illegitimate, to reestablish a sense of ethical, just governance, all of these things require time, the redesign of institutions, and government action (Jones Luong 2002). There are in fact many paths to the establishment of trustworthy government (Cook et al. 2003; Jones Luong 2002). In CEE, governments have turned to lustration laws as one way to tackle the daunting task of democratic state building. Yet, as this cursory account already indicates, the lustration process is ripe with dangers for establishing objectively trustworthy government. Over time the maintenance of lustration is likely to lose popular support and negatively affect citizen confidence in politicians.

Initial Support

Initially both the public and politicians might want lustration, believing it will foster trustworthy government. In many CEE countries, citizen demands for lustration motivated the initiation of vetting laws.

Central European Union surveys of citizens early in the transition process (1992 and 1994) show substantial citizen support for the removal of former Communist Party members from positions of influence in the new regime: 56.8 percent of Czechs, 38 percent of Poles, 44 percent of Slovaks, and 42.6 percent of Hungarians favored such policies.[17] Although Poland had the lowest citizen support of lustration early in the transition, between 1994 and 1997 there was a substantial rise, from 57 percent to 76 percent (Letki 2002).[18]

Popular calls for lustration have been a function of both domestic and international factors. Changes in information availability, economic conditions, and political freedoms have motivated popular desires for government-administered transitional justice. Moreover, political or economic uncertainty in neighboring countries has also affected the relative desirability of lustration legislation.

Changes in publicly available information can increase or decrease popular demands for lustration laws. For example, in East Germany (albeit an unusual case in terms of the implementation of lustration) the public sentiment initially favored a forgive-and-forget strategy. However, the publication of the Sauer Report in 1990, in which the mammoth scope of the secret police force (Stasi) was revealed, provoked mass protests and riots through the Stasi offices.[19] As additional information was released about the scope and depth of citizen collaboration, public opinion shifted, and the opposition began demanding the prosecution and punishment of Stasi members (Moran 1994: 98).

Economically disruptive policies, ubiquitous to transitions in CEE, have also affected the timing of popular demands for lustration. In Poland in 1991 there was relatively modest support for lustration policies, with 38 per cent of people polled supportive (Kritz 1995: 35). However, after a series of economic reforms in 1991, public concerns that former communist elites would continue to enjoy unequal benefits in the new economic system affected public perceptions about the desirability of lustration. When polled one year later, after the start of the privatization program, 64 percent of Poles supported lustration (ibid.: 35). In tandem with the economic and political reforms in Hungary in the 1990s, the identity of former informers and concern about the number that held seats in the democratically elected parliament continued to preoccupy the public, pressuring political parties to adopt a lustration law (ibid.: 663).

International shocks have also affected the timing of popular support for lustration policies. The failed hard-line communist coup against Mikhail Gorbachev in late summer 1991 fueled popular sentiment in both Czechoslovakia and East Germany for lustration by reigniting a fear of a potential communist revival (Boed 1999: 368; Moran 1994: 99).

This discussion is not meant to suggest that political entrepreneurs did not manipulate public sentiment to construct lustration laws to their own advantage in the jockeying for political supremacy among political parties at the start of the transition process. However, the preliminary evidence suggests that there was citizen support in favor of lustration early in the transition process. Citizens were concerned about the possibly negative effects of leaving former communist officials in power in the nascent democratic polities.

Decline in Popular Support and Confidence in Politicians

There is no good data available on recent public attitudes toward lustration. The trends we have already reported suggest there may still be a demand for some screening for those public officials who may have been involved with the secret police. Increasingly, however, it may take the active manipulation of lustration, by either political parties or the media, to inflame citizen concern, and the effort is not always successful. The attempt by the major opposition party, FIDESZ, to revitalize the lustration issue after the hotly contested 2002 Hungarian elections is a case in point. The surveys show little decline in support for the target, Prime Minister Péter Medgyessy (RFE/RL, August 12, 2002, Vol. 6, No. 150, Part II).[20]

There is just beginning to be country data that evaluates trust in politicians over time. The acquisition and analysis of this data will make it possible to evaluate our hypothesis that the maintenance of lustration will reduce trust and confidence in politicians, particularly politicians from those parties that advocate lustration practices or use the files to smear the opposition.

Conclusion

This review of the arguments and secondary evidence on post-1989 lustration processes in CEE suggests the need to modify our initial model and then to test its implications systematically. Although the tests will have to wait for the completion of future research, we can offer some preliminary conclusions about the political economy of the lustration process and the effects of lustration on trustworthy government.

It is obvious that there needs to be more precise specification of the interests and goals of the political actors, the key players in our model. The first step is a more realistic, albeit still simplified, catalogue of the key types of political parties in CEE.[21] The reemergence of socialist parties, on the one hand, and nationalist parties, on the other, complicates the political scene. Although many of their officials are as politically opportunistic as the candidates of any other party, their electoral and legislative strategies are more likely to lie in the termination rather than the continuation of lustration. They are outside the cycle of escalation we originally modeled.

We also need to have a clearer picture of the constitutional courts. Under what conditions are they likely to be autonomous, and under what conditions will that political insulation lead them to define certain lustration practices as unconstitutional? What is the evidence that would permit us to arbitrate among competing hypotheses about their role in the lustration process? Equally, we need a more refined model and better evidence about the conditions for effective pressure by the electorate. Although there is some evidence of citizen fatigue with lustration, do people actually vote against politicians who advocate lustration? Or is this an issue of secondary importance to voters?

Finally, there is the role of international organizations. Here again, we need a more nuanced classification. There are international organizations capable of exerting direct, virtually coercive pressure on CEE governments. For example, the EU requires governments to meet certain standards for membership, something most (but not all) CEE politicians seek. Other international organizations exert pressure through information intended to shame a government or to bring its abuses to the attention of other international organizations with more authority.

Understanding the lustration process is interesting in its own right but does not answer the question of its effect on the construction of trustworthy government. We hypothesize that the political manipulation of lustration laws by politicians undermines their trustworthiness in the eyes of citizens. We hope eventually to find the kind of survey evidence that will enable us to establish this observation as an empirical fact. The trustworthiness of politicians and governments are conceptually separable, however. Even if citizens sometimes conflate the two, we as scholars cannot.

One crucial factor in establishing post-transitional trustworthy government is its success in establishing a constitution that will in fact promote justice and fairness. This undertaking has both backward- and forward-looking components, which are often in contradiction with each other. There does need to be some break from the past while constructing a set of institutions that ensure human rights and fair processes in the years to come. Jon Elster (1999) warns of the complexities of sorting out the motives of the relevant actors in the transition. Arthur Stinchcombe (1995) eloquently argues that lustration ought to play a minor role in delegitimizing the past and building support for the new regime; he fears its constitutional consequences for opposing parties and other kinds of competitors. Here lies the danger of lustration for building trustworthy government. If, as Stinchcombe fears, it undermines the creation of a constitution credibly committed to due process and fairness, then it damages, possibly irretrievably, the possibility of trustworthy government.

Although we morally oppose the violation of anyone's civil rights, as social scientists we note that many democracies engaged in horrific or at least nondemocratic practices in their transitions (and later). These actions create untrustworthiness in some regards but not in all, and not forever. The CEE, too, may weather the less appealing acts associated with lustration.

Notes

* This essay benefited from the criticisms of János Kornai and Susan Rose-Ackerman, the organizers of the project, and the other participants in the workshop. We are particularly grateful to Antal Örkény, András Sajó, Péter Hack, György Péteri, Anna Grzymala-Busse, Pauline Jones Luong, Bo Rothstein, and Barry Weingast for their insightful readings and comments. Barna Ildikó helped us in our largely unsuccessful search for useful and current public opinion data. We thank her and the Budapest Collegium for supporting this research. Levi also thanks the Russell Sage Foundation for its continuing support of her research.

1. Oxford English Dictionary (2001) at http://dictionary.oed.com.
2. Natalia Letki helped clarify the details of the Polish process and Péter Hack the Hungarian.
3. For exceptions see Letki (2002) and Gonzales-Enriquez (2001).
4. These questions were asked of citizens in both 1990 and 1991 to gauge citizen wants with respect to transitional justice (Lex Zétényi-Takács, Hungary, December 5–10, 1991. Unpublished report).
5. Grzymala-Busse (2002) does an excellent job explaining electoral dynamics in the transitional societies of Hungary, Poland, the Czech Republic, and Slovakia and accounting for the reemergence of communist parties as viable political alternatives in the new democratic systems. See especially chapter 4 and the conclusion. See also Tworzecki (2003) who focuses on Hungary, Poland, and the Czech Republic.
6. János Kornai repeated this witty observation in conversation, October 13, 2002, Collegium Budapest. The actual source is unknown.
7. This discussion draws largely on Levi (1997, 1998). See also Sztompka (1999) and Rose-Ackerman (2001) for additional and important discussions of the conditions under which citizens are likely to believe their government is trustworthy or untrustworthy in post-communist states. Hardin (2001) offers a more general set of arguments.
8. The question of what citizens in a democracy expect of a government to consider it trustworthy is elaborated and explored empirically in Levi (1997).
9. We are indebted to Anna Grzymala-Busse for bringing this point to our attention.
10. Personal conversation with Margaret Levi in Budapest, November 19, 2002, which was followed by an e-mail correspondence with Levi on February 10, 2003.
11. This is similar to the German Gauck Commission model. One important difference should be noted. Unlike other CEE countries, the Hungarian law provided for the name of informants in the files to be blackened to protect their identities. See Tomiuc (2002).
12. This poll was conducted on September 11–12 by the Median Market Research agency, and was originally published in the daily *Népszabadság* on September 23, 2002.
13. See Brown (1991) for an excellent country-by-country discussion of the preliminary roundtable negotiations between the democratic opposition and the communist officials in power during the velvet revolutions.
14. Summary of polling information that was part of the Lex Zétényi-Takács report.
15. Personal conversations by the authors with János Kornai, October 2002.
16. The "policy of the thick line" was used in former Polish Prime Minister Tadeusz Mazowiecki's first speech, in which he talked about the need to draw a thick line between the past and the present (Michnik and Havel 1993: 21). The interpretation of the thick-line philosophy was influenced by comments from Adam Michnik, in which he couched Mazowiecki's policy in terms of setting the past to rest. Special thanks to Natalia Letki for pointing out Michnik's role in influencing the public's understanding of Mazowiecki's speech in which he introduced this policy.
17. The Central European Union Poll information for 1992 and 1994 is taken from Letki (2002).
18. The information regarding the polling is scant. There is no systematic information on who was polled, how individuals were polled, what definition of lustration was used at any point in time, or how citizens understood the question. There is no information regarding what exactly the term "lustration" meant for each poll. Despite information limitations, the polls are useful in presenting a general sense of citizen perceptions of the lustration process and constitute the only information available.
19. The Sauer Report revealed that the Stasi force consisted of 85,000 regular employees, of whom only 30,000 had been dismissed. It also included 109,000 informers, which means that one out of every eight citizens was a collaborator (Moran 1994: 98).
20. Medgyessy was the target of a major lustration campaign in summer 2002, which sparked the creation of investigatory commissions to review the backgrounds of parliamentarians (RFE/RL

Newsline, on-line research reports at http://www.rferl.org/newsline/Summer 2002). We benefited greatly from our conversations with fellow colleagues at the Budapest Collegium during fall 2002 who gave us firsthand information about the actual political manipulation of lustration laws in Hungary.

21. There is work on this, e.g., Kitshelt et al. (1999), Grzynrala-Busse (2002), and Tworzecki (2003), on which we shall build.

References

Ackerman, Bruce. 1992. *The Future of Liberal Revolution.* New Haven CT: Yale University Press.

Aguilar, Paloma. 2002. *Memory and Amnesia: The Role of the Spanish Civil War in the Transition to Democracy.* New York: Berghahn Books.

Barahona de Brito, Alexandra. 2001. "Truth, Justice, Memory, and Democratisation in the Southern Cone." In A. Barahona de Brito, C. Gonzalez-Enriquez, and P. Aguilar (eds.), pp. 119–60.

Barahona de Brito, A., Carmen Gonzalez-Enriquez, and Paloma Aguilar (eds.). 2001. *The Politics of Memory: Transitional Justice in Democratizing Societies.* Oxford: Oxford University Press.

Barahona de Brito, Alexandra, Paloma Aguilar, and Carmen Gonzalez-Enriquez, 2001. "Introduction." In A. Barahona de Brito, C. Gonzalez-Enriquez, and P. Aguilar (eds.), pp. 1–39.

Bates, Robert, Avner Greif, Margaret Levi, Jean-Laurent Rosenthal, and Barry Weingast. 1998. *Analytic Narratives.* Princeton NJ: Princeton University Press.

Berat, Lynn and Yossi Shain. 1995. "Retribution or Truth Telling in South Africa? Legacies of the Transitional Phase." *Law & Social Inquiry* 20: 163–90.

Bertschi, C. Charles. 1995. "Lustration and the Transition to Democracy: The Cases of Poland and Bulgaria." *East European Quarterly* 28: 435–51.

Boed, Roman. 1999. "An Evaluation of the Legality and Efficacy of Lustration as a Tool of Transitional Justice." *Columbia Journal of Transitional Law* 37: 357–402.

Brown, J. F. 1991. *Surge to Freedom: The End of Communist Rule in Eastern Europe.* Durham NC: Duke University Press.

Burns, Nancy and Donald Kinder. 2000. *Social Trust and Democratic Politics.* Ann Arbor MI: National Election Studies.

Cohen, Stanley. 1995. "State Crimes of Previous Regimes: Knowledge, Accountability, and the Policing of the Past." *Law & Social Inquiry* 20: 7–50.

Cook, Karen S., Russell Hardin, and Margaret Levi. 2003. *Trust and Its Alternatives.* Manuscript. New York: Russell Sage Foundation.

Darski, Jozef. 1993. "Decommunization in Eastern Europe." *Uncaptive Minds* Winter–Spring: 73–81.

Ellis, Mark. 1997. "Purging the Past: The Current State of Lustration Laws in the Former Communist Bloc." *Law and Contemporary Problems* 59: 181–96.

Elster, Jon. 1999. "Reason, Interest, and Passion in the East European Transitions." *Social Science Information* 38: 499–519.

Gibney, Mark. 1997. "Prosecuting Human Rights Violations from a Previous Regime: The East European Experience." *East European Quarterly* 31(1): 93–110.

Goldstone, Justice Richard. 2000. "Reconstructing Peace in Fragmented Societies." Paper presented at the Conference on Facing Ethnic Conflicts. Bonn, Center for Development Research, December 14–16.

Gonzalez-Enriquez, Carmen. 2001. "De-Communization and Political Justice in Central and Eastern Europe." In A. Barahona de Brito, C. Gonzalez-Enriquez, and P. Aguilar (eds.), pp. 218–247.

Grzymala-Busse, Anna. 2002. *Redeeming the Communist Past: The Regeneration of Communist Parties in East Central Europe.* New York: Cambridge University Press.

Gwiazda, Andrzej. 1991. "Justice is Not Revenge." *Uncaptive Minds* Spring: 81–2.

Hardin, Russell. 2001. *Trust and Trustworthiness.* New York: Russell Sage Foundation.

Huntington, Samuel. 1991. *The Third Wave: Democratization in the Late Twentieth Century.* Norman OK: University of Oklahoma Press.

Huyse, Luc. 1995. "Justice After Transition: On the Choices Successor Elites Make in Dealing with the Past." *Law and Social Inquiry* 20: 51–78.

Jones Luong, Pauline. 2002. *Institutional Change and Continuity in Post-Soviet Central Asia.* New York: Cambridge University Press.

Kitschelt, Herbert, Zdenka Mansfeldova, Radoslaw Markowski, and Gabor Toka. 1999. *Post-Communist Party Systems: Competition, Representation, and Inter-Party Cooperation.* New York: Cambridge University Press.

Kritz, Neil (ed.). 1995. *Transitional Justice.* Washington DC: United States Institute of Peace Studies.

Letki, Natalia. 2002. "Lustration and Democratisation in East-Central Europe." *Europe–Asia Studies* 54: 529–52.

Levi, Margaret. 1997. *Consent, Dissent and Patriotism.* New York: Cambridge University Press.

———. 1998. "A State of Trust." In V. Braithwaite and M. Levi (eds.), *Trust and Governance*, pp. 77–101. New York: Russell Sage Foundation.

Levi, Margaret and Laura Stoker. 2000. "Political Trust and Trustworthiness." *Annual Review of Political Science* 3: 475–507.

Los, Maria. 1995. "Lustration and Truth Claims: Unfinished Revolutions in Central Europe." *Law and Social Inquiry* 20: 117–61.

Michnik, Adam and Vaclav Havel. 1993. "Justice or Revenge." *Journal of Democracy* 4: 20–7.

Moran, John. 1994. "The Communist Tortures of Eastern Europe: Prosecute and Punish or Forgive and Forget?" *Communist and Post-Communist Studies* 27: 95–109.

Offe, Claus. 1992. "Coming to Terms with Past Injustices: An Introduction to Legal Strategies Available in Post-communist Societies." *Archives Européennes de Sociologie* 33: 195–201.

———. 1996. *Varieties of Transition: The East European and East German Experience.* London: Cambridge University Press.

Popkin, Margaret and Naomi Roht-Arriaza. 1995. "Truth as Justice: Investigatory Commissions in Latin America." *Law & Social Inquiry* 20: 79–116.

Rahn, Wendy and T. J. Rudolph. 2000. *Report on the NES 2000 Pilot Election Items.* Ann Arbor MI: National Election Studies.

Rose-Ackerman, Susan. 2001. "Trust and Honesty in Post-Socialist Societies." *Kyklos* 54: 415–43.

Rothstein, Bo. 2000. "Trust, Social Dilemmas and Collective Memories." *Journal of Theoretical Politics* 12: 477–501.

———. 2004. "Social Trust and Honesty in Government: A Causal Mechanisms Approach." In J. Kornai, B. Rothstein, and S. Rose-Ackerman (eds.), *Creating Social Trust in Post-Socialist Transition*, pp. 13–30. New York: Palgrave Macmillan.

Sciolino, Elaine and Emma Daly. 2002. "Spaniards at Last Confront the Ghost of Franco." *New York Times* November 11, p. A3.

Sieder, Rachel. 2001. "War, Peace, and Memory Politics in Central America." In A. Barahona de Brito, C. Gonzalez-Enriquez, and P. Aguilar (eds.), pp. 161–89.

Stinchcombe, Arthur L. 1995. "Lustration as a Problem of the Social Basis of Constitutionalism." *Law & Social Inquiry* 20: 245–73.

Stokes, Susan C. 2001a. *Mandates and Democracy: Neoliberalism by Surprise in Latin America.* New York: Cambridge University Press.

——— (ed.). 2001b. *Public Support for Market Reforms in New Democracie.* New York: Cambridge University Press.

Sustrova, Petruska. 1992. "The Lustration Controversy." *Uncaptive Minds* Summer: 129–34.

Sztompka, Piotr. 1999. *Trust.* New York: Cambridge University Press.

Tomiuc, Eugen. 2002. "Hungary: Government Proposes Further Opening of Communist-Era Files." RFE/RL Research Reports June 27 at www.rferl.org/nca/features/.

Tworzecki, Hubert. 2003. *Learning to Choose: Electoral Politics in East-Central Europe.* Palo Alto CA: Stanford University Press.

Tyler, Tom R. 1990. *Why People Obey the Law.* New Haven CT: Yale University Press.

Weschler, Lawrence. 1992. "The Velvet Purge: The Trials of Jan Kavan." *The New Yorker* October 19, pp. 66–96.

Wilson, Richard A. 2001. "Justice and Legitimacy in the South African Transition." In A. Barahona de Brito, C. Gonzalez-Enriquez, and P. Aguilar (eds.), pp. 190–217.

PART II

Corruption and State Capture

CHAPTER FOUR

Political Corruption: Conceptual and Practical Issues

Claus Offe[*]

The agenda of this essay is simple and unoriginal. First, I want to cut down the concept of corruption to a scope that minimizes its gray zones and fuzziness. An (incomplete) list of phenomena somehow neighboring (or perhaps forming subcases of) political corruption reads as follows: fraud, embezzlement, theft, nepotism, cronyism, gifts, tips, donations, clientelism, connections, networks, lobbying, bargaining, mafioso protection rackets, patronage, conflict of interest, kleptocracy. Given this vast range of phenomena associated with "corruption," it does not appear overly pedantic to ask for some demarcation lines. Here, I focus on "political" corruption, suggest a typology, and review some of its forms and aspects, including social stratification of corruption. Second, I discuss the damage caused by corruption. Finally, I offer some thoughts on how corruption might be controlled according to the precepts offered by economists, political scientists, and sociologists, and specifically on the role of social trust in anticorruption strategies.

Narrowing Down and Subdividing an Overextended Semantic Field

Corruption is an elusive phenomenon, both conceptually and empirically. It is a bag of concepts that academics, as well as organizations (such as Transparency International, TI), have filled with too many different things. One of the most widely used definitions is the one proposed by Nye (1967: 419). Its components are (a) the behavior deviating "from the formal duties of a public role" (which duties may be constituted by legal and/or social norms), (b) "because of private-regarding ... pecuniary or status gains"; such behavior includes (c) "bribery" but also (d) "nepotism" but excludes (e) other "behavior that might be regarded as offensive to moral standards," such as, supposedly, the killing of an opposition journalist by police officers.

There is a clear need to narrow down the scope of the concept. To do so, I suggest the following. Corruption is the voluntary violation of legal (and beyond that, social) norms performed by "public" actors.[1] But such norms can be violated in various ways. Not every instance of dishonest acts of public officials, or any self-serving act that knowingly harms the public good and violates social and legal norms is a case of corruption. Officials can do things falling under component (e) of Nye's definition. This is a crime, but not a crime of corruption: it is an abuse of office. Also, public officials can use the powers of their office to enrich themselves unilaterally (embezzlement) or extend illegal favors to persons close to them—component (d). Although such crimes are often included in the concept of corruption, I propose to exclude them as long as the illegal appropriation is *uni*lateral, such as theft, which is a subset of component (b).

Corruption in the strict sense (as I propose to define it) is *bi*lateral, a voluntary and deliberate illicit deal between two actors involving the exchange of official decisions for some payment, or promise of payment, be it in cash or kind. Corruption is *political* corruption if at least one of the two actors belongs to the public realm, widely understood. That is to say, the person must hold a public office or an electoral mandate or perform a professional service the execution of which is supposed (and normally trusted) to be guided by public-regarding and universalist considerations.

The reason to propose this definition derives from the following consideration. The universe of social action can be classified as belonging to one of three categories: it is either a *political* action, a *market* action, or a *communal* action (Goodin 2003; Offe 2000; Philp 1997: 448–9). Very briefly, political action is embedded in a state structure and framed within features such as the acquisition and use of legitimate authority, accountability, hierarchy, and the use of rule-bound power for giving orders and extracting resources. Its intrinsic standard of goodness is *legality*. Market action is recognized by the contract-based pursuit of acquisitive interests within the framework of legal rules that specify, among other things such as property rights, the universe of items that can be "for sale," and which cannot. Its standard of goodness is success or *profitability*. Finally, communal action is defined by a sense of reciprocal obligation among persons who share significant markers of identity and cultural belonging, that is, belonging to the same family, religious group, locality, and so on. The standard of goodness of communal action is shared *values and shared notions of virtue*. Now, in each of these three realms of social action, we can distinguish "appropriate," or consistent, modes from "hybrid" and inappropriate ones.

Limiting the discussion to the sphere of political action, there are three ways in which actors can engage in inappropriate forms of action. First, they can act politically yet break the frame of accountability, legal rules, and so on, and employ the powers of office for private and self-serving ends; they act in rent-seeking ways rather than according to their rules of office. That is to say, they tyrannize citizens, steal or embezzle public assets, and impose arbitrary "taxes" in order to increase their personal income. In sum, they overstep the institutional rules and constraints and thereby "privatize" the state power that is attached to their office; they act as if they *were* "the state," rather than representatives of the people, or civil servants.[2] This type of inappropriate political action, however, must be conceptually distinguished from the two other hybrids. In the case of "corruption" (as defined here) politicians and public officials act as if they were merchants of decisions. And in the case of nepotism, "contacts," "connections," and other kinds of informal influence, politicians and public officials behave as if they acted in a communal or family context. The phrase "as if" suggests the idea of the action being misplaced and inappropriate, with the logic of one sphere of action spilling over into, infiltrating, or contaminating another sphere.

To be sure, the verdict that the exercise of power or familial relations or commercial calculations occur "in the wrong place" can only emerge in "modern" societies, defined as societies with a strong functional differentiation of these spheres and their respective modes of action. Hence in societies where this differentiation is weak—as is the case in (former) state-socialist economies (cf. Ledeneva 1998) or tribal polities—the contamination of spheres of action will not raise the same objections of inappropriateness and disorder. These societies do not have a "moral theory" of corruption. Note that this caveat leads us into two paradoxes which are, however, hard to avoid. First, if there exists neither functional differentiation of the three spheres nor a widely shared recognition of the distinctive standards of proper action within each of them, there also exists no "corruption" as an objectionable pattern of action. As long as the pattern is "normal," it disappears from the cognitive map of the society in which it *is* normal (Rose-Ackerman 1999).[3] In such societies, which lack standards of separation between political, economic, and communal modes of action, it is only from an external perspective of observers applying such standards that corruption becomes visible as such. A second and related paradox is this: In societies where the separation of spheres and related modes of appropriate action is present, corrupt deals will be considered violations of legal and other social norms, and hence sanctioned. As a consequence, actors involved in corrupt deals will try to hide their deals, thus rendering the phenomenon hard to observe. If it were openly carried out and thus easily observable, we would no longer speak of "corruption," as the term connotes a sense of inappropriateness or illegality that gives rise to feelings of indignation and anger over unjust acts and thus leads the partners of corrupt deals to hide as well as they can. In contrast, political corruption that is routinely, openly, and ubiquitously practiced by, for instance, tax, customs, health, or education officials without being monitored, sanctioned, or even complained about by its victims ceases to be "corruption." Instead, it is more accurately described as the normal mode of operation of a thoroughly "uncivil" economy (Rose 1992). If the widespread incidence of corruption is commented upon by the majority of its direct victims with a sense of fatalism, realism, cynicism, and resignation (cf. Transparency International 2001b: 27), it ceases to be conceived of as a disorder with the potential of being controlled and eventually overcome. Rather, it is taken for granted as an unpleasant fact of life. People may well know that corruption is bad in terms of its economic consequences; but they still may not consider it worth of moral protest or legal complaint in most cases.[4] Thus in societies that have a moral theory of corruption, corruption is virtually impossible to observe and measure; and vice versa, the phenomenon is easily detected (by external observers) where the concept does not exist.

Concentrating on corruption as the selling and buying of public decisions implies that the empirically often related, though conceptually distinct, phenomena of unilateral "embezzlement" and "nepotism" will not count as "corruption" here. Who are the agents involved in corrupt deals? In political science we are used to the rough distinction between "elites" (comprising all roles committed to the making of collectively binding decisions and performed in legislatures, the state executive at its various levels, and the judiciary) vs. nonelites, or "masses." Applying this binary code to corrupt deals, we get four kinds of corrupt transaction. First, private corruption as an illicit act of "selling what is not for sale," for example, a businessman who bribes an employee of a competitor in order to have him reveal a commercial secret of his employer or a bookmaker bribing a cricket team to produce a highly unlikely outcome of a game.[5] Such cases are of no interest in the present context of "political" corruption. Second, nonelite actors bribing elite actors, which will be the focus of the present discussion. Third, elite actors bribing other elite actors, as in the case when an incumbent government buys votes from members of the opposition party in order to save legislation contested internally (within the governing coalition).[6] Here, we enter a gray zone between the phenomena of corruption and bargaining: An incumbent government may not explicitly buy votes from the opposition but rather engages in vote trading or budgetary concessions across levels of government. For example, it may offer benefits to the governments of federal states, whose support in the second chamber may be decisive to getting federal legislation passed.[7] Fourth, elite actors can also try to "purchase" private support, namely the votes of segments of the electorate through preelection favors. This is where we enter another gray zone between political corruption and "clientelism." However, and as long as the ballot is secret, bribers in the political elite cannot possibly know who exactly has voted for them in exchange for such favors. The only case when it makes unambiguous sense to political elites to pay bribes to private actors (as opposed to collecting bribes from them in exchange for favors) is when the leadership of protest groups can be secretly bought off and induced to abandon their mobilization efforts. In contrast to this case, what makes ordinary preelection favors just marginally interesting in the present context is the fact that they are rarely concealed from public perception as is the case with the (by definition) clandestine deals of the second type, namely illegal transactions across the private/public divide where private actors purchase public decisions in illicit ways.

As public officials are involved, we speak of "political" corruption, regardless of whether the "price" for the decision purchased (the bribe) ends up in the private pocket of the official, or in the election campaign budget of a candidate, or the bank account of a political party.[8] In the latter case,[9] political corruption is "political" in the double sense that (a) at least one and possibly both of the partners are holders of public office *and* that (b) the revenues from the deal are also used for political purposes, the standard case being that of illegal political party and campaign finance.[10] Note that the term "purchase" also covers the notion of investment, as when I purchase the title to a future stream of income, the actual amount and point in time of which remains more or less uncertain at the point of paying. For instance, if a business association provides (illegal) campaign funding to a political party, the opportunity for the party to reciprocate (and thus to provide a motivation for the continuation of donations) may yet be quite uncertain as to its timing and substantive content. Nor is political corruption restricted to cash payment as the currency in which desired decisions are being purchased. Such purchases can also be made in kind.[11] It suffices that the payment is motivated by the expectation that some kind of private return will be forthcoming (Rose-Ackerman 1999: 92). A corrupt interaction is one that follows the logic of *quid pro quo* or *do ut des*. In the absence of that motivation, the payment becomes either a personal gift or a donation for a public cause. When used within a social science context, the term "corruption" should be stripped of its overtones of moral disapproval of acts and persons. Corruption is something that results from (and must thus be explained in terms of) incentives, opportunity structures, and social norms, not the character deficiencies or inherent dishonesty of the persons involved in it.

Political Corruption: A Typology

Even if we strictly exclude, as I have proposed to do, any unilateral action of officials (such as embezzlement, nepotism) or, for that matter, unilateral acts of clients (such as gifts and tips) from the universe of political corruption proper, a variety of types of corrupt exchanges remains.[12] Let me distinguish four of them:

1. Inherently "illegal" sale of goods and services. State agents allow an illegal business to operate and receive a bribe in return; army officers sell firearms, customs officials sell confiscated drugs to private clients— transactions in which neither side is permitted by law to do what it does. The legal prohibition of intoxicating liquors and gambling in the United States did not make these markets disappear, instead, it created "pervasive corruption of law enforcement officers" (Rose-Ackerman 1999: 40).

2. Arbitrary distortion of principal–agent relations. This applies if agents are making decisions that they have a right to make, but due to the bribes involved, they do this in inappropriate ways and with inappropriate outcomes. In a constitutional liberal democracy, the entire body of members of the legislature and public officials can be thought of as "agents" of the principal, "the people," as well as the judiciary and executive branch of

government as the agent, with the legislature as their principal. Any deviation from the proper course of action as prescribed by the procedural rules of this principal–agent relationship, to the extent it is premised upon payments (in cash or kind), or promises of payments, made to any of the agents constitutes a case of political corruption. Note that, in contrast to type 1, the legislature is perfectly *entitled* to make laws, and the officials within the administration to make decisions on public procurements, provision of services, and so on. What makes these decisions corrupt is the improper course of decision making caused by bribes, thus breaking the trust that the principal has extended to him. Examples include the granting of contracts to less efficient suppliers, or the charging of special levies on government services that are meant to be provided free of charge or according to professional judgment (e.g., of teachers in the case of grades), or the distortion of waiting lines in favor of those willing to pay "speed money." Legally undeserved access to benefits granted by officials for a bribe applies to goods and services such as government contracts, privatization deals, import/export licenses, academic exams, recruitment to public sector positions, professional licenses, and the allocation of telephone services, passports, driver's licenses, visas, and so on. This type of political corruption also includes the taking of bribes for services that are legally free, which results in the restriction of access to those willing to pay. It can also involve the purchasing of *relative* advantage, such as bribing an official into harassing one's competitor through inspections, and so on.

3. The sale and purchase of selective favors through commission and omission. The first means giving people, for a price, what they are not entitled to according to a properly functioning principal–agent relation, as in all variants of type 2. The second, type 3, involves *relieving* citizens, again for a price, *from performing duties* that they are legally obliged to perform. What the private actor gets in return for the money spent is *in*action or a *non*decision (Bachrach and Baratz 1970). The official refrains from applying measures that imply negative consequences for the client, although such measures are mandated by the rules governing the conduct of his office. Although political corruption that consists in the illegal *failure* of officials to act is rarely studied (as it is exceedingly hard to pin down), there seems to be a huge market potential for this kind of inaction or nondecisions and the purchase of exemption from legal duty. The majority of political corruption cases that have been brought to German courts belong to this category. For instance, officials can turn a blind eye to profitable violations of legal standards designed to protect consumers' interests, workers' interests, or environmental concerns; police officers and the judiciary can avert negative sanctions in return for a bribe; tax office clerks can postpone the processing of files;[13] the leadership of political parties can silence legislative initiatives that are unwelcome to some specific benefactor of that party (Crenson 1971); issues can be removed from the agenda, decisions postponed, and incriminating documents made to disappear from the files of the administration. Examiners in ancient China are reported to have accepted bribes for

failing to scrutinize the knowledge and competence of those applying for public office. Even if uncovered, excuses such as lack of time, lack of staff, lack of competence, errors, and so on, are easily available and hard to disprove.

Such opaqueness of the transaction suggests that political corruption through inaction is less costly for the official in terms of his risk of being caught and sanctioned. If this asymmetry between decisions and nondecisions/inaction were to be generalized, the relative size of this variety of political corruption could be explained in terms of the low cost of its supply. But that raises the question of the determinants of demand. It is a cliché in the literature that high levels of regulation breed corruption.[14] Highly regulated political economies impose many and costly restriction upon private actors, which these actors will be interested in circumventing, if need be, by paying a price for officials' acts of omission. This is the static hypothesis. The dynamic hypothesis is this: In order to expand the market for nondecisions, political actors will attempt to increase the level of regulation,[15] and/or change regulations frequently, and/or put them in ambiguous or incomprehensible language so as to misguide clients as to what is permitted and what is not. All this adds to the probability of private actors being in need of, and ready to pay for, the services of officials who are willing to "look the other way," thus refraining from enforcing duties and sanctions. As a result, officials would put themselves in the power position[16] of determining both supply and demand in the corruption market.

4. Extracting payment for the arbitrary enforcement of *fictitious* duties—a mirror image of the usurpation of fictitious rights in type 1. This is the case of a *coerced* deal, or extortion. An extreme case is police officers stopping bicycle riders and fining them for the nonpossession of a drivers' license for bicycles even though no such licenses are legally required. Less extreme is the case of sanitation inspectors visiting (and each time closing down for half a day) a restaurant no less than 18 times per year, thus creating a source of income as the victim pays for an end to such visits (Transparency International 2001b). As long as the law does not state how often inspections must be performed or that they must be equally performed on all relevant businesses, such exploitative arbitrariness is impossible to control. A standard technique that allows for the establishment (and remunerated nonenforcement) of made-up duties is to keep legal obligations ambiguous, inconsistent, or incomprehensible. The less clear-cut and transparent the citizens' duties are, the more arbitrarily can authorities act and the easier it becomes for them to coerce citizens to pay a ransom.

On the Social and Organizational
Stratification of Corruption

Corruption is a deal that takes place—at least as far as the supply of corrupt decisions is concerned—among persons, not organizations. The officials selling decisions for a bribe, however, derive their ability to engage in corrupt interaction from their position within some state organization. The initiator can be either the private agent or the public official, except in cases of type 4 where predatory officials always take the first step. The interaction itself is premised upon a relationship of personal trust. Perversely enough, the perception of political corruption being widespread does not only *destroy* trust at a general level, such as trust in the fair conduct of business and administrative practices; it also *presupposes* trust of a more specific kind, namely trust between the participants in the corrupt deals, at least those of type 2. Each of the two partners needs sufficient reasons to believe in two things. First, each must believe that the other side will not expose the agent to third parties who may be capable and willing to sanction the corrupt wrongdoing. Second, trust is needed to generate some subjective assurance on the part of the briber that the bribed will actually deliver what he has been bribed for, and vice versa, as there is obviously no recourse to the court system to enforce the *quid pro quo*.[17] Such trust, or the standards of (something equivalent to) "thieves honor," is all the more called for if the decision by which the bribe is to be reciprocated or the bribe itself (as to kind and point of payment) are poorly specified or delayed into the future. It is therefore to be expected that corrupt interaction thrives particularly well under conditions where the partners "trust each other because of close personal ties that depend on kinship, business links, or friendship" (cf. Rose-Ackerman 1999: 97–8). It also helps if both sides anticipate that their respective partner will be around for the foreseeable future, as he "cannot easily exit the market and move to a less corrupt community elsewhere" (ibid.: 101).[18]

There are, however, surrogates for trust. If the briber and the bribed have reasons to *dis*trust the state as to its *capacity* for sanctioning corruption, they need less trust of the first type (trust in not being exposed) in order to enter into the deal, as the risk of being caught is reduced under such conditions even if the trustworthiness of the partner cannot be fully ascertained. Alternatively, personal trust can be limited if not just the supplier of the corrupt decision, but his hierarchically superior supervisor as well is also being bribed. In this case, part of the bribe is converted into "hush money," or second-order bribes, which is used to undermine the *willingness* of potential sanctioning agents to act.[19] This points to one of the many mechanisms through which corruption breeds corruption, or corruption becomes addictive. If supervisors (as well as the supervisors of supervisors) need to be bribed into silence, bribe takers are under constant pressure to expand the volume of trade; inversely, the increased volume of trade requires an increased volume of second-order bribes, thus leading to the upward proliferation of corruption. The willingness of the superiors of the briber to sanction can be deactivated if the decision that is being purchased serves some interest of the organization to which the briber belongs. If an employee of a private company manages to bribe a public official, and if that transaction results in a procurement contract given to the company, the employee's supervisors do not have a strong incentive to sanction the employee's wrongdoing. The same applies to the corrupt acquisition of funds for a political party. The incentive to sanction bribing will be even weaker if the superior can claim, according to the logic of "rational ignorance," to be unaware of the details of the employee's action (Rose Ackerman 1999: 57). If the exchange is initiated by an official, he can sometimes leave it open whether the payment requested is a fee, a donation, or a bribe. For example, the parents of high school students in Moldova are asked by teachers for a payment to help buy teaching materials. The understanding of parents is, however, that failure to pay such "fees" will result in their sons and daughters getting poorer grades (Transparency International 2001b).

But such collusion and ambiguity will help to solve just one of two problems: the protection of the parties involved from external sanctions. It does not solve the other problem, the internal risk, that the bribe is not reciprocated by the decision promised, or vice versa. Here, the surrogate for trust is the threat of violence through private enforcement agents that substitute for what in legal exchanges is performed by civil courts. Mafia-type enforcement agencies make corrupt deals possible even among partners who have no reason to trust each other (cf. Varese 1994).

The alternative to lower participants in an organization—that is, those operating at the interface with clients (like customs officers)—engaging in corrupt deals is corruption at the top of state agencies or political parties. This presupposes that their partners in the private sector are also located at the top, for example, of some corporation or a business interest association. This alternative involves the advantage that fewer people will have access to knowledge about the corrupt deal, and that it typically can be performed on a larger scale corresponding to the greater scope of decisions made at the top. Here, decisions on "big" deals of type 2 are being made, such as decisions on arms procurements, large privatization projects, the granting of a license to exploit a mine or oil field. High-level corruption is harder to expose, as the top personnel can take precautions in order to protect themselves from being detected. That advantage, however, is partly offset by the greater publicity and more severe consequences that are likely to follow if the deal is uncovered.

Let me suggest three hypotheses concerning the organizational and social stratification of corruption. First, the higher up in the hierarchy of the state organization, the more likely it is that decisions of type 2 (e.g., the allocation of tangible benefits, such as construction or procurement contracts) are being traded. In contrast, the nonenforcement of duties through acts of omission—type 3—is what agents at the lower end of the hierarchy can perform without risking sanction. Second, the standards of public condemnation (and, as a consequence, the standards of moral inhibition) differ widely depending on the hierarchical position of the officials and the social position of bribers. Those closer to the bottom of the hierarchy, those with lesser income and job security, and those who are in direct contact with clients (policemen, customs officers, border guards, tax office clerks) can count upon a more lenient public assessment and greater forgiveness for their corrupt acts than those at the top, and particularly so if the low-level officials' clients also belong to the ranks of "ordinary people." This is likely to be so regardless of the fact that, arguably, the aggregate damage inflicted upon society as a whole and its capacity for developing "formal rational" economic and political structures is greater in the case of low-level than in high-level corruption. A third hypothesis is that in type 2 corruption, where decisions concern tangible benefits, the private-demand side will take the initiative in order to obtain the desired privilege, whereas with type 3 the initiative is more likely to be taken by the supply side.

Are those in the higher ranks of status, wealth, and power more likely to engage in corrupt activities than their less privileged fellow citizens? On the one hand, powerful and wealthy actors are likely to have the resources at their disposal that are needed to purchase major decisions. If need be, they can offer benefits that none but the most honest officials can resist. Similarly, monopoly power will be needed on the supply side in order to extort bribes. However, the socially powerful may not even *need* to invest their plentiful resources in corruption, because the reputation they enjoy for being powerful may suffice for them to get the decisions they desire for free. For example, a former mayor of a Central East European capital told me that when he needed special services from a well-known medical specialist (within the public health system of the socialist state), he would simply call the specialist, confidently expecting that the service would be delivered by him within hours. In contrast, normal patients would have to wait for months for the same service and pay a substantial bribe to get it at all. Similarly, in the rich capitalist democracies, the most powerful economic actors may not need to "purchase" decisions that they can get anyway and for free, provided that the economic interests they pursue are sufficiently salient for policy makers. The example suggests the possibility that, rather than being the preferred strategy of the rich and powerful, corruption may also be a coping strategy of the less advantaged who must pay to obtain what the privileged can expect to get "for nothing."

Whom or What Does Corruption Damage?

It is well known and widely documented in the academic as the well as the political literature on corruption that many of the symptoms of economic and political backwardness are caused by political corruption. In a static perspective, corruption interferes with the efficient allocation of resources, in general, and the inflow of foreign direct investment to poor countries, in specific. In a dynamic perspective and concerning second-order effects, it hinders the development of "formal rational" patterns of economic and political organization (cf. Rose-Ackerman 1999). The damage consists in the "moral externalities" of such illegal deals as they are routinely perceived or suspected by third parties. Such perception (or even unsubstantiated suspicion) will increase the level of temptation and lower the threshold of inhibition for others to engage in the same kind of behavior: corruption feeds upon itself, as a kind of "me-tooism" spreads on either side with the actors asking themselves why they should be the only ones (the "suckers") adhering to clean practices.[20] Older claims that corruption (functioning as the payment of "speed money") might positively enhance efficiency (Leff 1964) are no longer being given any credit. Taken together, negative distributional patterns, erosion of the tax base, inefficiencies of allocation, decline of domestic as well as foreign direct investment, the failure of regulatory policies and the resulting damage to the natural environment, foreign trade problems caused by smuggling and illegal exports/imports, and the obstruction of governance and democratic accountability are all attributed to corruption as a major cause. Advocates of anticorruption policies try to break two vicious circles: (a) poverty leading to corruption leading to poverty and (b) poor governance leading to corruption leading to poor governance. The link between political corruption and economic growth works both ways: corruption hinders economic growth *and* "corruption has generally declined with economic growth," as the "process of economic growth ultimately generates enough forces to reduce corruption" (Bardhan 1997: 1329).

The negative effects of corruption on efficiency, investment, growth, and innovation are mostly studied and documented with a focus on less developed countries and countries undergoing a transition from state socialism. Although the presence of political corruption in the advanced capitalist democracies of the OECD world has received wide scholarly and media attention during the 1990s, I do not see any claims being made that corruption in the core capitalist countries negatively affects their overall economic performance and/or their governing capacity to the same extent as it does in the less prosperous regions of the globe. This may be due to the fact that the level of corruption in the wealthy countries appears to be comparatively low and largely limited to the misallocation of public resources and the distortion of the democratic political process according to type 2. This is perhaps due to the better mechanisms of corruption control or to the higher level of generalized trust we find in place in these countries that may strengthen the moral inhibitions of potential type 3 perpetrators.

Although in theory corruption is conceived of as a hen-egg-problem with circular causation—corruption breeds a poor economy and poor economic performance breeds corruption—much of the literature clearly emphasizes just one of the causal links (which occasionally and to a certain extent borders on victim-blaming): Corruption is an obstacle to efficiency, development, modernization, and formal rationality. What has drawn much less attention is the reverse causal link: In order to be able to restrain corruption, a country has to be relatively rich already. For instance, it has to have a tax base that allows the state to build a sufficiently dense public administration staffed with trained personnel who are paid an adequate wage. The economic structure must be sufficiently diversified and competitive to allow the state to resist the attempted blackmail of monopolistic industries trying to buy protection and privilege that would further undermine efficiency.

And the political culture must be sufficiently informed by universalist principles (as well as sufficiently noncynical concerning the possibilities of effective corruption control) to generate the support of voters for effective anticorruption policies, even if these run counter to local and tribal interests in protection and traditionalist survival strategies.

What about the link between liberal democracy and corruption? Is there also a symmetrical negative relation, as there is between growth and corruption? As corruption curtails the right of the popular sovereign (the "principal") to an unbiased implementation of the law and conduct of the state administration (the "agent"), it always violates accountability as the basic principle of democracy. Moreover, it has been argued that in the post-communist context corruption causes the "political damage" of "undermining the purpose of public institutions" of diminishing popular support for the transition to democracy and its consolidation (Karklins 2002: 24). The perception of elections, law making, and court proceedings all being distorted by corrupt deals can breed the fatalistic attitude that democracy, rather than being an antidote to corruption, just multiplies opportunities for corrupt deals as well as for covering them up. According to Karklins, "corruption is the chief obstacle to democratic...progress in the post-communist region" (30–1).

Inversely, it is not certain whether or not the achievements of liberal democracy do have the desired negative impact upon the level of corruption. On the one hand, rule of law, the publicity of the political process, and the division of power seem to facilitate the enforcement of accountability and the control of corruption. Also, the promise of "fighting corruption" has been a powerful device of populist electoral mobilization in developed as well as underdeveloped and post-communist countries (Holmes 1999: 9). However, if *both* of the major contenders in a competition of parties or party alliances are perceived to have been involved in corruption scandals, or if both of them share an interest in leaving loopholes for corruption in the legal regulation of party finance, the campaign issue of "fighting corruption" loses much of its credibility and priority (cf. Seibel 2001: 88). Moreover, party competition generates an insatiable appetite for campaign funds (the appetite being "insatiable" because it is not the absolute volume of funds a party can spend on its campaign that is thought to count, but the margin by which it surpasses the other party).

The focus on party finance is also due to the steeply increased costs of political competition in a "media democracy," where opportunities for communicating with a highly volatile electorate must be purchased from commercial suppliers.[21] Given the sensitivity of the issue of party finance, each party is permanently interested in both acquiring additional funds *and* in exposing opposing parties for allegedly illegitimate sources of their funding. Also, party competition gives rise to a phenomenon normally not counted as "corruption," namely the open "purchase" of the decisions of voters through clientelistic promises and policies on which budgetary resources are being spent, often arguably at the expense of long-term and collective interests. In several developed countries donations are commonly given by powerful economic agents to *both* of the major parties. This effect allows the donor to "punish" recipients who fail to reciprocate by simply discontinuing his donations. In order to avoid this unwelcome event, the recipient party or politician will think twice before moves are contemplated that might hurt the assumed interests of the donor—interests which do not even need to be spelled out by the donor. Thus, what the donor gets in return for his investment may consist not so much in what the recipient does as in what, according to the logic of nondecisions, the recipient *refrains* from doing, proposing, or initiating. It is only by reference to this logic— investing in the self-interested discipline of politicians and parties—that one can explain the major funding scandals in Germany and in Italy. In both cases donors donated not just to their most preferred party but simultaneously gave to several of the major political parties.[22]

One of the virtues of competitive party democracy is rightly believed to be the medium-term uncertainty of electoral outcomes. This is so the rules of political competition are fixed, and its outcome is not, as Adam Przeworski observed (1991: 10–14). This effect exposes any democratically elected politician to a degree of uncertainty of his or her career prospects that is uncommon within the ranks of any other comparable sectoral (e.g., administrative, judicial, academic, media, or corporate) elite. Democratic politicians have difficulty securing the equivalent to what in other institutional sectors is known as job tenure. To be sure, part of this uncertainty is often compensated for by rather generous provisions for public retirement payments for politicians who fail to be reelected. But that will not effectively discourage them during their tenure of elected office from making additional autonomous investments in the security and continuity of their own status—be it in the form of the sale of decisions they promise to make in case of reelection or of alternative sources of status security (e.g., promises of consultancy contracts). It is in the nature of the electoral political process itself, its configuration of uncertainties, incentives, and opportunities, that each of these two options involves the temptation of political corruption—a temptation that can hardly be ruled out by any devices suggested by economists and political scientists. The extent to which it can be ruled out depends on the strength of "character," the availability of "moral resources," and the sense of "politics as a vocation."[23]

The second-order damage inflicted by such democracy-induced kinds of "advanced" corruption does not so much undermine state capacity or economic growth as it affects the political culture and the perceived legitimacy of the democratic political process. Publicity and scandalization of corruption cases can cut both ways. It can alert the public and political elites to a problem that must be remedied, and it can also serve to confirm cynical mass attitudes and lead elite actors to abandon their moral inhibitions. "Perceived political corruption has contributed to growing popular disillusionment with the established parties and with 'money-driven' political systems. Declining levels of voter turnout are eloquent testimony to this" (Transparency International 2001a: 146). The narrower the margins by which the winning party or party coalition beats the loser,[24] the more plausible becomes the cynical view that it was not the "will of the people" that determines the outcome of elections, but the balance of campaign funds and other politically irrelevant contingencies. What is thus arguably being purchased in OECD democracies is not some decision of some official or minister (as in "backward" types of corruption), but the decision of the popular sovereign itself. A spreading perception that this might be the case is bound to breed cynicism, and it undermines the credit of the "political class." It contributes to the condition of "democratic disaffection" (Pharr and Putnam 2000). For these reasons, the reform and stricter control of the funding of political parties has become a major issue in the politics of OECD democracies.

Fighting Corruption: Formal Control vs. Building Trust

We can conveniently divide anticorruption strategies into three classes that correspond not only to the three spheres of social action (the economy, politics, community) but also to the respective branches of the social sciences. Economists would fight corruption by making it more costly, political scientists would think about rearranging the institutional opportunity structure for corrupt action, and sociologists would propose policies that are designed to strengthen trust, solidarity, and normative standards such as honesty, as well as the differentiation of spheres of economic, political, and communal action.

Economic thinking will operate with incentives and propose making corruption more costly and less beneficial for the parties involved. One way to do so is paying officials better salaries in order to reduce the demand for extra income (heroically assuming that there is a decline in the marginal utility of money income). Generous salaries for officials will also increase the loss they must face in case they get fired as a consequence of corrupt deals.[25] More severe criminal punishments will also work as a negative incentive. Also, the market for corrupt deals can itself be constrained. That might happen if regulations are abandoned, and with them the opportunities removed to sell/buy exemption from the conditional burdens of these regulations. The illicit use of bribes to accelerate administrative processes can be legalized, so that faster service will be made available at a perfectly legal additional fee rather than the corrupt payment of "speed money" (Rose-Ackerman 1997: 46).

Political science thinking will use the institutional opportunity structure for corruption as its preferred lever of reform. What is needed in order to fight corruption is good governance. An improved selection and recruitment of officers, greater precision of procedural rules, the limitation of discretion, the rotation of officers, the increased choice made available to citizens among service-providing officials, rewards and protection for whistle-blowers, a more stringent review of the administrative process through auditing and other investigative agencies, and the reform of the procurement process are just some of the items in the rich arsenal of institutional devices by which the opportunity space of political corruption can be constrained and thus the quality of governance improved (cf. Rose-Ackerman 1999: ch. 4 and Bardhan 1997: 1338).

However, what corruption-immune good governance actually means remains controversial. On the one hand, the neoliberal view enjoys considerable acclaim under which every state-owned facility, any state regulation, any state bureaucracy, as well as any but the most simple and transparent scheme of taxation provide an entry point for corrupt deals. The obvious policy implication is deregulation, privatization, and the reshaping of public institutions according to the logic of "quasi markets," as recommended by the "new public management" doctrine. On the other hand, it has also been argued that the spread of managerial (as opposed to bureaucratic) modes of running state agencies will undermine the professional ethic of administrators and their standards of impartial service. The new "cult of performance targets" might even increase the susceptibility of officials to make deals and exchanges with powerful clients and undermine the distinctive standards of action in the public (as opposed to the market and communal) sphere(s) (Theobald 2002: 438; Mény 1996: 315; Nelken and Levi 1996: 2; Holmes 1999).

Nevertheless, there can be little doubt that reform measures, as suggested by economists and political scientists, could change much about the realities of political corruption if adopted and implemented. But the question still remains which motives, values, and political forces would actually push forward the reform project, valuing it as being both worth the effort and assessing it as having a chance to succeed. The question remains: What are the incentives to introduce incentives designed to control corruption or to redesign opportunity structures? Political elites, as well as their private sector partners with whom they have participated in (supposedly) lucrative corrupt deals, would have to change their minds in order to accomplish a basic change of the hitherto established and taken-for-granted rules of the game. Voters would have to put leaders into positions of authority who have both the will and a road map to promote reform. The question is what might drive these reform efforts. Although it is a compelling idea—arguably the most fundamental one that supports both the economic and political version of liberal theory—to "economize on virtue," the capacity to implement it presupposes a measure of virtuous motivations, as well as the requisite cognitive disposition of actors, and some degree of material independence. Even the best economic and institutional designs alone would not be sufficient to help the recovery of corruption-infested societies. Such designs need to be advocated and implemented by social and political actors who consider them intrinsically just and valuable, and not just instrumentally advantageous for the sake of a better government or a more efficient economy.

In some of the literature, the options available for controlling corruption are classified as "changing situations" vs. "changing participants" (see e.g., Miller et al. 2002: 188). But this dualism appears overly simplistic, as it misses the interaction and overlap between the two. For instance, political institutions (such as a state-funded and compulsory school system) will not only establish a set of opportunities and constraints; what institutions do, in addition, is to provide participant actors (and, beyond that, third parties) with a cognitive map, which indicates to them the kind of behavior expected as normal. They can also motivate the courses of action of participants, and provide trust and assurance (concerning the likely behavior of everyone else) that is needed in order for social norms to be enacted and complied with. Thus, institutionally shaped situations will exert a formative impact upon participants, their cognitions, and motivations. But we know little about the dynamics through which material conditions and incentives, as well as institutional patterns, translate into particular cognitive and normative dispositions of actors—and vice versa.

It is to these crucial questions that the sociological perspective may provide an answer. Although most people might, in principle, prefer to live in a society where they do not have to pay bribes for government services that are nominally free for all, where officials treat clients with impartiality and fairness, and where citizens' duties are effectively enforced even against the rich, the moral resources that are needed to bring about this state of affairs are not always easily mobilized. First, although it may be widely understood that a corruption-free interaction between state and society is in the best interest of "all of us" in the long run, "each of us" may feel helpless to bring it about in the short run. In a society where corruption is considered a normal fact of everyday transactions, individuals fighting corrupt practices will not automatically promote the common good of a corruption-free government because it will expose them to reprisals or the self-exclusion from service. Widespread corruption can thus discourage the motivation to resist or to overcome corruption.

In order to escape from this trap, people must be able to invoke standards of fairness and similar *moral norms* that are inherent in—and can be invoked as being part of—their cultural tradition. Beyond that, it is not well understood which institutional contexts can serve as a source of encouragement and moral mobilization in support of anticorruption reform efforts. International actors, NGOs (such as Transparency International), and third sector organizations may play a role, as may the institutions and traditions of professional training to the extent they can inculcate an ethos of professional honor and loyalty to the law in public officials (cf. Holmes 2001). The media and popular arts may have a role to play, as well as religious institutions (cf. Transparency International 2002). Leslie Holmes speaks of "methods for reducing corruption" that include programs "to educate people, especially young people at an impressionable age" (1999: 29). He also reports, "Poland introduced ethics classes for its customs officers . . . in response to apparently high levels of corruption among them" (ibid.). In order for such sources of moral motivation and critique to have a conceivable impact, however, the institutional system of the society in question must be relatively open already. If it is not, a sense of demoralization, cynicism, apathy, resignation, anomie, and passivity will prevail, and the support will be missing that any reform effort critically depends upon.

Second, any progress toward the control of corruption presupposes a suitable and widely shared *cognitive frame*. Most importantly, people must perceive their personal future as intertwined with the collective future of society. They must also believe that they are not entirely powerless and have some measure of "voice" in the shaping of that future. One or the other of these cognitive premises is certainly absent in countries where major parts of the younger generation hope for (or often just fantasize about) opportunities for emigration, as it has often been reported from Africa and the poorer post-communist societies.[26] Moreover, generalized trust—both "horizontal" trust in fellow citizens and "vertical" trust in the officials in public agencies—is a cognitive frame that is conducive to the successful fighting of corruption. Such generalized trust prevails if people operate on the assumption that most people (and not just those "I" know or who belong to "my" group) can most of the time be relied upon not to deceive "me," nor to take unfair advantage of others, as well as show a measure of respect for the rules and laws that are supposed to bind "all of us." Again, these perceptions are not likely to be formed in an environment where corrupt deals are a ubiquitous experience.

Social trust is both called for and destroyed in corrupt deals. The participants in the deal need to trust each other. Belonging to a shared political, regional, tribal, local, and so on "micro-milieu" facilitates trust. But the greater the opportunity for developing trust between partners in a corrupt interaction, the less reason there is for macro-trust, which is the belief that most transactions between most people, throughout a national political community and even beyond, are reliably corruption-free. If this is right, an obvious method to fight corruption would be to increase macro-trust and to weaken the kind of micro-trust that can give rise to and facilitate corrupt deals. Policy makers can do the latter by manipulating the structure of opportunity for building such micro-trust between the parties involved, which can always violate the terms of the deal by either failing to deliver or by exposing the deal and triggering sanctions coming from outside actors. Rotation in public administration is a means to increase the risk of trusting, and the facilitation of whistle-blowing and tightening controls are means to increase the risk of disclosure and sanction. Taken together, these measures can well undermine the conditions for the formation of micro-trust between partners of corrupt deals (Lambsdorff 2002).

In contrast, macro-trust, or the generalized belief that most people will behave in trustworthy and fair ways most of the time cannot be built and conditioned in the same way. Note that such macro-trust is not just experiential, that is, derivative of the experience and perception of the widespread occurrence versus the rareness of corrupt deals. It is not just counterfactual, but depends on positively generated social facts. Macro-trust can work as a moral force that *shapes* the social reality of which it is more than just a reflection. This follows as a possibility because extending trust to other persons can imply obliging that person to honor that trust and to confirm the trustworthiness she or he is credited with. Yet building macro-trust that has this capacity for self-confirmation is an activity that can have at best indirect results. To be sure, institutional devices that credibly prevent and detect corrupt deals will help to nurture macro-trust and macro-trust will in turn oblige policy makers to put into effect further such devices. Yet macro-trust differs from the imposition of formal controls, which, as it were, can be turned on and off at will, while trust can only be deliberately turned off, not on (Offe 1999). There is an asymmetrical temporal pattern in the building and destruction of macro-trust. Trust building as the formation of a cognitive frame is a time-consuming process—trust must "grow." In contrast, the decay of trust tends to be a rapid process: it "breaks down" if it confronts an overdose of evidence pointing to the lack of trustworthiness of others.

Finally, and in order to resist corruption and to support reforms designed to contain it, people must be minimally independent and self-sufficient so they can afford to refrain from corrupt deals. If the immediate life interest of people—in obtaining and keeping a job and income, in getting access to services, in protecting themselves from repression—all depend on their willingness to pay bribes, such self-sufficiency is absent. Analogous material prerequisites apply to the suppliers of corrupt decisions. If people are very poor, if their life chances depend upon the decisions and services of predatory public officials, and if a neoliberal economic culture prevails that suggests and condones unrestrained acquisitive opportunism, it is simply unrealistic to expect that transactions will be conducted in an honest, fair, and corruption-free manner. And even if heroic individuals were willing to live up to those standards, they are likely to be discouraged by the fact that they have no reason to expect that the moral principles they follow will also be followed by others. In such conditions, people are trapped in corruption, as they cannot cope with the necessities of day-to-day life without engaging in it. Under such extreme conditions, what external observers do when they attribute the absence of development and the failure of political and economic modernization to corruption is little more than victim-blaming. On both sides of the corrupt transaction, officials and their clients, proposals for good governance may simply be far from incentive compatible.

In order to control corruption, the right arrangement of formal controls, incentives, and opportunities, is not enough. It cannot even start to operate without the moral commitment of elites who put the arrangements in place. People must bring an "ethical project," that is, the right configuration of motives, beliefs, and conceptions of legitimate interests to bear on the problem, a configuration the emergence of which can in turn be constrained by the prevalence of high levels of corruption itself. In the absence of such an ethical project, formal controls are neither likely to be adopted nor can they fully be relied upon to do the job once adopted.

Virtue is thus indispensable. In conclusion, let me illustrate this point using party finance in advanced societies as a model case (cf. Alemann 2002).

The number of instruments by which formal controls of party and campaign finance operates is limited. Political parties can be granted tax money for campaigns so that they become less dependent on private donations. Anonymous donations can be made impermissible beyond a relatively low threshold. Parties must make public the amount and origin of the revenues they receive. In case a party is found to have violated these rules, it has to pay painful penalties. So much is stipulated by the German law on political parties passed in 1967, a law that, incidentally, took 18 years for the federal parliament to pass after an unambiguous mandate to do so was established by the 1949 *Grundgesetz* (Article 21). But the capacity of the law to neutralize the financial influence of private donors through enforcing publicity is known to be limited. As the German Federal Constitutional Court argued in a 1992 decision, legal regulation can only approximate that goal. In the final analysis, it depends upon the leadership of political parties to what extent party operatives will comply with the law (rather than opt for the various remaining possibilities of circumvention). Parties have found it easy to stay at least one step ahead in terms of the sophistication of their financial tactics relative to the effectiveness of formal controls. For instance, funds are accumulated abroad, donations are made into private accounts of party leaders, and larger amounts of donated money are divided up into numerous small and anonymous payments. The calculus of what use to make of these options, in turn, will be made with a view to the perceived virtuousness of competing parties and in accordance with an assessment of how seriously the electoral fortunes of the party will be damaged in case corrupt modes of finance are uncovered and made public (cf. Isensee 2000; Seibel 2001). The more common corrupt campaign financing becomes, the easier it is for hitherto noncorrupt parties to excuse their participation, the more the public will supposedly get used to it, and the less choice remains for voters anyway to sanction corrupt party finance in the voting booth. Evidently, the only force that might bring this escalating dynamic to a halt is not formal regulation, but the robustness of standards of political virtue, as observed by elites and nonelites alike.

The need for virtuous dispositions even increases as complexity makes formal control more costly and less effective. Constraining the opportunities for corruption and assigning negative sanctions to it become costlier as complexity increases. Also, maintaining tight and intense control will send a signal of strong distrust to those being controlled, which in turn will arguably tend to undermine their loyalty. Moreover, the presence of strong supervision and control sends the message that corruption must be very common in the respective country or organization, a perception that may well lead to the spread rather than the containment of corruption. No doubt, a very weak control structure will make corruption cheap for the corrupt agent, and all the more tempting. But it is a *non sequitur* to conclude that very heavy policing will make it prohibitively costly. Once corruption has taken hold, it is unlikely to be deterred by formal controls alone. In highly complex conditions with limited means of direct observation and control, there seems to be a strong case for relying on loyalty, trustworthiness, reliability, and other kinds of endogenous sources of discipline, such as virtue, instead of an exclusive reliance on formal control.

All political corruption depends upon the deal being hidden from the public eye, or the absence of transparency. It is covered up by false appearances: The official acts as if he were providing a service to a citizen in accordance with his duties, when in reality he is handing over a favor in exchange for a bribe. The manipulation of institutional opportunity structures and incentives can accomplish a great deal by making it harder to build the cover of false appearances. The emphasis of these strategies is on inducements to *truth* telling. They make it either impossible or imprudent (unreasonably risky) for agents to rely on lies and to create untrue appearances. But, as the case of party finance shows, formal arrangements can virtually always be subverted by corrupt agents resorting to practices that these arrangements are incapable of detecting. The more elaborate the system of opportunities and incentives, the greater the temptation to "beat the system" through ever more refined methods of corruption. What can help here is not better arrangements for *truth* telling through the preclusion of lies, but a strengthened moral commitment of actors to truth *telling*, or the internal controls of shame and guilt, the preparedness to confess wrongdoing, as well as the courage to complain, a sense of dignity and loyalty, and a perceived duty to act and speak sincerely. Although people can be "made" to desist from lying by external controls, it requires the internal controls of civic virtue to motivate agents to be sincere—to *tell* the truth as opposed to keep silent.

Corruption control based on a sense of shame, regret, and a loss of honor and self-respect is more powerful than corruption control through external sanctions that depend on the expectation of being caught. A person experiences moral costs if he keeps reticent about something he knows he is morally obliged to tell or admit. The desire not to burden one's conscience by concealing something that one's duty of loyalty to others makes it mandatory to tell provides an anticorruption motivation that may be as strong—or even stronger—than the desire to avoid a situation in which one suffers a sanction. The difference between the two is the same as that between paying a fine and fulfilling a duty, or the external conditioning of behavior versus the internal commitment to honor the demands of sincerity. People will avoid corrupt dealings, not when they understand that corruption is (or can be) costly to them, but only if they understand that it is wrong.

Notes

* I wish to thank Susan Rose-Ackerman, Federico Varese, and John Uhr for their helpful comments and suggestions.

1. Legal and social norms are indispensable benchmarks of "corruption," but sometimes they do not coincide. In international relations, the attempt of a government to purchase a foreign government's decision is perfectly legal, although it may lead to an outburst of moral indignation in the target country. Conversely, a bribe paid to a police officer to protect a relative from torture will be considered illegal, but morally laudable; a case for "benign" violations of the law has been made in connection

with political party finance. Cf. Heidenheimer et al. (1989), Mény (1996), and Philp (1997: 441) for discussions of ethical vs. legal standards of corruption.

2. As such, they can engage in "asset stripping" or in the "diverting of public funds." By doing so, they arrogate to themselves illegal taxation powers (Karklins 2002: 25), which is different from corruption due to its "unilateral" nature.

3. The relativity of what corruption "is" and how it is contingent upon public opinion, legal norms, and "standards derived from modern western democratic systems" is extensively discussed by Philp (1997).

4. Cf. Holmes (1999: 4) where the author reports that 57% of respondents surveyed in a study on Bulgaria "claimed it was a 'waste of time' to report cases of corruption."

5. These and many other cases of illegal or arguably immoral exchanges among private parties are included in the very broad definition of corruption that is employed in the documentary and advocacy work of Transparency International. Cf. Transparency International (2001a).

6. Cf. Heywood (1997: 421) and his proposed solution of the "definitional dilemma" of political corruption.

7. The buying of parliamentary votes is a common practice in international relations, though probably rarely as explicit as the deal offered to—and eventually rejected by—the Turkish parliament by the U.S. administration in early March 2003 in connection with the intended use of Turkish military bases for the Iraq war.

8. It has been suggested by some German commentators (cf. Isensee 2000) that the former kind of political corruption is characteristic of Left-of-Center politicians who put the proceeds of their deals into their private pockets, while Right-of-Center politicians (perhaps because they normally do not depend upon additions to their household income) tend to spend corruption revenues on campaigns and donations to their political party. Although the Left–Right equation is confirmed by some of the recent German corruption scandals, there are both types of deviant cases. An interesting problem is posed by the question which one, if any, is worse—worse in (a) political and (b) moral terms. Note that misusing public money for private gain need not involve a deal; it can simply be theft or embezzlement. In contrast, the misuse of private money to influence public policy or to purchase decisions will always involve a deal.

9. A rather spectacular case of such "doubly political" corruption is that of Germany's ex-chancellor and the Christian Democratic Union's (CDU) honorary president, Helmut Kohl. Although he illegally acquired several millions of deutschmark for his party, even his staunchest critics "assume that Kohl's illegal action was not motivated by personal corruptibility" (Seibel 2001: 85).

10. Heywood (1997: 426) speaks of "personal" vs. "institutional" corruption.

11. For example, according to the French criminal prosecution authorities, Elf Aquitaine paid for the luxury apartment of the lover of Mr. Dumas, the French foreign minister. Or a consultancy job may be promised to a ranking official after retirement. In the interest of camouflaging corrupt deals, the currencies used can vary widely and imaginatively.

12. The two axes of this classification of corrupt deals are rights vs. duties and arbitrary extension vs. arbitrary curtailment. Thus, type (4) represents an arbitrary extension of duties, and type (2) an arbitrary curtailment of the rights of the popular "principal." This classification is inspired by, but different from, the one suggested by Rose-Ackerman (1999: 56–7).

13. Just to illustrate: A wealthy Italian lady tells me casually that she pays a certain amount of money to an official in the local tax authority in order to have him keep the folder containing her real estate tax documents (for the several buildings she owns in town) near the bottom of the pile on his desk, thus making sure that they will not be processed in the foreseeable future.

14. Yet equally well known is the fact that deregulation and privatization can also breed corruption. But that is not of interest in the present context.

15. Elsewhere, I have quoted reports from the *Wall Street Journal* from the early 1970s that argued that the U.S. Occupational Safety and Health Administration (OSHA) issued stricter regulations of the work environment not in order to have them implemented, but in order to allow violators to escape statutory fines by paying into the campaign fund of the incumbent administration. Cf. Rose-Ackerman (1999:129) for a similar observation.

16. This power position is comparable to that applying to medical doctors and to the information asymmetry obtaining between doctor and patient. Doctors, too, operate on both sides of the market for medical services, as they can decide both what the patient "needs" (the diagnosis, which determines demand) and what must be done in order to satisfy this need (the therapy, or supply of medical services). But this game can be institutionalized, and the exploitative temptations inherent in it mitigated. Neither of which is the case with political corruption.

17. "There is many a slip between the bribing transaction and the actual delivery of the good or the service involved. The control rights on the latter are often arbitrary and uncertain, leaving a lot of leeway for the bribee to renege on his understanding with the briber, or to come back and demand another bribe" (Bardhan 1997: 1324).
18. This assurance effect of anticipated immobility may be a key to understanding why corruption appears so widespread in the essentially "localized" construction industry.
19. The following extreme example is based upon a personal communication of the victim. It is reported to have taken place in the capital of a Latin American Andean state in 1993. A visibly short-sighted visitor is robbed of his spectacles in a busy street. The next day, someone alerts him of an advertisement in the local paper which says that "the person who lost his glasses yesterday" is welcome to call a phone number. The number turns out to be that of the director of the local prison. He tells the visitor that an inmate of the prison, while being on daytime leave, "found" the glasses that now can be picked up at the prison for a ransom of 200 dollars. It was obvious from the circumstances that the thief of the glasses not only had the permission of the prison adminis-tration to do what he did, but even a mandate to contribute in this way to the income of the staff of the entire organization.
20. Contrary to the intentions of advocacy groups who are engaged in uncovering, publishing, and scandalizing cases of corruption, they may thereby in effect breed cynicism about—rather than enhanced compliance with—"good" business and governance practices. "Too much" publicity can counter-intentionally lead to corruption being framed as a thoroughly normal phenomenon. This double-edged impact of corruption publicity is nicely captured by former Indian Prime Minister Nehru: "Merely shouting from the house-tops that everybody is corrupt creates an atmosphere of corruption. People feel that they live in a climate of corruption and they get corrupted themselves" (quoted in Bardhan 1997: 1334).
21. It has always been true that "the democratic political process costs money" (Heywood 1997: 430); but we do not seem to have good comparative and longitudinal data on the increased costliness of the process.
22. This pattern of giving to more than one party, famously called "cultivation of the political land-scape" (*politische Landschaftspflege*) in the German Flick affair in the 1980s, can also be motivated by the precautionary consideration that recipient parties will develop a common interest in keeping the donation a secret.
23. Compare Max Weber's famous speech of this title (reprinted in Weber, 1965), where he draws the distinction between civil servants living "off" politics and politicians living "for" politics.
24. This margin was a record low, namely one-ten-thousandth of the German electorate, in the federal elections of September 22, 2002.
25. Reportedly, this efficiency wage logic has been successfully applied in Singapore. Cf. Bardhan (1997: 1339).
26. The widespread longing for exit is itself an important source of corruption, namely the corrupt market for forged passports, visas, and favors of the border police.

References

Alemann, Ulrich von. 2002. "Party Finance, Party Donations and Corruption. The German Case." In D. Della Porta and S. Rose-Ackerman (eds.), *Corrupt Exchanges: Empirical Themes in the Politics and Political Economy of Corruption*, pp. 102–17. Baden-Baden: Nomos.
Bachrach, Peter and Morton S. Baratz. 1970. *Power and Poverty. Theory and Practice*. New York: Oxford University Press.
Bardhan, Pranab. 1997. "Corruption and Development. A Review of Issues." *Journal of Economic Literature* 35: 1320–46.
Crenson, Matthew. 1971. *The Unpolitics of Air Pollution*. Baltimore MD: Johns Hopkins University Press.
Goodin, Robert E. 2003. "Democratic Accountability: The Third Sector and All." *Hauser Center for Nonprofit Organizations, John F. Kennedy School of Government*, Working Paper No. 19, Harvard University, Cambridge MA.
Heidenheimer, Arnold J., Michael Johnston, and Victor T. LeVine. (eds.). 1989. *Political Corruption. A Handbook*. New Brunswick NJ: Transaction.
Heywood, Paul. 1997. "Political Corruption: Problems and Perspectives." *Political Studies* 45: 417–35.

Holmes, Leslie. 1999. "Corruption, Weak States and Economic Rationalism in Central and Eastern Europe." Manuscript, University of Melbourne.

———. 2001. "Crime, Corruption, and Politics." In J. Zielonka and A. Pravda (eds.), *Democratic Consolidation in Eastern Europe*, pp. 192–230. Oxford: Oxford University Press.

Isensee, Josef. 2000. "Das System Kohl—Das System Rau." *Frankfurter Allgemeine Zeitung*, January 28, p. 41.

Karklins, Rasma. 2002. "Typology of Post-Communist Corruption." *Problems of Post-Communism* 49(4): 22–32.

Lambsdorff, Johan Graf. 2002. "What Nurtures Corrupt Deals? On the Role of Confidence and Transaction Costs." In D. Della Porta and S. Rose-Ackerman (eds.), *Corrupt Exchanges: Empirical Themes in the Politics and Political Economy of Corruption*, pp. 20–36. Baden-Baden: Nomos.

Ledeneva, Alena V. 1998. *Russia's Economy of Favours: "Blat." Networking and Informal Exchange.* Cambridge: Cambridge University Press.

Leff, Nathaniel. 1964. "Economic Development through Bureaucratic Corruption." *American Behavioral Scientist* 8: 8–14.

Mény, Yves. 1996. " 'Fin de siècle' Corruption: Change, Crisis and Shifting Values." *International Social Science Journal* 149: 309–20.

Miller, William L., Åse B. Grødeland, and Tatyana Y. Koshechkina. 2002. "Values & Norms *versus* Extortion & Temptation." In D. Della Porta and S. Rose-Ackerman (eds.), *Corrupt Exchanges: Empirical Themes in the Politics and Political Economy of Corruption*, pp. 165–93. Baden-Baden: Nomos.

Nelken, David and Michael Levi. 1996. "The Corruption of Politics and the Politics of Corruption." *Journal of Law and Society* 23: 1–17.

Nye, Joseph S. 1967. "Corruption and Political Development: A Cost-Benefit Analysis." *American Political Science Review* 61: 417–27.

Offe, Claus. 1999. "How Can We Trust Our Fellow Citizens?" In M. E. Warren (ed.), *Democracy and Trust*, pp. 42–87. New York: Cambridge University Press.

———. 2000. "Civil Society and Social Order: Demarcating and Combining Market, State and Community." *Archives Européennes de Sociologie* 41: 71–94.

Pharr, Susan J. and Robert D. Putnam (eds.). 2000. *Disaffected Democracies. What's Troubling the Trilateral Countries?* Princeton NJ: Princeton University Press.

Philp, Mark. 1997. "Defining Political Corruption." *Political Studies* 45: 436–62.

Przeworski, Adam. 1991. *Democracy and the Market. Political and Economic Reforms in Eastern Europe and Latin America.* New York: Cambridge University Press.

Rose, Richard. 1992. *Monitoring Socio-Economic Trends in Eastern Europe: A Survey-Based Approach.* Report to the World Bank. Strathclyde: CSPP.

Rose-Ackerman, Susan. 1997. "The Political Economy of Corruption." In K. A. Elliott (ed.), *Corruption and the Global Economy.* Washington DC: Institute for International Economics.

———. 1999. *Corruption and Government. Causes, Consequences, and Reform.* New York: Cambridge University Press.

Seibel, Wolfgang. 2001. "Institutional Weaknesses, Ethical Misjudgment: German Christian Democrats and the Kohl Scandal." In J. Fleming and I. Holland (eds.), *Motivating Ministers to Morality*, pp. 77–90. Dartmouth UK: Ashgate.

Theobald, Robin. 2002. "Can the State Deliver?" *New Political Economy* 7: 435–41.

Transparency International. 2001a. *Global Corruption Report.* Berlin: Transparency International.

———. 2001b. *Corruption and Quality of Governance: The Case of Moldova.* Moldova: Transparency International.

———. 2002. *Artists Against Corruption.* Moldova: Transparancy International.

Varese, Federico. 1994. "Is Siciliy the Future of Russia? Private Protection and the Rise of the Russian Mafia." *Archives Européennes de Sociologie* 35: 224–58.

Weber, Max. 1965. *Politics as Vocation.* Philadelphia PA: Fortress Press.

CHAPTER FIVE

The Inequality of Influence

JOEL S. HELLMAN AND DANIEL KAUFMANN[*]

There is now a substantial literature demonstrating the negative impact of inequality on economic growth and on a wide range of intermediate social and economic outcomes that affect growth.[1] Linking these results to another well-established literature—the quality of institutions—Glaeser et al. (2002) have argued that inequality affects growth by subverting the institutions that guarantee secure property rights. The rich can use their superior resources to manipulate political, legal, and regulatory institutions to preserve and extend their privileged positions through inefficient redistributions, anticompetitive measures, and other discriminatory practices. This subversion of institutions undermines the security of property rights for those less well-endowed and thus weakens investment and growth. Yet to the extent that inequality leads to the subversion of institutions, it is not necessarily through the inequality of wealth per se, but the inequality of influence, though the two are obviously closely interrelated. The rich are assumed to be able to convert their greater wealth into greater political influence over both the formation and functioning of institutions. However, the extent to which inequalities of wealth can be converted into inequalities of influence will be mediated by different configurations of the political system. In order to understand the mechanisms linking inequality and growth, we need a much deeper investigation into the inequality of influence in developing countries.

Building upon the extensive literature on special interest politics in developed countries, recent work has begun to examine the impact of the inequality of influence on economic performance, both at the macro and micro levels, with a particular focus on transition economies.[2] Hellman et al. (2000) use firm-level survey data to investigate the effects of different forms of influence activities on firm performance, emphasizing the strong gains to firms that engage in state capture, that is, paying bribes to influence the basic laws, rules, and regulations governing their activity. Slinko et al. (2003 and this volume) have created an extraordinary dataset identifying instances of preferential treatment for individual powerful firms in thousands of pieces of regional legislation in Russia to demonstrate how these preferences affect performance at the firm and the regional levels. The transition economies constitute an extremely rich set of cases for such research, because the simultaneous processes of economic liberalization, redistribution of state property, and building the political, legal, and regulatory institutions of a market economy place these interrelationships into much sharper relief than in those countries with a more established institutional order.

To date, empirical work on the inequality of influence has focused on identifying "winners" of the influence game and demonstrating the strong performance gains that such firms enjoy as a result. There is also some evidence suggesting that such inequalities do generate negative externalities in the form of less secure property rights and reduced sales growth for the less influential firms (Hellman et al. 2002) and higher barriers to entry for small firms and lower growth in regions where state capture is particularly pronounced (Slinko et al. 2003 and this volume). Nevertheless, we do not have a clear picture of the mechanisms by which the inequality of influence imposes costs on noninfluential firms. If inequalities of influence lead to the subversion of institutions, then we should find differences in the performance and credibility of institutions among firms with different degrees of political influence.

This essay develops a proxy measure for the inequality of influence on the basis of survey evidence from the 2002 Business Environment and Enterprise Performance Survey (BEEPS) conducted among 6,500 firms in 27 transition countries. Firms were asked to compare the influence of their collective representative, for example, business or trade association, on recently enacted laws, rules, or regulations that had a direct impact on their business with the influence of conglomerates, firms, or individuals with close ties to political leaders. We refer to the resulting inequality as a perceived "crony bias" in the political system that can be measured at both the firm and country level. This measure gives us a crude indication of the extent to which firm managers believe that there are other actors with more or less influence than their own collective voice on the basic rules shaping their business environment. If managers believe that the rules of the game are biased in favor of political cronies, then this might be expected to have an impact on how they interact with public institutions, especially those whose reputation for impartiality is critical to their credibility and effectiveness.

We examine the impact of crony bias at both the firm and country levels on four indicators of institutional subversion: (1) perceptions of and interaction with courts; (2) security of property rights; (3) tax compliance; and (4) bribery. Following Glaeser et al. (2002), we assume that courts are the public institution most susceptible to subversion as a result of severe inequalities of influence, because their effectiveness is so closely based on expectations of impartiality and their ability to enforce decisions on all participants. Firms that perceive their environment as being sharply skewed in favor of more politically influential players are likely to have greater doubts that courts can render fair and impartial verdicts, as well as enforce such verdicts on more influential firms. As a result, such firms should have more negative perceptions of courts and be less likely to use them. This should, in turn, lead to greater insecurity of property rights among less influential firms.

Tax compliance is a broader indicator of the subversion of public institutions as it reflects both the firm's willingness to contribute to the development of public institutions as well as the effectiveness of the state's capacity to collect taxes and to punish tax cheats. Though few firms are eager to pay taxes, those that believe that the system is skewed in favor of a privileged few should be even less willing to pay taxes in support of biased state institutions. Given the limited capacities of any state to enforce tax provisions, tax compliance becomes a much broader measure of confidence in state institutions. Bribery is also a good indicator of weak state institutions.

We find a consistent pattern in which the inequality of influence has a negative impact on assessments of public institutions that ultimately affects the behavior of firms toward those institutions. Crony bias at both the firm and the country level is associated with a much more negative assessment of the fairness and impartiality of courts and the enforceability of court decisions, even for those firms that have never been involved in a court case. Moreover, firms that perceive a crony bias are significantly less likely to use courts to resolve business disputes. Such firms are shown to have less secure property rights than more influential firms. We also find that crony bias is associated with lower levels of tax compliance and significantly higher levels of bribery.

The evidence suggests that the inequality of influence not only damages the credibility of institutions among weak firms, but affects the likelihood that they will use and provide tax resources to support such institutions. By withholding tax revenues, paying bribes, and avoiding courts, these firms ensure that such state institutions are likely to remain weak and subject to capture by more influential firms and individuals. The inequality of influence thus appears to generate a self-reinforcing dynamic in which institutions are subverted, further strengthening the underlying political and economic inequalities.

The Dataset

The BEEPS questionnaire for the transition economies was developed jointly by the World Bank and the Office of the Chief Economist at the European Bank for Reconstruction and Development (EBRD). The survey was conducted on the basis of face-to-face interviews with high-level firm managers or owners through site visits by local surveyors trained according to a standardized methodology. The first round of BEEPS was conducted at over 4,000 firms during the period June through August 1999 in 25 transition countries. The second round of BEEPS was conducted at nearly 6,500 firms in the first half of 2002 in all of the transition economies except Turkmenistan,[3] as well as in Turkey. This essay makes use of only data from the second-round survey as the questions driving the analysis of influence were not included in the first-round survey instrument.

In each country, between 150 and 500 firms were interviewed based on the size of their economies. The sample was structured to be fairly representative of the domestic economies with specific quotas placed on size, sector, location, and export orientation.

The BEEPS survey instrument is structured around multiple objectives: (1) to measure managers' perceptions of the investment climate and their interactions with the state; (2) to develop quantitative indicators of various obstacles to business and aspects of market structure based on the direct experiences of firms; and (3) to obtain simple measures of firm performance across a variety of dimensions that can then be related back to varying perceptions and experiences.

Measuring the Inequality of Influence

To develop a proxy measure for the inequality of influence, we rely on a question in the survey designed to ask firms about the relative influence of different actors on the development of laws, rules, and regulations. In the survey, firms were asked: "How much influence do you think the following groups actually had on recently enacted national laws, rules, and regulations that have a substantial impact on your business?" It is important to note that the question is structured not to ask about all laws and regulations, but just those directly affecting their business. Of course, firms cannot be expected to know the actual level of influence of different groups on legislation; the question simply elicits their perceptions of the gaps in influence. Their answers are expected to be more a function of their larger worldview than their detailed knowledge of the legislative process.

After assessing their own influence, firms were asked in direct succession to compare the influence of a large set of other actors including their domestic competitors, foreign firms, their business association, other business associations, dominant firms or conglomerates in key sectors of the economy (other than theirs), labor unions, organized crime, regional or local government, military, international development agencies or foreign governments, and individuals or firms with close personal ties to political leaders. For each category, firms could select from a 0–4 range with 0 = no impact and 4 = decisive influence.

Using factor analysis to assess how the perceived influence of these different actors are related to each other, we find what might be called an "us versus them" pattern of the inequality of influence. Not surprisingly, firms lump most of the institutions listed earlier into the "them" category with a particularly high correlation among foreign firms, other business associations, dominant firms in other sectors, international development agencies, and individuals or firms with close ties to political leaders. More surprising is who the firms put in the "us" category. Given the concerns often expressed about the uneven playing field for competition in transition countries, one might have expected firms to see their domestic competitors as more influential than themselves, that is, that their business rivals take advantage of

political influence to gain competitive advantages. But instead, firms see a
reasonably high correlation between their own influence and that of their
competitors in contrast to everyone else. Firms seem to be making a distinction between the political playing field in which their influence relative
to the other players is quite small and their own competitive playing field
where their political influence is not substantially different from that of
their competitors.

To measure the inequality of influence in the broader political playing
field, we identify the extent of crony bias, as perceived by the firm, as the
difference between the firm's characterization of the influence of individuals or firms with close, personal ties to political leaders and the influence
of its own business or trade association on recently enacted laws, rules, and
regulations affecting their business. Given that the majority of the firms in
the BEEPS sample are small and medium-sized enterprises—though there
is a quota of 15 percent of the sample in each country for firms over
250 workers—we chose to compare the power of political cronies to some
collective representative of the firms rather than their own individual influence. However, the results reported later are not substantially different if we
use an index of crony bias based upon the firm's own influence.

Crony bias scores are calculated for each firm ranging from values of -4
to 4 with 0 suggesting equal influence and negative scores indicating firms
who see their collective representatives as more influential than political
cronies. The distribution of crony bias scores across the sample is shown in
figure 5.1. Only 16 percent of the firms in the sample assessed the influence of their business association as greater than that of individuals or firms
with close ties to political leaders. Nearly 40 percent of the firms did not
report any inequality of influence between their business associations and
political cronies. Of the remaining 44 percent of firms that did report an

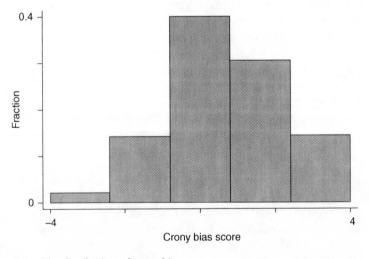

Figure 5.1 The distribution of crony bias

inequality of influence, there is considerable variation in the extent of this perceived inequality.

There is not a strong correlation between the crony bias score and any standard firm characteristics. Not surprisingly, the strongest correlation is with firm size, as firms with a larger number of employees tend to perceive a lower crony bias ($r = -0.1$). Crony bias is also negatively, but weakly, correlated with state ownership ($r = -0.06$). Across the sample, there is no significant correlation between sectors and crony bias. The inequality of influence does not appear to be strongly driven by basic firm-level characteristics.

We can also aggregate the firm-level crony bias scores to construct country-level aggregates for the perceived inequality of influence. These country averages are presented in figure 5.2.[4] There is considerable variation in the extent of crony bias across the transition economies. It is interesting to note that at the low end of the crony bias scale are both some of the most democratic (Slovenia, Estonia, the Czech Republic, Lithuania) and some of the least democratic (Azerbaijan, Belarus, Kazakhstan, Kyrgyzstan, and Uzbekistan) countries in the region. Slovenia stands out as the only country in which firms believe the influence of their business associations exceeds the influence of political cronies (hence the negative crony bias). In contrast, Poland is a significant outlier in comparison with all the transition countries and, in particular, with the other more advanced, democratic reformers. Though the influence of the firms' business association in Poland is on par

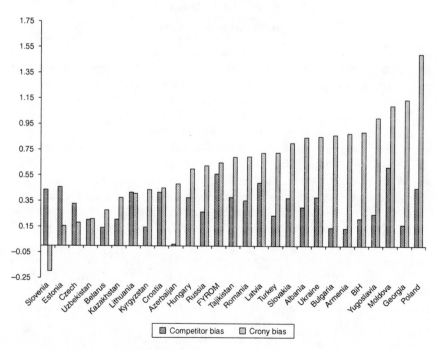

Figure 5.2   The inequality of influence

with other countries in the region, the perceived influence of political cronies is extremely high exceeding all other countries in the sample.[5]

For comparative purposes, figure 5.2 also presents the country averages of another form of inequality of influence: the difference between the firm's own influence and that of its direct competitors, which we refer to as competitor bias. At the firm level, there is a positive, but weak, correlation between competitor bias and crony bias ($r = 0.08$). Inequalities associated with crony bias are generally seen as more significant across the region than competitor bias, as might be expected. But surprisingly, these biases are not correlated across countries. At the country level, there would appear to be different dynamics shaping perceptions of the inequality of influence in different dimensions of the firm's experience. Firms shape their views about the inequality of influence at higher levels of the political system independently of their views about the inequality of influence in their own competitive playing fields.

Though these patterns are interesting at the country level—and we will later try to link them to measures of institutional quality—the main challenge is to link these perceptions of the environment to the actual behavior of firms. If perceptions of the inequality of influence play a role in subverting institutions, then we should see firms act differently according to their perceptions of these inequalities. For this, we turn to a firm-level analysis.

The Inequality of Influence and the
Subversion of Courts

If the quality of any institution is likely to be susceptible to the impact of the inequality of influence, it is the courts. The effectiveness of courts is predicated to a large extent on their fairness and impartiality. If individuals can take advantage of inequalities of political and economic power to unduly influence courts, their fairness and impartiality can be undermined.

The link between the inequality of influence and the subversion of institutions such as courts should be highly dependent upon perceptions of both the extent of such inequality and of the institution. If individuals perceive that the political or economic playing field is skewed by severe inequalities of influence, then they are likely to be more concerned about the likelihood of receiving fair and impartial treatment through institutions susceptible to such influence. This should, in turn, affect their behavior in terms of their use of courts to settle disputes and to enforce their property rights.

The BEEPS survey incorporates questions on the perceptions of courts and the use of courts. This provides an opportunity to test empirically the extent to which the inequality of influence subverts the effectiveness of courts in transition economies, as well as the impact on the security of property rights.

Firms were asked to assess the following attributes of the court system in their countries in resolving business disputes: (1) fairness and impartiality; (2) honesty and incorruptibility; and (3) ability to enforce decisions. They could choose from a scale of 1–6, in which 1 denotes that such attributes "never" apply to the court system and 6 denotes that such attributes "always" apply. We run separate regressions on each of the three attributes of the court system listed earlier. Crony bias is included in two forms—the individual firm score and the country average. This allows us to test the impact of general country conditions with regard to the perceived inequality on perceptions and use of courts, as well as the perceptions of the manager of the individual firm.

Since the firm's assessment of courts will also be affected by its experience of interacting with courts, we add a dummy variable (court exposure) if the firm identified itself as either a plaintiff or defendant in a civil or commercial arbitration court in the three-year period covered by the survey. Just over 37 percent of the firms in the sample used the court system in this period.[6] We include an interaction term between crony bias at the country level and court exposure (crony bias × court) to see if the experience of interaction with courts has a different impact in countries with higher levels of inequality of influence. This will also allow us to determine if crony bias has an impact on perceptions of the court even for firms that do not use the courts. Included in the regressions are control variables for firm size, sector, and ownership (state vs. private), as well as country-fixed effects. The results are presented in table 5.1.

Table 5.1 The inequality of influence and the court system

	Fair	Honest	Enforce decisions	Court use	Security of property rights
Crony bias (firm level)	−0.07 (−5.17)***	−0.09 (−6.23)***	−0.06 (−4.54)***	−0.02 (−1.56)*	−0.10 (−7.50)***
Crony bias (country average)	−0.36 (−2.21)**	−0.70 (−4.17)***	0.03 (0.16)	−1.01 (−6.14)***	0.06 (0.37)
Court exposure	0.15 (1.72)**	0.12 (1.36)	0.11 (1.26)		−0.01 (−0.17)
Crony bias (country average)×court exp.	−0.13 (−1.17)	−0.10 (−0.87)	−0.38 (−3.22)***		−0.18 (−1.62)*
State-owned	0.29 (4.67)***	0.32 (4.91)***	0.26 (3.95)***	0.03 (0.53)	0.25 (3.96)***
Size	0.11 (7.31)**	0.11 (7.29)***	0.08 (5.41)***	0.22 (15.54)***	0.08 (5.37)***
Sector dummies	Yes	Yes	Yes	Yes	Yes
Country dummies	Yes	Yes	Yes	Yes	Yes
Constant	2.47 (11.36)***	2.52 (11.43)***	2.98 (12.87)***	−0.64 (−3.10)***	3.14 (14.57)***
R-squared	0.10	0.11	0.10	0.13 (pseudo-R^2)	0.09
Observations	4,340	4,281	4,306	4,692	4,483
Mode	OLS	OLS	OLS	Probit	OLS

Notes: *t* statistics in parentheses; *significant at 10 percent; **significant at 5 percent; ***significant at 1 percent.

Firm managers and owners who see a higher level of bias toward political cronies have a consistently more negative assessment of all attributes of the court system. In addition, higher average scores on crony bias at the country level have a strong negative impact on perceptions of the fairness and honesty/incorruptibility of the courts across all firms in the country. The country-level effects of high crony bias are particularly pronounced on the perceptions of the honesty/incorruptibility of the court system: A one standard deviation increase in the country crony bias average is associated with a quarter-point fall in the assessment of the honesty of the court system. It is important to note that the negative impact of crony bias holds regardless of the firm's exposure to the court system.

Exposure to courts does bring some small improvement in the assessment of the fairness of courts, though for the honesty and enforceability dimensions this has only borderline significance. Yet exposure to courts has the opposite effect on perceptions of the enforceability of court decisions in countries with a high level of country bias, as evidenced by the significant negative coefficient on the interaction term (crony country avg × court). Those firms that do have experience with courts in crony-dominated systems are even more pessimistic that the courts are able to enforce their decisions.

So far, the results have linked measures of underlying inequalities of influence to perceptions about the various attributes of courts. Yet to the extent that such perceptions subvert institutions, they need to be linked to some aspect of firm behavior. One would expect that perceptions of the credibility of courts influence the likelihood that firms will use courts to resolve disputes. To measure the propensity to use courts, we use a modified variable from the court exposure variable included in the regressions mentioned earlier. Instead of exposure to courts as both a plaintiff and a defendant, we define a dummy variable called "court use" based exclusively on whether the firm had ever been a plaintiff in a court case. Being a plaintiff implies a voluntary decision to bring a case to court that entails costs and is thus a better measure of the extent to which a firm is inclined to use courts to resolve disputes. The probit model reported in the penultimate column of table 5.1 uses the same specifications as the previous regressions without the court exposure variable and the interaction term. The results show that in countries with a high crony bias, all firms are less likely to use courts to resolve business disputes. In addition, firms that perceive the business environment as skewed toward political cronies are even less likely to make use of courts. The inequality of influence undermines the credibility of courts and, in so doing, deters firms from using courts. This should only serve to further weaken the courts and increase their susceptibility to undue influence from more powerful firms.

These regressions suggest that the inequality of influence is associated not only with lower perceptions of the credibility of the court system, but also with the firm's willingness to use the courts. Perceptions and behavior are closely interrelated and mutually reinforcing.

If the courts cannot be relied upon to adjudicate disputes impartially and honestly and are subject to manipulation by influential firms, then the security of property and contract rights for all should be diminished, but especially for noninfluential firms. This can be tested using the survey results. Managers were asked to what degree they agree with the statement: "I am confident that the legal system will uphold my contract and property rights in business disputes." Again, respondents could choose from a 1–6 scale with 1 = never and 6 = always. Using the same specification as the court attributes regressions, we find that crony bias at the firm level has a significant negative impact on the firm's security of property rights, though the country-level effects of crony bias are not significant. Exposure to courts, in general, does not increase the security of property rights for firms. Indeed, for firms that have used courts in countries with a high level of crony bias, the security of property rights is even lower.

These results suggest some insights into how the inequality of influence can subvert institutions. The effectiveness of courts in guaranteeing property rights is based on the credibility among potential court users that the courts can be expected to make decisions in a fair and honest manner and that such decisions can be enforced on all participants, regardless of any differences in their economic strength or political influence. Yet in countries where firms on average see a significant inequality of influence, the firms are much less likely to place credibility in these attributes of the court system, regardless of their direct interaction with the court system. In other words, crony bias systematically weakens firm's perceptions of the credibility of the courts. Although direct exposure to courts does mitigate these negative perceptions at least with regard to the fairness of courts, it actually exacerbates the problem with the enforceability of court decisions. Firms who do use courts in countries with a high inequality of influence find that these courts are less able to enforce their decisions. Experience thus reinforces perceptions, further weakening the credibility of courts. The result is that the inequality of influence creates disincentives for firms to use the courts with negative implications for the security of their property rights. This is largely consistent with the model of institutional subversion proposed by Glaeser et al. (2002).

To Bribe or Pay Tax?

Perceptions of the inequality of influence should not only affect attitudes and behavior toward the courts, because one's view of all state institutions should be, to some extent, affected by the extent to which they are anticipated to make decisions and provide services in an impartial, honest, and reliable manner. One possible indicator of firm managers' broader attitudes toward state institutions is their willingness to pay taxes.[7] If a manager believes that the inequality of influence subverts the functioning of all state institutions then she should be less willing to pay taxes to support state institutions that are skewed to someone else's advantages. If the inequality of influence does lead managers to conceal more of their revenue from tax authorities and, hence, reduces the state's tax revenue, then such behavior might further subvert the effectiveness of state institutions.

Although tax compliance is obviously a difficult phenomenon to measure, previous business surveys have had some success in estimating relative compliance levels across countries. The BEEPS survey asks managers the following question: "Recognizing the difficulties that many firms face in fully complying with taxes and regulations, what percent of total annual sales would you estimate the typical firm in your area of business reports for tax purposes?"[8] On the basis of this question, we develop a tax compliance variable and measure the impact of different types of inequality of influence. Tax compliance rates should also be affected by the level of tax rates, problems of tax administration, and the performance of firms. To measure the impact of tax rates and tax administration, we add variables created from the firm's own assessment of the extent that tax rates and tax administration represent a problem for the operation and growth of their business measured on a 1–4 scale, with 1 = no obstacle and 4 = major obstacle. To measure firm performance, we include a variable indicating the percentage change in sales in real terms from 1998 to 2001. We also include the standard controls for firm characteristics and country-fixed effects. The results are reported in table 5.2.

As might be expected, firm managers that see high tax rates as more of a problem for their business report a lower share of annual sales for tax purposes. Neither the firm's own sales growth nor problems associated with tax administration (though this is highly correlated with the tax rates variable) have a significant impact on tax compliance.

Table 5.2   The inequality of influence and tax compliance

	Tax compliance
Crony bias (firm level)	−0.60
	(−2.43)***
Crony bias (country average)	−4.86
	(−1.96)**
Tax rates	−1.41
	(−2.86)***
Tax administration	−0.34
	(−0.71)
Sales growth	0.002
	(0.41)
State-owned	5.37
	(4.73)***
Size	1.59
	(6.17)***
Sector dummies	Yes
Country dummies	Yes
Constant	80.75
	(20.59)***
R-squared	0.13
Observations	3,981

Notes: t statistics in parentheses; ** significant at 5 percent; *** significant at 1 percent.

Higher levels of crony bias at both the country and the firm levels are associated with lower rates of tax compliance. At the firm level, a one standard deviation increase in the crony bias score leads to a one percentage point decrease in tax compliance. The impact of crony bias at the country level is greater with a one standard deviation in the country average score leading to a nearly two percentage point decline in tax compliance across all firms in the country.

The relationship between the inequality of influence and tax compliance would appear to reinforce the underlying imbalance of power that subverts institutions. If firms pay less in taxes in countries where they believe that political cronies subvert state institutions, this ensures that such institutions will remain weak (through low pay, low investment, low capacity, etc.) and, therefore, more subject to capture and political influence.

In addition to taxes, there are other payments that firms make to state officials, namely bribes. How does the inequality of influence affect the other main flow of transfers from firms to the state? BEEPS provides a detailed picture of the extent and the types of bribery across the region.[9] One would expect inequalities of influence to increase the incidence of corruption, and hence bribery, because this is one of the main mechanisms by which such inequalities are created. Firms invest in influence, just as they invest in other assets, to secure advantages arising from the legal, regulatory, and distributional powers of the state. At the same time, existing inequalities of influence could lead state officials to target weak firms. In either case, the inequality of influence should be associated with higher levels of corruption.

We look at two different aspects of corruption: (1) the extent of unofficial payments and gifts to public officials as a percent of the firm's annual sales revenues and (2) the frequency of unofficial payments and gifts to public officials in a given year. Corruption should be a function of certain firm characteristics, such as size, ownership, and sector, as previous work has shown. We also add two more dynamic variables—amount of senior management time spent with government officials and firm sales growth. Corruption is often linked to the extent of intervention by bureaucrats at the firm level, so the government "time tax" on management should lead to higher corruption.[10] Firms that perform well are more likely to attract the attention of predatory officials. Finally, we test for the impact of crony bias at the firm and country level on the extent and frequency of corruption. The results are reported in table 5.3.

The results are consistent across both regressions. As previous studies have shown, state-owned and large firms consistently pay less of their revenues in unofficial payments and make such payments less frequently than smaller, private firms. Senior management time spent with government is associated with a greater level and frequency of corruption payments. Firms perceiving a high inequality of influence pay more in corruption as a share of their revenue and pay more frequently. Moreover, in countries where the average level of crony bias is high, firms again pay more bribes, more frequently. The effects at both the firm and the country level are quite

Table 5.3   The inequality of influence and corruption

	Bribe share	Bribe frequency
Management time spent w/state	0.03	0.02
	(7.86)***	(8.35)***
Sales growth	−0.0005	−0.0002
	(−0.80)	(−0.48)
Crony bias (firm level)	0.12	0.14
	(3.82)***	(9.37)***
Crony bias (country average)	0.58	0.45
	(1.77)**	(3.18)***
State-owned	−1.00	−0.72
	(−6.73)***	(−10.56)***
Size	−0.17	−0.03
	(−5.03)***	(−1.65)*
Sector	Yes	Yes
Country dummies	Yes	Yes
Constant	2.19	2.54
	(4.43)***	(11.16)***
R-squared	0.12	0.15
Observations	4,009	4,089

Notes: t statistics in parentheses; *significant at 10 percent; **significant at 5 percent; ***significant at 1 percent.

substantial. A one standard deviation increase in the country crony bias average increases the mean "bribe tax" on all firms by nearly 15 percent. Similarly, a one standard deviation increase in the firm's crony bias score increases its mean bribe tax by an additional 12 percent.

The results in table 5.3 also suggest that firms that perceive themselves as more influential (i.e., with a negative crony bias score) pay a smaller share of their revenues in corruption and pay less frequently.

There are several possible interpretations for the causal link between the inequality of influence and corruption. One possible interpretation is that predatory officials prey upon weak firms extracting greater bribes from them, while influential firms can use their power to shield themselves from such demands. Such behavior on the part of officials would then exacerbate the firms' perception of inequalities. Another possible interpretation is that firms choose to bribe on the basis of their perceptions about inequalities in the broader environment. Less influential firms may bribe more because they are seeking to redress those power imbalances rooted in the greater size, employment, or personal political connections of influential firms. It is also possible that influential firms are just better bribers, getting more influence with a lower overall investment in corruption.

Surely, the causal relationship goes in both directions. It is important to note, however, that the impact of these perceptions about the inequality of influence have an additional impact on the level and frequency of corruption even beyond such differences in firm characteristics as size and ownership that might be expected to affect the extent to which firms are preyed upon by predatory state officials.

These results suggest that the inequality of influence affects not only the perception and use of courts, but influences more broadly the firm's relationship to the state. At lower levels of the inequality of influence, firms are more willing to invest in supporting state institutions through their tax contributions. At higher levels of inequality, firms are more likely to invest in bribery of individual public officials—either to gain advantages or to protect themselves—rather than in the support of state institutions. Naturally, such behavior further reinforces the weakness of state institutions in highly unequal environments.

Impact on Firm Performance

If the inequality of influence subverts state institutions, then it should affect the performance of all firms in highly unequal environments. By subverting courts, undermining tax revenues, and weakening the security of contract and property rights, significant inequalities of influence should reduce overall growth performance at the country level, even as it generates concentrated advantages for particular firms with close ties to political authorities. If so, then we need to turn to an examination of the effects of such inequalities at the country level to identify the externalities associated with varying levels of crony bias across countries.

Given the impact of the inequality of influence on the security of property rights and the quality of public institutions, we would expect this to have a negative impact on the firm's investments in restructuring. Restructuring is a form of investment of financial and human capital that should be quite sensitive not only to the security of property and contract rights, but to distortions in market structure that might limit or otherwise distort competition. Like all other forms of investment, the potential benefits of restructuring will be heavily discounted if there are significant risks that property rights and associated returns are subject to unpredictable expropriation by the state or by other powerful competitors. Moreover, if state institutions intervene in the economy to provide selective advantages to favored firms and to erect all sorts of barriers to market entry and competition, then firms might be wiser to invest in trying to influence or capture state institutions than in restructuring to improve performance. Even influential firms that enjoy considerable rents as a result of their capacity to capture the state are likely to face less substantial market pressures or other incentives to engage in restructuring. As a result, high levels of inequality of influence at the country level should have a negative impact on restructuring for all firms.

The BEEPS data provide evidence on a wide variety of restructuring activities, such as changing suppliers and customers, developing new products, opening new plants, insourcing or outsourcing production activities, forging new partnerships, and exporting to new markets—14 different activities in all. On the basis of these questions, we can develop an unweighted index of restructuring at the firm level measuring the likelihood that firms have engaged in any of these activities during the period 1998–2001.

Then we can test for the impact of the inequality of influence at the country level on restructuring, controlling for a variety of firm-level factors.

In addition to the standard firm-level characteristics, we expect the propensity to engage in restructuring to be influenced by the pressures of competition as seen by the firm and by its managers' perceptions of the investment climate. The measure of the investment climate is based on the extent to which a wide range of factors in the areas of finance, infrastructure, regulation, macroeconomic instability, and the rule of law are seen by the firm to pose obstacles for the operation and growth of their business. Competition is measured by two variables—price elasticity of demand and competitive pressure. The price elasticity is based on a question assessing the likely response from customers of a 10 percent increase in the price of the firm's main line of products or services.[11] An index of competitive pressure is based on the firm's assessment of pressure from a wider range of sources—such as domestic and foreign competitors, customers, creditors, and shareholders— on decisions to develop new products/services and markets as well as to reduce production costs.[12] Finally, we also add a variable denoting the age of the firm, because the propensity to engage in restructuring might also be related to the lifecycle of firms. The results are presented in table 5.4.

Table 5.4   The determinants of restructuring

	Restructuring index
Crony bias (firm level)	−0.05
	(−2.04)**
Investment climate (firm level)	0.36
	(4.13)***
Price elasticity of demand	−0.16
	(−4.89)***
Pressure	0.32
	(5.23)***
State-owned	−0.003
	(−0.14)
Size	0.22
	(8.52)***
Age	0.004
	(1.84)*
Sector dummies	Yes
Country dummies	Yes
Constant	−28.07
	(−6.86)***
R-squared	0.17
Observations	2,957

Notes: t statistics in parentheses; *significant at 10 percent; **significant at 5 percent; ***significant at 1 percent.

The restructuring index was created from a set of survey questions that asked firm managers if they have taken 14 different types of activities within the past year. On each of the 14 activities, they could respond positively or negatively. The index is the sum of all the positive responses at the firm level with a maximum of 14 and a minimum of zero.

Regarding firm characteristics, it is not surprising that larger firms and those in manufacturing and industry are more likely to engage in restructuring than smaller firms in the retail and trade sectors. That state ownership does not have a statistically significant effect on the propensity to engage in restructuring is particularly interesting, suggesting perhaps that sharper differences between state-owned and privatized firms in the earlier years of transition are beginning to weaken over time. Older firms are also less likely to restructure, perhaps reflecting the fact that the bulk of their restructuring was accomplished at an earlier stage of the transition. Firms that cite greater pressure from competitors, customers, creditors, and shareholders are significantly more likely to restructure.

As expected, firms that cite a higher level of crony bias are less likely to invest in restructuring. An uneven playing field skewed in favor of political cronies creates disincentives for less influential firms to make long-term investments in restructuring their business.

Conclusions: Political Institutions and the Inequality of Influence

The inequality of influence is clearly generated by the quality of existing political institutions. One could suggest a very long list of specific institutions, laws, regulations, and practices that shape the market for influence across countries.[13] Our understanding of what shapes inequalities of influence in developing countries is at a particularly early stage. Though explaining why countries have different levels of crony bias is beyond the scope of this essay, it is worth pointing out some initial, speculative relationships between broad regime types and the inequality of influence.

In reviewing the country averages for crony bias across the transition countries, an interesting pattern emerges. The lowest crony bias averages are in some of the most democratic and the least democratic regimes in the region. Indeed, figure 5.3 shows a simple correlation between the average crony bias and a standard measure of democratic political regimes, the Freedom House political liberties index for the period 1998–2001, suggests a bell-shaped curve. The Freedom House index ranges from one to seven with seven being the least free. We could speculate that political inclusion and participation mitigate severe inequalities of influence in more democratic systems, while political exclusion in personalistic dictatorships ensures that most actors outside the government are equally uninfluential. In general, perceived inequalities of political influence are greatest in those countries with partial political reforms, what some are referring to as "semiauthoritarian regimes" or "managed democracies" (though this gives us some idea of how firms would answer the question "managed by whom?"). Such regimes might be liberal enough to allow some competition for political influence, but the market for influence is still highly segmented and distorted with significant entry barriers and monopolistic practices.

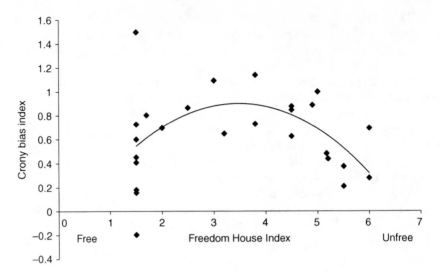

Figure 5.3   Crony bias and democracy

This relationship between political regimes and the inequality of influence extends beyond the transition economies. Data from about 5,000 firms from the global Survey of Executives carried out for the Global Competitiveness Report (GCR) for 2002–03, with a much broader coverage of 80 countries, allow us to construct a similar crony bias index and relate it to regime type in a larger sample of countries. The same bell-shaped relationship holds between the crony bias index in the Global Competitiveness Survey (GCS) with a broad measure of political voice and accountability from the "governance matters" database (Kaufmann and Kraay 2002).[14]

Though these simple correlations are very speculative, they suggest that we need to explore further how different regimes of competition, voice, and accountability shape the market for influence in developing countries. It is clear that political competition itself does not prevent the development of severe inequalities of influence. Rather, we need to understand how different rules, regulations, and practices generate a robust and reasonably transparent competition for political influence in developing countries.

Notes

*   The authors would like to thank the members of the Project on Honesty and Trust: Theory and Experience in the Light of Post-Socialist Transition at the Collegium Budapest for extremely helpful comments and support, and to the participants of the conferences Corruption: Its Consequences and Cures, held at Stanford University, and The Unobserved Economy: Measurement and Policy Issues, held at Tor Vergata University in Rome. János Kornai, Margaret Levi, Martin Raiser, Susan Rose-Ackerman, and Randi Ryterman, in particular, provided extensive and insightful feedback on earlier drafts of the chapter. Jana Kunicova not only provided expert research assistance on this project, but also made an important contribution to the development of the empirical work through her

analysis of the BEEPS dataset. The authors write in their personal capacity and do not necessarily reflect the views of the World Bank or its Board of Directors.

1. The extensive theoretical literature on inequality and growth includes Aghion and Williamson (1998); Alesina and Rodrik (1994); Banerjee and Newman (1991, 1993); Benabou (1996, 2000, 2002); Murphy et al. (1989); Perotti (1993); Persson and Tabellini (1994); Piketty (1997); and Rajan and Zingales (2002).

2. For previous work on transition countries, see Hellman (1998); Hellman et al. (2000); Hellman and Schankerman (2000); and for an application to Russia, Hellman (2002). Similar arguments have been developed in the EBRD's *Transition Report* (1999) and the World Bank's (2001) retrospective on the first decade of transition. For an analysis of these dynamics on a much broader range of countries, see Kaufmann and Kraay (2002).

3. The survey was terminated mid-course in Turkmenistan due to political harassment of the local survey firm.

4. We could create these indices by dividing the influence of political cronies and competitors by the firm's own influence and that of its business association, but this would lose valuable information about the overall level of influence perceived across the transition countries. Nevertheless, we have tested this alternative version of the indices on all the results presented in this essay and found similar, albeit occasionally less robust, effects.

5. One of the possible reasons for this unusually high perception of political cronyism in Poland is that the survey was conducted exactly when a very high profile case of influence peddling at the top levels of the Polish political establishment dominated the media. This, combined with a downturn in Poland's macroeconomic performance, contributed to an extremely pessimistic outlook regarding corruption in Poland that is evident in other surveys in the country.

6. This number itself is revealing, especially given that most of the firms in the sample are small and medium-sized enterprises and that the question only covered the period from January 2000 until the survey in early 2002. Given the low regard with which many in the region hold the court system, it is still actively used.

7. In the transition economies, such a decision has much more of an element of choice than obligation, as in other countries with more effective tax enforcement mechanisms.

8. The assumption, of course, is that firms base their estimate on their own practices. The evidence presented in this essay that firms do not see a vast gap between themselves and their direct competitors (i.e., "the typical firm in your area of business") suggests this assumption is not implausible.

9. For more on this issue using the first round of BEEPS, see Hellman et al. (2000) and World Bank (2000).

10. Of course, both corruption and time spent with government officials could be a function of the same underlying variable of excessive government regulation of the economy. However, we have no simple direct measure of such regulation other than what might be captured in the country and sector dummy variables. As a second-best alternative, the "time tax" can be seen as proxy for the regulatory burden.

11. Responses could range from continuing to buy from the firm in the same quantities, at slightly lower quantities, at much lower quantities, or buy from one's competitors instead.

12. Firms were asked to assess the importance of pressure from each of the actors described above on a 1–4 scale with 1 = not at all important to 4 = very important on the decisions to introduce new products and to reduce production costs separately. An unweighted average of these components is used to develop the index.

13. A good starting point to review the many factors that affect special interest politics is Grossman and Helpman (2001). Becker (1983) also takes a very broad and comprehensive approach to this issue.

14. The preliminary nature of the exposition of the global results based on the survey for the GCR is due to this data being still under analysis. Initial analysis suggests that, consistent with the results on transition based on the BEEPS survey detailed earlier, the evidence from global survey for the GCR indicate that where crony bias is more prevalent, the judiciary, property rights protection, and tax compliance are significantly more likely to be subverted. For the country average results, similarly strong and robust statistical results emerge from firm-level regressions with similar controls. For details on this worldwide firm-level dataset and its analysis, see also Kaufmann (2003).

References

Aghion, Philippe and Jeffrey Williamson. 1998. *Growth, Inequality, and Globalization*. New York: Cambridge University Press.

Alesina, Alberto and Dani Rodrik. 1994. "Distributive Politics and Economic Growth." *Quarterly Journal of Economics* 109: 465–90.

Banerjee, Abhijit and Andrew Newman. 1991. "Risk Bearing and the Theory of Income Distribution." *The Review of Economic Studies* 58: 211–35.

———. 1993. "Occupational Choice and the Process of Development." *Journal of Political Economy* 101: 274–98.

Becker, Gary S. 1983. "A Theory of Competition Among Pressure Groups for Political Influence." *Quarterly Journal of Economics* 98: 371–400.

Benabou, Roland. 1996. "Inequality and Growth." *NBER Macroeconomics Annual 1996*. Cambridge MA: MIT Press.

———. 2000. "Unequal Societies: Income Distribution and the Social Contract." *American Economic Review* 90: 96–129.

———. 2002. "Tax and Education Policy in a Heterogeneous-Agent Economy: What Levels of Redistribution Maximize Growth and Efficiency." *Econometrica* 70: 481–518.

EBRD (European Bank for Reconstruction and Development). 1999. *Transition Report: Ten Years of Transition*. London: EBRD.

Glaeser, Edward, Jose Scheinkman, and Andrei Shleifer. 2002. "The Injustice of Inequality." National Bureau of Economic Research Working Paper No. 9150, Cambridge MA.

Grossman, Gene M. and Elhanan Helpman. 2001. *Special Interest Politics*. Cambridge MA: MIT Press.

Hellman, Joel. 1998. "Winners Take All: The Politics of Partial Reform in Postcommunist Nations." *World Politics* 50: 203–34.

———. 2002. "Strategies to Combat State Capture and Administrative Corruption in Transition Economies." Background paper for the International Conference on Economic Reform and Good Governance: Fighting Corruption in Transition Economies, Beijing, China, April 11–12.

Hellman, Joel, Geraint Jones, and Daniel Kaufmann. 2000. *Seize the State, Seize the Day: State Capture, Corruption and Influence in Transition*. World Bank Policy Research Working Paper No. 2444, Washington DC: World Bank.

———. 2002. "Far From Home: Do Investors Import Higher Standards of Governance in Transition Economies?" World Bank, draft working paper, Washington DC.

Hellman, Joel and Mark Schankerman. 2000. "Intervention, Corruption and Capture: The Nexus Between Enterprise and the State." *Economics of Transition* 8: 545–76.

Kaufmann, Daniel. 2003. "Governance Crossroads." In P. Cornelius (ed.), *Global Competitiveness Report 2002–2003*, pp. 329–53. New York: Oxford University Press.

Kaufmann, Daniel and Aart Kraay. 2002. "Growth Without Governance." *Economia* 3: 169–229.

Murphy, Kevin, Andrei Shleifer, and Robert Vishny. 1989. "Income Distribution, Market Size and Industrialization." *Quarterly Journal of Economics* 104: 537–64.

Perotti, Roberto. 1993. "Political Equilibrium, Income Distribution, and Growth." *The Review of Economic Studies* 60: 755–76.

Persson, Torsten and Guide Tabellini. 1994. "Is Inequality Harmful for Growth?" *American Economic Review* 84: 600–21.

Piketty, Tomas. 1997. "The Dynamics of the Wealth Distribution and Interest Rate with Credit Rationing." *Review of Economic Studies* 64: 173–90.

Rajan, Raghuram and Luigi Zingales. 2002. "Property Rights and the Taming of Government." Manuscript, University of Chicago, Chicago IL.

Slinko, Irina, Evgeny Yakovlev, and Ekaterina Zhuravskaya. 2003. "Institutional Subversion: Evidence from Russian Regions." CEFIR Working Paper No. 31. Moscow.

World Bank. 2000. *Anticorruption in Transition: Confronting the Challenge of State Capture*. Washington DC.

———. 2001. *Transition—The First Ten Years: Analysis and Lessons for Eastern Europe and the Former Soviet Union*. Washington DC.

World Bank and European Bank for Reconstruction and Development. 2003. *Business Environment and Enterprise Survey (BEEPS)*. http://info.worldbank.org/governance/beeps/.

CHAPTER SIX

Effects of State Capture: Evidence from Russian Regions

IRINA SLINKO, EVGENY YAKOVLEV, AND
EKATERINA ZHURAVSKAYA[*]

Oligarchy ... throws a close network of dependence relationships over all the economic and political institutions of present-day bourgeois society without exception.

Lenin
("Imperialism: The Highest Stage of Capitalism," 1916)

Introduction

Ever since the emergence of the post-Washington consensus, striking differences in economic performance among transition countries and provinces within transition countries have been attributed to differences in the institutional environment. A wide range of institutions has been listed as important for transition to go smoothly, including federalism, political regime, property-rights protection, presence of an outside anchor, social norms, and trust.[1] Institutions, however, are not exogenous. Vested interests often influence the evolution of the very rules of the game in the economy. The literature labels this phenomenon *state capture* or *institutional subversion*.

A cross-country study done by the World Bank and the European Bank for Reconstruction and Development (EBRD) in 1999 confirmed that state capture is deeply rooted in the economic and political processes of Russia, which ranked fourth in the composite index of state capture among 20 transition countries.[2] Indeed, the first decade of Russia's transition was notorious for the intervention of *oligarchs* in determining the direction and speed of institutional reforms.[3] Russia provides a good case for investigating the effects of state capture not only because the problem is clearly present, but also because the high political autonomy of Russia's regions resulted in wide variations in regional institutions that one can use to explore the phenomenon. In addition, all regional laws are in the public domain. This allowed us to construct a reliable measure of state capture by studying preferential treatments of particular firms in regional legislations. This essay draws on the results of the formal econometric analysis done by Slinko et al. (2003), which examines the effects the capture of regional legislature exercises on the budgetary and regulatory policies of regional governments, aggregate growth, the growth of small businesses, and the performance of captor firms.

The theoretical literature on state capture was originated by Olson (1965), Stigler (1971), Pelzman (1976), and Becker (1983), and developed further by Laffont and Tirole (1991). Seminal work by Grossman and Helpman (1994, 1995) created the contemporary framework for studying interest groups politics. Persson (1998) studied interest-group-specific government spending. Glaeser et al. (2003) analyzed the effects of state capture on law and order, property rights protection, capital accumulation, growth, and inequality. Benedssen (2000) and Sonin (2003a) applied ideas from that literature to the context of transition. Theoretical literature identified the following determinants of state capture: cohesiveness of interest groups, level of voter awareness, electoral competition, electoral uncertainty (Bardhan and Mookherjee 1999), political centralization (Blanchard and Shleifer 2000), and initial inequality (Glaeser et al. 2003).

Empirical studies of state capture are scarce. The main reason is the difficulty in finding direct measures of influence because neither firms, nor bureaucrats would like to be caught engaged in high-level corruption. To the best of our knowledge, most of the empirical research on state capture in transition countries is based on the data from the BEEPS 1999 and BEEPS 2002 enterprise surveys that asked firms if they engage in activities that can be characterized as extending political influence or feel that other firms do so (see Hellman, Jones, Kaufmann, and Schankerman 2000; Hellman and Schankerman 2000; Hellman, Jones, and Kaufmann 2000; Hellman and Kaufmann this volume). These works show that, first, there is a sizable variation in the levels of capture among transition countries and, second, the speed and success of reforms is partly explained by the interplay of capture and democratization in the transition economies. Firm-level analysis with BEEPS data proved that in (and only in) high-capture countries, captor firms showed superior performance in the short run compared to similar noncaptor firms but did not expect their advantage to be sustained in the long term. Survey evidence produced by BEEPS is very interesting and insightful but has limitations—such as the small number of observations, incomparability of most policy variables, possible discrepancy between perceptions and reality—common to cross-country studies and studies based on survey data.

We take another approach—a panel data analysis of regional variation in one country based on objective publicly available data. It turns out that measuring the extent of institutional subversion based on the official information is a challenging but feasible exercise. We use the fact that Russia, as many other countries, has a system that allows legislation to be enacted only after its publication. We study regional legislation to find laws that treat economic agents unequally. It is worth mentioning that in some transition countries (e.g., Uzbekistan) this kind of legislation is a state secret.

We construct a measure of state capture that takes account of direct evidence of vested interests' influence on regional legislation. To construct this measure we take the following steps. First, we count the number of regional legislative acts that contain preferential treatments (tax breaks, investment credits, etc.) for the largest regional firms in each of 73 regions between 1992 and 2000. These are laws that explicitly mention the names of particular firms. The following are typical examples of legislation that contains preferential treatments. In 1998, Volgograd regional duma adopted the law "On a special economic zone on the territory of the Volgograd Tractor Plant (VTP)." The law relieves all firms from paying regional and local taxes for the period of ten years if they operate on the territory of VTP and at least 30 percent of their assets is owned by VTP. In Adygeya Republic in 1999 a law was enacted "On the preferential tax treatment of the meat-packing plant Li-Chet-Nekul." The law relieves this plant from paying regional property taxes for a period of two years. The budget law of Kamchatskaya Oblast of 2001 contained a special budgetary item called "support of fishing industries." It postulated that only one firm, Akros was to receive a large sum of money under this budgetary item. Needless to say, there are many fishing firms in Kamchatskaya Oblast but no other firm is mentioned directly in the budget law.

Second, we take concentration of the resulting number of persistent preferential treatments among firms as a measure of regional state capture controlling for the total number of preferential treatments. Thus, for two regions with the same number of legislative acts that contain preferential treatments, the region where preferential treatments go to only one (or a few) large firms is considered to be more captured than the one where preferential treatments are uniformly dispersed across firms. We compare the concentration of preferential treatments across regions and not their total number because the total number of preferential treatments may just reflect the general level of paternalism of the regional governments, while we are interested in the effect of *unequal* treatment of similar economic agents (in our case, firms) by rules and institutions. Similarly, we take the share of preferential treatments that go to a particular firm among the five largest recipients of preferential treatments as a proxy for the likelihood that this firm is a captor because "the regional rules of the game" treat it most preferentially.

Although these measures are quite intuitive because they account for unequal treatment of firms by legislation, they have serious drawbacks. First, we cannot compare the importance of different preferential treatments, thus we just count the number of "subverted" legislative acts. Second, we can only identify preferential treatments when the text of the law directly mentions a particular firm. An example of legislative preferential treatment that we cannot systematically account for can be drawn from the Briansk regional legislature. In 1997 the regional duma adopted the law "On the regulation of the alcohol market" that stated that alcohol was to be sold only by accredited firms. Any firm could get accreditation from the regional administration if it satisfied a list of criteria (e.g., being present on the market for several years, having storage place of a certain size, etc.). Products sold by firms without accreditation were subject to confiscation. There were many firms in the market in the region at that time, but only one satisfied the criteria outlined in the law.

Despite all the imperfections of our measure of preferential treatment, it is fairly correlated with the Transparency International (TI) and Information for Democracy (INDEM) state capture rating available for 39 regions in 2001 (the correlation coefficient is 0.5, significant at 5 percent significance level).[4]

Our main findings are as follows: At the regional level, state capture has an adverse effect on small-business growth, tax collection, federal tax arrears, and regional public spending on some social services. At the micro level, it generates substantial performance gains to firms that exercise regional political influence both in the long and the short run. In the long run, captor firms lack efficiency incentives but continue to grow: The profitability and market shares of captor firms grow faster, and labor productivity grows slower compared to their noncaptor counterparts.

This essay proceeds as follows. The next section describes the measures of institutional subversion. That is followed by a section presenting data sources and summary statistics. Then the essay goes on to formulate hypotheses and present results. The final section concludes.

How Did We Measure State Capture?

The measurement of state capture plays a central role in our analysis.

In order to construct a proxy for state capture at the regional level and identify captor enterprises in each region, we took the following steps. First, we limited ourselves to the largest firms in the regions: We constructed a list of firms that includes the five largest nonstate regional firms and all state regional firms that are among the five largest firms in any of the years 1992–2000. The resulting list contained 978 firms (up to 20 of the largest regional firms in each of 73 regions). We considered these firms as potential candidates for being captors. Second, we searched the comprehensive database of Russia's regional laws "Consultant Plus"[5] for any preferential treatment for each of these enterprises in the regional legislation in each year between 1992 and 2000. We deemed an enterprise to have been treated preferentially in a particular year if it received any of the following benefits: tax breaks, investment credits, subsidies, subsidized loans and loans with a regional budget guarantee, official delays in tax payments, subsidized licensing, state property given away for free, and creation of a "Special Open Economic Zone" on the territory of the enterprise. We then counted the number of regional laws that grant different (distinct) preferential treatments to each of the 978 firms each year. Preferential treatments are a persistent phenomenon. If an enterprise receives preferential treatments in any particular year, there is an over 60 percent chance that this enterprise also receives preferential treatments in the subsequent or the previous year. If an enterprise does not get preferential treatments in any particular year, there is an over 80 percent chance that this enterprise does not get preferential treatments in either the subsequent or the previous year. Of the firms in our sample, 56 percent did not have one single preferential treatment throughout the whole period.

Third, we constructed a measure of regional capture. We took the concentration of preferential treatments for the five enterprises in each region each year that received the largest number of preferential treatments.[6] Thus, preferential treatment concentration is our measure of state capture at the regional level. Holding the total number of preferential treatments constant (that may reflect other forms of paternalism by the regional authorities), higher persistent preferential treatment concentration is an indication of a higher extent of legislative capture because few firms receive disproportionate amount of preferential treatments by the regional legislature. At the firm level, the higher share of all regional preferential treatments that go to a particular firm for a given level of regional institutional subvention (measured by preferential treatment concentration) is an indication of a higher likelihood that this particular enterprise is a captor. We compare the concentration of preferential treatments across regions and the shares of preferential treatments across firms instead of comparing their total numbers because we are interested in the effect of the *inequality* in treatment of similar large firms by regional legislations. If, for example, all firms in a region receive preferential treatments, we do not think of this region as captured because, essentially, all firms in this region are treated equally.

The concentration of preferential treatments is an indication of merely one aspect of institutional subversion because it takes into account only what is reflected in the text of regional legislation. The institutional environment affected by vested interests is much richer. In addition to legislation, their influence extends over law enforcement and regulation. For example, captor firms may directly affect court decisions or licensing and registration policies. Thus, we also use regional size concentration among the ten largest nonstate regional enterprises as an alternative measure of *potential* capture. There are two theoretical stories behind the motivation for the potential capture measure. First, in the model by Grossman and Helpman (1994), everyone is assumed to have different interests; and big agents can organize their interests more easily. Concentration matters for potential capture because it makes organization cheaper. Second, Friebel and Guriev (2002) assumed all agents (local firms) to have similar interests (e.g., attracting high-skilled workers to the locality), thus everyone benefits if the preferred policy occurs. In this case, the free-rider externality is smaller for larger firms because they receive a significantly larger portion of the total benefits when favorable regulations are adopted. Glaeser et al. (2003) argued that there is a feedback in the relationship between concentration and institutional subversion: Inequality leads to subversion and weak institutions allow only the rich to protect themselves in order to become even richer. As proxies from potential capture measure we use the firm's employment and output as proxies for size.

Data and Summary Statistics

Apart from the state capture measures the following data were used for hypothesis testing. Financial and other statistical data on enterprises comes from the Russian Enterprise Registry Longitudinal Data (RERLD) covering the most basic financial statistics on (45,000) large- and medium-size firms in Russia that produce over 85 percent of Russia's official industrial output. The data span the period from 1992 to 2000 for 77 regions. Detailed regional budgetary figures for the period 1996–2000 come from the Ministry of Finance of the Russian Federation, while the source of some other regional level statistical data is Goskomstat, Russia's official statistical agency. The panel spans the period 1996–2000.

The average annual preferential treatment concentration equals 0.395. It corresponds to the common situation where in a particular year one regional enterprise receives two preferential treatments, another two enterprises receive one each, and all other regional firms do not receive any. The mean value of output concentration is 0.226. On average, the first firm's output is twice as large as the output of the second largest firm and three times as large as the output of the third largest firm. The mean value of employment concentration is 0.160. On average, employment in the largest enterprise is 70 percent larger than in the second largest; in the second largest it is 35 percent larger than in the third; in the third it is 20 percent larger than in the fourth, and so on. Figure 6.1 shows the median regional

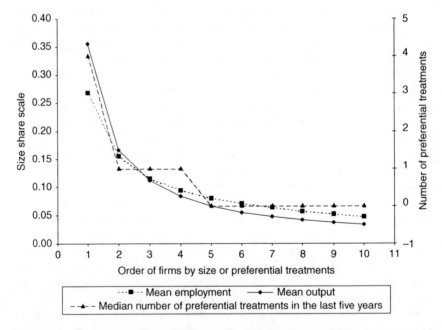

Figure 6.1 Average output and employment shares for the largest regional enterprises and preferential treatment for their largest regional recipients

Source: Slinko et al. 2003.

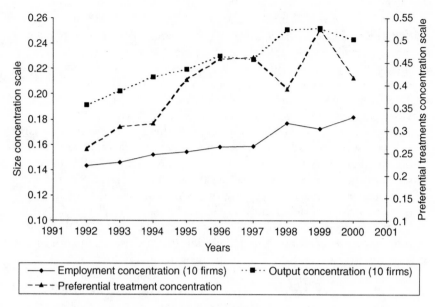

Figure 6.2 Means of state capture measures through time
Source: Slinko et al. 2003.

distribution of preferential treatments among the largest ten recipients of preferential treatments and the average relative size of the ten largest regional enterprises. Measures of legislative and potential capture are positively, significantly, but not very highly correlated. Despite the low correlation between the legislative and potential capture, the results using the two alternative measures turned out to be similar. Figure 6.2 shows the dynamic aspect of our capture measures: Throughout the 1990s all the measures grew more or less steadily.

Effects of State Capture

This section presents the results that we rigorously derived from our analysis.

Effects of State Capture at the Regional Level

Small-Business Growth

On the one hand, large powerful firms may be interested in small and medium-size enterprises (SME) growth because they may have excessive employment and would like to lay off workers, but they cannot do so for political reasons unless there are small firms to hire these workers.[7] In this case, politically powerful firms may lobby for creating a favorable regulatory environment for small businesses. On the other hand, SME growth may be against interests of managers of large politically connected firms if they compete with the small firms for scarce skilled labor on the labor market (Friebel and Guriev 2002) or for scarce government budgetary resources (Gehlbach 2003). In the case of direct competition, vested interests may put pressure on regional authorities to harden the regulatory environment for small businesses. Regional authorities can directly affect the small-business environment, for example, by changing the costs of registration, certification, inspections, licensing, and leasing premises. There is also a possibility (outlined by Gehlbach 2003) that there is no hostility of large businesses toward small-business development, but the fact that vested interests capture budgetary resources implies that there are fewer resources left to be spent on infrastructure for small businesses or salaries of bureaucrats in order to prevent them from preying on them. Thus, if either of the arguments set forth by Friebel and Guriev (2002) and Gehlbach (2003) are empirically relevant, we would observe smaller SME growth in the regions with higher levels of institutional subversion because in these regions more SMEs would be driven out of the market or to the unofficial sector.[8]

We use three measures of small-business development: the number of small businesses per capita, the share of small-business employment, and retail turnover per capita. We find that changes in preferential treatment concentration have a significant negative effect on the changes in the share of small-business employment in the short run.

To illustrate the magnitude of the short-run effects of capture on regional macroeconomic performance, consider a region N that experienced an increase in the concentration of preferential treatments in some particular year. Initially, region N had the following distribution of preferential treatments among their largest recipients: The largest received two preferential treatments, the second and the third largest obtained one each, and no other enterprises received any. Next year, the largest recipient of preferential treatments got three, the second largest got one, and other firms in region N got no preferential treatments. Regression results imply that the share of small-business employment would fall by 2.4 percent in region N when the described change occurred.

The long-run relationship between legislative capture and small-business growth is even stronger. In the long run, two of the three measures of small-business growth (the number of small-businesses and the share of small business employment) are significantly related to state capture. The magnitude of the long-term effect can be illustrated by comparing the two regions X and Y over a period of nine years. These regions are similar in all respects except that in two out of nine years they differ in their preferential treatment concentrations. For seven years both regions have the following distribution of preferential treatments: The largest recipient gets two preferential treatments, another two enterprises receive one each, and no other firm receives any. In the other two years, in region X the distribution of the number of preferential treatments remains unchanged, but in region Y, in each of those two years only one firm receives four preferential treatments.[9] Clearly, region Y is more captured because it has a slightly higher nine-year-average concentration of preferential treatments. Long-run regression results imply that the average number of small businesses per capita is 13 percent higher and the share of small-business employment is 7 percent higher in region X than in region Y.

Retail turnover is not significantly affected by state capture. This fact points to the possibility that some small businesses do not exit the market completely under regulatory pressure from the regional governments; instead, they are driven to the unofficial sector. Overall, the hypothesis that vested interests get in the way of small-business growth finds strong support in the data.

GRP Growth and Investment

Theoretically, the effect of capture on Gross Regional Product (GRP) growth and investment is ambiguous. On the one hand, capture improves growth prospects and return on investments in captor enterprises because they successfully bargain for investment credit, tax breaks, and protection from competitors. On the other hand, the subversion of institutions by vested interests leads to lower growth and investment by the rest of the economy because producers outside vested interests groups are discriminated against. Thus, captor firms are the major potential source of growth in a captured state both in the short and the long run. There is an additional consideration in the long run: State capture may lead to deterioration of investment and growth even in captor firms because they lack incentives for efficient production because of the very high profitability of their rent-seeking activities. Our analysis shows that the annual changes in GRP per capita are significantly positively associated with changes in preferential treatment concentration. Thus, in the short run, the positive effect of state capture on growth within vested interests dominates the negative effect on the rest of the producers. The size of the effect is such that region N experiences an additional 1 percent economic growth when its preferential treatment concentration increases as described earlier. There is no statistically significant relationship of state capture to growth or investment in the long run. The fact that the short-run positive effect on growth is not sustained in the long run is consistent with the view that the rent-seeking activities of captor enterprises destroy value in the long run, and we just do not have a sufficient time horizon to observe the negative correlation.

Tax Collection and Arrears

Tax collections should decrease with an increase in state capture for a given level of tax base because large captor enterprises lobby to decrease their own tax burden. This effect should be seen in the aggregate because large enterprises contribute the most to regional tax collections. Indeed, we find a strong negative association between regional tax collection and state capture, such that the share of region N's annual tax revenues as a share of the regional product would fall by 1.2 percent when it experiences an increase in preferential treatment concentration of a magnitude described earlier.

One also should expect tax arrears to be higher in more captured regions because captor firms lobby for delays in tax payments. Moreover, federal arrears should increase to a larger extent than regional arrears because regional authorities often protect captor firms from paying federal taxes. Mechanisms of such regional protection have been extensively studied in the literature. For example, Ponomareva and Zhuravskaya (2001), Shleifer and Treisman (2000), Treisman (1999), Lambert-Mogiliansky et al. (2000), and Sonin (2003b) present theory and evidence on protection of regional firms from paying federal taxes. The regression results we presented in our 2003 paper show that, first, federal arrears in the region N would increase by 2.7 percent when preferential treatment concentration increases as described earlier, and second, regional arrears would not be significantly affected by the change in preferential treatment concentration (Slinko et al. 2003). This evidence supports the view, expressed, for instance, by Sonin (2003b) and Ponomareva and Zhuravskaya (2001), that Russia's regional governments protect regional firms from paying federal taxes.

Social Spending

The theoretical link between capture and social spending in our analysis is motivated by Friebel and Guriev (2002) who argue that large enterprises in Russia attract skilled workers by paying them in kind (e.g., providing them with corporate housing, health care, education, and daycare for their children) in order to prevent savings that are sufficient for the workers to leave. One implicit assumption of their model is that workers value privately provided social services. This could happen only when public provision of social services is poor. Public access to high-quality social services would undermine the captor's attachment strategies. Thus, public spending on the provision of such social goods as housing, health care, daycare centers, and so on should be lower in regions with higher level of state capture.

There are two other stories that are consistent with the negative correlation between social spending and state capture. First, vested interests may not be concerned with social services at all; instead, they are more interested in other budgetary items (e.g., expenditures on industry, police, and the media). Therefore, they may lobby for the reduction of expenditures on social infrastructure services relative to spending on these other budgetary items. Second, large enterprises and regional governments may agree to private provision of social services in exchange for tax breaks in order to avoid paying federal tax obligations.

The test of whether regional variation in any of the budgetary items can be partly explained by differences in state capture lead to findings consistent with Friebel and Guriev's story as well as the story of federal tax evasion (Lavrov et al. 2001). Holding other things constant, legislative capture is significantly negatively correlated with expenditures on the construction of some social service facilities. The magnitude of the effect is such that region N would experience cuts in expenditures on construction of new housing by 5 percent, and cultural facilities by 14 percent in the same year when preferential treatment concentration increases as is described earlier. There is no evidence of significant correlation in any other budgetary items with our measures of state capture.

Regional-level results prove to be robust enough to be used to measure potential rather than legislative capture.

Effects of State Capture at the Firm Level

Hellman, Jones, and Kaufmann (2000) pointed out that in countries with an active market for capture (of which Russia is an example) captors received short-term benefits of capture in terms of increases in sales, employment, and investment. They also showed that captor firms did not expect to outperform other firms in the long run. In addition, capture should increase the market power of captor firms. There are two channels through which this can happen. First, captor firms should grow as a result of their preferential treatment, and second, captors' competitors should decline as a result of the discrimination against them (e.g., because of any excessive regulatory burden). Friebel and Guriev (2002) predict that captor firms have more bargaining power vis à vis their employees compared to other firms; therefore, wage arrears in captor firms should be higher. Also, the political power of captor enterprises may allow them to run higher arrears to suppliers compared to other enterprises because subversion of the institutions responsible for enforcement of the payments may occur; and, as was discussed earlier, tax arrears should be higher in captor firms as well.

The evidence of microeconomic effects of capture we derived are consistent with these hypotheses. Holding other things constant, in the short run captors experience significantly higher investment, employment and sales growth, and growth of their shares both on the regional and national markets. A 1 percent increase in the share of preferential treatments given to a particular firm in any particular year increases employment and sales by approximately 2 percent and fixed assets by 1.5 percent in this firm in the same year. In addition, regional market share increases by one-tenth of a percentage point and national market share by one-hundredth of a percentage point.

In the long run the results are even stronger. Holding other things constant, captors continue to outperform noncaptor firms in terms of sales and employment growth, investment in fixed assets, and national and regional market shares. In addition, in the long run, captors have higher profits and higher bargaining power vis à vis employees, suppliers, and government that allows them to run higher wage, trade, and tax arrears. A very important finding is that in the long run, firms that engage in state capture have significantly lower labor productivity growth than their counterparts despite higher profitability. This means that the long-run gains to captor firms are a result of rent-seeking activities and not driven by efficiency improvements. The magnitude of the effect is as follows: If the average share of preferential treatments over a decade is 1 percent higher, sales grow by 1.7 percent, average employment by

0.5 percent, average fixed assets by 3.6 percent, profitability by 1.4 percent, arrears to suppliers by 1.4 percent, wage arrears by 2 percent, and tax arrears by 3 percent. Labor productivity falls by 1 percent. In addition, the firm experiences one-tenth of a percentage point increase in its regional market share and two-hundredth of a percentage point increase in its national market share (both effects are statistically significant).

Comparison with BEEPS

These findings by and large are consistent with BEEPS evidence (Hellman, Jones, and Kaufmann 2000; Hellman and Schankerman 2000). Cross-country comparisons based on BEEPS show that in countries with higher levels of capture, firms from the BEEPS sample have on average lower investment, output, and employment growth. We find that there is a short-run positive association between GRP growth and capture in Russian regions and that it disappears in the long run. How can one reconcile these pieces of evidence? The variation in state capture across countries is much higher than across Russia's regions. So, the evidence from BEEPS and our study are not inconsistent because the relationship between the level of capture and growth may be different within the group of high-capture environments (i.e., countries or regions) and between the high- and low-capture environments. We also find a negative relationship between the level of regional capture and small-business development. This finding is in line with Hellman and Schankerman's (2000) result that reform is slower in high-capture countries.

There is a slight dichotomy between BEEPS and our findings at the micro level: There is universal evidence that sales and investment grow faster in captor firms compared to noncaptors in the short run. Hellman, Jones, and Kaufmann (2000) found that captor firms do not expect these gains to be sustained in the long run. We find, however, that captors are too modest in their expectations, at least according to their answers; actual long-run growth in sales, investment, and market share is higher in captor firms, but their productivity growth is lower.

Conclusions

We find that the most important effect of state capture is that environments with higher levels of state capture have greater obstacles to small-business growth. This effect has particularly significant consequences in a transition economy because institutional subversion becomes an impediment to asset reallocation from the old to the new sector. Despite the negative effect of state capture on small business, institutional advantages for captor firms result in short-term aggregate economic growth that is not sustained in the long run. The tax capacity of the state deteriorates with capture: Tax revenues fall and arrears grow for a given level of GRP. In addition, the structure of fiscal expenditures is affected by the level of regional capture: Construction of new social facilities is smaller in high-capture regions.

On the micro level, capturing the state brings great advantages to firms. Captors exhibit faster growth in employment, sales, market share, and investment both in the short and the long run. In addition, higher bargaining power gives captors the ability to maintain higher arrears to suppliers and employees in the long run because local officials protect captors from legal enforcement of these payments. The source of the long-run captors' growth is rent seeking as they win market share from their counterparts and lose to them in efficiency measured by labor productivity.

Notes

* We thank Akhmed Akhmedov, Erik Berglof, Scott Gehlbach, Sergei Guriev, Andrei Illarionov, János Kornai, Rory MacFarquhar, participants at the Center for Economic and Financial Research (CEFIR) seminar, participants of the 2001 New Economic School (NES) research conference, and the Honesty and Trust 2002 workshop in Budapest for helpful comments and suggestions. We are grateful to Evgenia Kolomak for the help with data collection and to NES for financial support in the early stages of this project.
1. For an excellent survey of the literature, see Roland (2000).
2. The study is called Business Environment and Enterprise Performance Surveys (BEEPS). Two rounds of BEEPS surveys were conducted in 1999 and 2002 jointly by the World Bank and the European Bank for Reconstruction and Development in transition countries. See http://info. worldbank.org/governance/beeps/ for survey description, data, and research.
3. Russian oligarchs were called so for a reason. According to Encyclopedia Britannica, "*oligarchy* is especially despotic power exercised by a small and privileged group for corrupt or selfish purposes."
4. Transparency International and INDEM data are available at http://www.anti-corr.ru/rating_regions/index.htm.
5. www.consultant.ru/Software/Systems/RegLaw.
6. As our concentration measure we use the Herfindahl-Hirsman formula (a sum of squared shares of the numbers of preferential treatments).
7. Needless to say, managers of large firms may be interested in SME growth because they want to eat in good restaurants and shop in nice stores.
8. See, e.g., Johnson et al. (1998) and Frye and Zhuravskaya (2000).
9. The changes of preferential treatment concentrations in region N and between regions X and Y correspond to one standard deviation increases of preferential treatment concentration from the mean in the short and the long run, respectively.

References

Bardhan, Pranab and Dilip Mookherjee. 1999. *Relative Capture of Local and Central Governments. An Essay in the Political Economy of Decentralization.* CIDER Working Paper C99-109. University of California, Berkeley CA.

Becker, Gary S. 1983. "A Theory of Competition Among Pressure Groups for Political Influence." *Quarterly Journal of Economics* 98: 371–400.

Bennedsen, Morten. 2000. "Political Ownership." *Journal of Public Economics* 76: 559–81.

Blanchard, Olivier and Andrei Shleifer. 2000. *Federalism With and Without Political Centralization. China Versus Russia.* NBER Working Paper No.w7616. Cambridge MA.

Friebel, Guido and Sergei Guriev. 2002. *Should I Stay or Can I Go? Worker Attachment in Russia.* CEFIR Working Paper No. 8. Moscow.

Frye, Timothy and Ekaterina Zhuravskaya. 2000. "Rackets, Regulations and Public Goods." *Journal of Law, Economics and Organization* 16: 478–502.

Gehlbach, Scott. 2003. *Taxability, Elections, and Government Support of Business Activity*. CEFIR Working Paper No. 30. Moscow.

Glaeser, Edward, Jose Scheinkman, and Andrei Shleifer. 2003. "The Injustice of Inequality." *Journal of Monetary Economics: Carnegie-Rochester Series on Public Policy* 50: 199–222.

Grossman, Gene and Elhanan Helpman. 1994. "Protection for Sale." *American Economic Review* 84: 833–50.

———. 1995. "Politics of Free Trade Agreements." *American Economic Review* 85: 667–90.

Hellman, Joel S. and Mark Schankerman. 2000. "Intervention, Corruption and Capture." *Economics of Transition* 8: 545–79.

Hellman, Joel S., Geraint Jones, and Daniel Kaufmann. 2000. *Seize the State, Seize the Day: State Capture, Corruption and Influence in Transition*. World Bank Policy Research Working Paper No. 2444. Washington DC.

Hellman, Joel S., Geraint Jones, Daniel Kaufmann, and Mark Schankerman. 2000. *Measuring Governance, Corruption, and State Capture: How Firms and Bureaucrats Shape the Business Environment in Transition Economies*. World Bank Policy Research Working Paper No. 2312. Washington DC.

Johnson, Simon, Daniel Kaufmann, and Andrei Shleifer. 1998. "The Unofficial Economy in Transition." *Brookings Papers on Economic Activity* 2: 159–239.

Laffont, Jean-Jacques and Jean Tirole. 1991. "The Politics of Government Decision-Making: A Theory of Regulatory Capture." *Quarterly Journal of Economics* 106: 1089–127.

Lambert-Mogiliansky, Ariane, Konstantin Sonin, and Ekaterina Zhuravskaya. 2000. "Bankruptcy Capture: Theory and Evidence from Russia." CEFIR Discussion Paper No. 2488. Moscow.

Lavrov, Aleksei, John M. Litwack, and Douglas Sutherland. 2001. *Fiscal Federalist Relations in Russia: A Case for Subnational Autonomy*. OECD Center for Co-operation with Non-members Working Paper at http://www.imf.org/external/pubs/ft/seminar/2000/fiscal/lavrov.pdf.

Olson, Mancur. 1965. *The Logic of Collective Action*. Cambridge MA: Harvard University Press.

Pelzman, Sam. 1976. "Toward a More General Theory of Regulation." *Journal of Law and Economics* 9: 211–40.

Persson, Torsten. 1998. "Economic Policy and Special Interest Politics." *Economic Journal* 108: 310–27.

Ponomareva, Maria and Ekaterina Zhuravskaya. 2001. *Do Governors Protect Firms from Paying Federal Taxes?* CEFIR Working Paper No. 10. Moscow.

Roland, Gerard. 2000. *Transition and Economics: Politics, Markets and Firms*. Cambridge MA: MIT Press.

Shleifer Andrei and Daniel S. Treisman. 2000. *Without a Map: Political Tactics and Economic Reform in Russia*. Cambridge MA: MIT Press.

Slinko, Irina, Evgeny Yakovlev, and Ekaterina Zhuravskaya. 2003. "Institutional Subversion: Evidence from Russian Regions." CEFIR Working Paper No. 31. Moscow.

Sonin, Konstantin. 2003. "Why the Rich May Favor Poor Protection of Property Rights?" *The Journal of Comparative Economics* 31: 715–31.

———. 2003b. "Provincial Protectionism." Mimeo. CEFIR. Moscow.

Stigler, George J. 1971. "The Economic Theory of Regulation." *Bell Journal of Economics* 2: 3–21.

Treisman, Daniel S. 1999. "Model of Regional Protectionism." Mimeo. UCLA. Los Angeles CA.

CHAPTER SEVEN

Regulation and Corruption in Transition: The Case of the Russian Pharmaceutical Markets

ALEXANDRA VACROUX

Most research on corruption in transition countries focuses on how entrepreneurs exploit and evade the regulatory environment (e.g., Johnson et al. 2000). Surveys of firms have been used to identify corrupt mechanisms (e.g., Hellman et al. 2000) and country-specific analyses have estimated the cost of such practices (e.g., Satarov 2002). However, we lack case studies that illustrate why bureaucrats engage in corruption, how corrupt systems evolve, and why corruption varies from place to place. To meet this need, this chapter presents the preliminary findings of a study of the Russian pharmaceutical sector. This chapter and the larger project of which it is a part complement earlier work done on firm behavior by concentrating on the incentives that encourage civil servants to engage in corruption. The conclusions are based on interviews conducted with regional health care officials and business people.

The collapse of the Soviet Union demanded that Russia's Yeltsin government address many urgent tasks. The need to simultaneously build a viable independent state, stabilize the economy, and privatize state property put tremendous pressure on the narrow circle of reformers in the Yeltsin government. Overwhelmed and inclined toward federalism, Moscow counted on regional leaders to solve local problems, and granted governors greater autonomy. Strained finances meant that the regions received not only sovereignty but also the responsibility for sustaining key programs, including the constitutionally protected health care system. Provincial leaders cobbled together reforms on an ad hoc basis that produced many inconsistencies and inefficiencies. As a result, in the early 1990s poorly considered regulatory decisions were often passed down to lower-level officials for implementation. These officials had to figure out for themselves how to execute new policies, and found that the proposed rules could frequently be modified in ways that made them more appropriate for the task at hand, easier to implement, or more likely to promote bribery.

Decentralized and uneven reforms introduce instability into organizations, thereby increasing opportunities for corruption. Corruption may develop even if the initial reforms themselves are not deliberately written to create red tape and allow for petty corruption. This chapter looks at how regulatory agencies responded to the retail and wholesale pharmaceutical markets that emerged as part of Russia's post-communist transition. It begins with a discussion of the incentives presented to bureaucrats and entrepreneurs in this environment, and moves on to examine how these are affected by the reform process. Throughout the chapter, the focus is on shifts in incentives that may foster corruption, where a corrupt transaction is defined as an unsanctioned exchange between two actors: a bureaucrat and the representative of a private firm.[1]

Overview of the Case Study

A case study on corruption should offer not only a rich illustration of a corrupt environment, but also an explanation for why the extent and form of corruption may vary. The Russian pharmaceutical industry is an ideal subject for this kind of analysis: It is—and should be—highly regulated, and therefore offers many instances in which the public and private sectors interact. Concentrating on a single economic sector (but treating each market within that sector separately) allows one to hold constant the type of regulation required. At the same time, one can compare the activities of the bureaucracies involved in regulating pharmacies and drug distributors. Bureaucratic behavior depends on institutional rules and functions but may also reflect local conditions. Because the relevant regulatory agencies exist in each of Russia's regions, one can also ask whether a given agency behaves identically in different environments.

The research underlying this chapter was conducted in summer 2002 in four Russian cities: Samara, Volgograd, Ufa, and Ioshkar-Ola.[2] It encompassed interviews and surveys of public officials, drug distributors, and pharmacy directors. Conversations with public officials and market participants did not focus on specific cases of corruption but rather on uncovering patterns of behavior and expectations.

The framework used here to explain bureaucratic behavior in transitions builds on three complementary studies of the Soviet and post-Soviet state. Philip Roeder (1993) applied the new institutionalism to the Soviet Union's authoritarian system to explain why the country collapsed. His emphasis on the informal side of Soviet institutions and their place in larger state structures is echoed in this analysis. Steven Solnick's (1998) book on the behavior of bureaucrats in disintegrating state institutions adds a role for financial motives. Solnick found that agile bureaucrats used the uncertainty created by Gorbachev's partial reforms to profit from their access to state assets. His discovery sets the stage for the post-Soviet period reviewed here, in which public officials are confronted with even greater instability. Joel Hellman (1998) examined the "winners" in the early transition period and their incentives to block further reforms that eliminate rent-producing distortions in the economy. Hellman was concerned primarily with the activities of the nascent private sector, but his approach can be productively applied to the study of bureaucrats.

The Corrupt Transaction

In this essay corruption will be defined as "the abuse of public office for private gain." Three types of corruption are relevant here: petty corruption, grand corruption, and capture. Petty corruption involves the regular sale of decisions (such as licenses) by low-level officials to private actors. Grand corruption occurs when a high-ranking official abuses his authority over major programs to reap significant monetary benefits (Moody-Stuart 1997). If the rules for awarding government contracts have been altered to favor specific firms, the purchasing agency and responsible officials may have been captured. Evidence that state orders are repeatedly filled by one seller does not itself demonstrate capture—the seller may indeed be offering the best terms or products. Administrative capture can be proven only if (a) a firm or industry is repeatedly favored by a public official or agency; (b) the favoritism is not justified by legitimate qualitative or quantitative parameters; and (c) the favoritism has been institutionalized.[3] In practice, actors are inclined to hide unfair procedures, which makes it difficult to meet these criteria even when rumors of capture abound. Legislative capture, in which laws are written to explicitly favor a given company, is easier to identify (see Slinko et al. this volume).

The extent to which a public official and private actor are able and willing to participate in a corrupt transaction will be determined by the bureaucratic context, market conditions, and ethical considerations. More precisely,

1. The public official's incentives depend on:
   a. His ability to dispense services in a way that produces private income. The bureaucratic context in which he operates determines his authority and discretion, the chances that he will be caught and punished for his transgression, and the degree to which he holds a monopoly in dispensing the services required by the individual (Shleifer and Vishny 1993).
   b. His personal understanding of whether corruption is acceptable. This depends on his code of ethics and the actual (vs. formal) ethical standards proposed by his employer. These concerns will also be shaped by the culture in which he lives, which may or may not see private compensation of bureaucrats as inappropriate.
2. The private actor's incentives depend on:
   a. The benefits of a corrupt transaction and his ability to pay the bribe in question. If he is representing a firm, the size of the transaction will be determined by the potential gains to the firm and the market in which the firm is operating.

b. His personal understanding of whether corruption is acceptable. This will depend on his individual code of ethics and fear of being caught and punished. This attitude will be rooted in the same cultural context as that of the bureaucrat, with differences reflecting education, religious beliefs, and other individual attributes.

This chapter will consider only the noncognitive incentives outlined in points 1a and 2a.

The past experience of actors will also be relevant. An actor who has never tried to obtain the services in question will approach the bureaucrat with a different attitude than the person who knows how the system works, and who may "specialize" in obtaining these services.[4] Likewise, the new bureaucrat is likely to approach his responsibilities differently from the wizened official who has been dispensing government services for years.

In countries with established state administrations, the incidence of novice public officials will not be very high. Bureaucracies will be staffed with civil servants who are familiar with how rules are implemented and who will, in an environment of widespread corruption, understand that many of their colleagues are corrupt.[5]

From a strictly financial viewpoint, a private actor, the source of the funds that grease a corrupt transaction, has an incentive not to pay. Public officials have reason to attract the payment. And yet, some officials are corrupt and others (presumably) are not. What explains variations in the behavior of bureaucrats and the incidence of corruption? The rest of this chapter looks for answers to this question by focusing on the Russian regional officials responsible for monitoring drug supply.

Formal and Informal Institutions

Bureaucrats who supervise the activities of Russian drug distributors and pharmacies are close to the ground. They work in local (regional or municipal) Health Committees[6] or in branch offices of federal ministries. Three federal ministries play a role in regulating the wholesale and retail trade in pharmaceutical products. The Ministry of Health is the most involved, with partial authority over Health Committees and full control over the local Sanitary and Epidemiological Service (SES). The other two ministries monitor all businesses, including pharmacies and drug distributors; they are the Ministry of Extraordinary Situations (which oversees Fire Departments) and the Ministry for the Collection of Taxes (which oversees local Tax Inspectorates).[7] There are important differences between these federal and regional entities, the most important of which concerns their sources of funds. Branch offices are supposed to be supported by federal ministries. Often, however, they receive inadequate funding, and must find alternative ways of financing their operations. Health Committees are funded from regional budgets that cover administrative costs and policy expenditures such as vaccination programs and subsidized drug supply. The Health

Committee specializes in health care issues and has access to far greater resources than branch offices. It plays a larger role in determining regional health care policy than any other agency, including the national Ministry of Health.

The public official serves as an agent of a public bureaucracy. His authority and discretion are determined by the formal and informal rules of his employer. Formal rules are specified in laws and internal documents that specify the functions of an agency, its hierarchical structure and the responsibilities of various departments, the systems to be used in executing these responsibilities, and relationships with other agencies. These rules may be set at the federal, regional, or municipal level and may complement or contradict each other. Municipal rules, for example, can be used to clarify procedures for implementing centrally designed policies, or may consist of rules that supplement those designed at higher administrative levels.[8]

The bureaucrat's behavior may also be constrained or conditioned by formal rules that apply to all local civil servants, but which are generated outside of his particular bureaucracy. Similarly, he works within an informal "corporate culture" that is specific to his organization, but which is naturally influenced by other organizations, individuals, and events. He will, however, be most influenced by those aspects of the bureaucracy that have a direct impact on him: his compensation level, his supervisors, and his colleagues. We can assume that most people would rather have more money than less. The official considering corruption is likely to begin by calculating the shortfall between his salary and his desired standard of living. He will consider the proximity of his supervisor and the latter's interest in fighting corruption as he estimates the chances of being caught and punished. (Here both the formal hierarchy and its rules, as well as the attitude of supervisors are important. The line between formal and informal constraints is artificial.) The official will factor in his job opportunities elsewhere, on the off chance that he is fired. Finally, he will ask whether his colleagues in the same position would take a bribe and how much they might charge.

Interviews with Russian bureaucrats and pharmaceutical firms suggest that agency leadership plays a key role in determining whether or not corruption is a problem in a given organization. Bureaucratic managers influence their subordinates via formal institutions and through informal understandings of what constitutes acceptable behavior. Formal rules determine the likelihood that corrupt exchanges will be exposed (supervisors have more or less authority to monitor behavior, sit closer or further away, and are aware of internal anticorruption measures, if any). But informal signals seem to determine whether or not lower-level officials choose to engage in corruption in the first place. Managers of industry-specific bureaucracies are often drawn from regulated firms. In Russia, many do not abandon their ties with these firms as they ascend to political power. Moreover, bureaucratic leaders frequently do not disguise their preferences for some market participants over others. As a result, it is not unusual to find government policies consistently benefiting a small number of regional companies. Lower-level bureaucrats allude (albeit euphemistically) to their superiors' conflict of interest to explain why they feel comfortable favoring certain private actors over others. The fact that agency leaders appear to be profiting from abuse of their authority creates an environment in which corruption is acceptable.[9]

Specifying the mechanism by which leadership influences employees highlights the difficulty of distinguishing between formal and informal rules. In many cases, formal rules explain how an organization is meant to function, while informal constraints, defined by Douglass C. North as "codes of conduct, norms of behavior, and conventions," describe how an organization really works (1990: 36). The process of registering, licensing, or certifying a firm may be outlined in official instructions, but the system actually used may differ substantially from what was intended. A study of the administrative barriers facing small and medium-sized enterprises found, for example, that the cost of registering a small company often exceeds the officially prescribed limit of 2,000 rubles, and that roughly half of the time, the one-month time limit for such a procedure is not observed (CEFIR and World Bank 2002). The divergence between formal and informal rules often extends beyond the logistical and well into the substantive: Required signatures may be collected out of order, problems with an applicant overlooked, connections deployed to speed up a procedure, and bribes paid. Informal requirements may be greater or smaller than the formal ones and may change more rapidly than official regulations. Ambiguity in the authority of public officials encourages instability in relations between the public and private sector, and sows the seeds for corruption.

In Russia informal "ways of getting things done" can be far more important than the official, formal procedures that describe how things should be done. Vadim Radaev (2004) has described a five-step process he calls the "informalization of the rules" to explain how official rules are replaced with informal arrangements.

> First, formal rules are imposed by the public officials in a way which leaves room for their discretion and creates a high level of uncertainty for market actors. Second, confronting high costs of compliance with the formal rules, economic agents create specific governance structures to avoid formal rules on a systematic basis. Third, public officials establish selective control, in which formal rules are used for extortion and selective pressures on economic agents. Fourth, economic agents, in turn, bargain with the public officials on terms and conditions of the implementation of formal rules. Fifth, multiple arguments and interpretations are produced to legitimate practices of informalization. (p. 94)

A system in which officials can manipulate rules gives them leeway to bargain with private actors. But how does this bureaucratic condition come about?

The Evolution of Bureaucratic Institutions

The bureaucracy does not exist in a vacuum. It has internal rules and operating procedures with their own momentum, but it is affected by the transition process and targeted reforms. As the Soviet state has morphed into the Russian state it has acquired new roles commensurate with democratic government and capitalism. How does institutional reform change the behavior of individual bureaucrats? In this section, I propose a causal chain that describes how the reforms of the early 1990s affected bureaucratic incentives and actions.

In the early days of the Russian transition, the need for dramatic reforms was evident, but the appropriate means and objectives of these reforms were unclear. At the national and regional level, new responsibilities required new institutions and policies but most leaders had no experience with democracy and the private sector, and had but a vague idea of how the state should relate to independent political and economic groups. The Communist Party no longer organized political and economic life, and state institutions at all levels of government were confronted with strident demands for decentralization, democratization, and development of a functional market economy.

Organizations had to be created or modified to meet these demands. In policy areas not relevant under communism, new agencies were created at the federal, regional, and municipal level.[10] In other areas, like health care, the required bureaucracies existed but had to adapt to a radically different environment. Over the 1990s, branch offices of federal bureaucracies were subjected to multiple reorganizations, some of which remain in force, others of which were reversed.[11] Unenforced reforms eroded the center's authority (Shleifer and Treisman 2000: 18). The inability of Moscow-based ministries to adequately finance local offices further reduced their control over subsidiary organizations they were reluctant to close. To maintain these regional offices, they gave them the "freedom" to survive on their own instead (Radaev 2002: 294). As a result, many underfunded regional offices launched their own reforms. Some created new departments, while others introduced local requirements or procedures ostensibly in line with their mission. In some cases, reforms were precipitated by regional or municipal leaders who did have funds—even though the branch offices of federal bureaucracies were not primarily subordinated to local government.

When it became clear that the federal government could no longer support the old health care system, much of the burden of maintaining public health fell to the regions.[12] Regional governors were overwhelmed with the diversity and complexity of the problems they faced and used an ad hoc approach in many policy areas, including health care. Monitoring the nascent pharmaceutical markets was one of the most urgent tasks confronting both federal and regional authorities at the beginning of the transition. In Soviet days, the diffusion of drugs from producer to consumer had been managed from Moscow by a single state distributor. The demise of the Soviet Union and Comecon trade agreements cut off the flow of medicine into Russia and private distributors were allowed to come into being. In the early 1990s, these companies were small and loosely controlled. Lower down on the drug distribution chain, local retail markets were dominated by state-owned pharmacies until the mid-1990s, when the number of privatized and new pharmacies began to rise. In addition to other policy problems, Russian authorities confronted desperately needed, rapidly developing, and poorly regulated pharmaceutical markets with the attendant risk to public health.

Some components of the system that had overseen the Soviet drug delivery system remained relevant. The Health Ministry, for example, had a Sanitary and Epidemiological Service that regularly inspected pharmacies to check hygiene and drug storage conditions. The Health Ministry itself remained an important source of information and federal regulation for the sector. Its small budget, however, meant that it had little ability to control the development of the health care sector in the regions or to influence the regional committees that were only partially under their control through an old and ineffective system of "dual subjugation." Regional governors decided how extensively they could finance local health care systems of hospitals and clinics, and how much money they could devote to pay for drugs on the subsidized essential drug list. Most of the spending on health care in the Russian Federation now came from regional rather than federal budgets, and the locus of power for health care reforms shifted to regional oblast, krai, and republican administrations.

As the transition progressed, new rules governing committees, branch offices, and their internal departments were drawn up, sometimes with guidance from Moscow. For the most part, however, the organizations and the bureaucrats within them figured out how to organize their activities by trial and error. The great variety in the structure of regional and municipal pharmaceutical-related bureaucracies testifies to the independence given to the regions to address this issue. Federal ministries and committees contributed to the decentralization of the regulatory regime by abdicating varying degrees of control over branch offices. Required to "self-finance" their operations, the "numerous departments and controlling agencies [built up] a lot of administrative barriers and started to live on their formal rent and informal bribes" (Radaev 2002: 294).[13] Regulated local businesses, both private and state-owned, became the source of funds for these local bureaucracies. Several of the officials interviewed happily waved around "price lists" for services (though they refused to give out copies).[14] Their reluctance to fully reveal official and unofficial means of collecting revenues illustrates the ambivalent result of these bureaucratic reforms. Branch bureaucracies adapted to uncertainty and underfinancing, and modified their rules to deal with problems as they arose. In the process, they developed new regulations for the local businesses they were supervising. Some rules, for instance, the licensing of pharmaceutical warehouses, were undoubtedly very necessary. But others, such as the mandatory certification of drugs not only at the federal level, but also in many regions in which they are sold, appear to have been created for the sake of collecting revenues and excluding undesirable companies.[15] Visits to SES offices in four regions found some of them housed in nicely renovated premises, and others in frigid and decrepit conditions. Certain organizational leaders had proven to be more adept at devising "self-financing" systems for their organization than others. This skill level varied from bureaucracy to bureaucracy within a city, and from city to city for a given bureaucracy, implying that the revenue-generating procedures were indeed created within each branch office.

To understand how bureaucracies implemented new rules, let us consider the evolution of the rules governing licenses for pharmacies, warehouses, and distributors. Regional health committees established licensing procedures, usually through recently created Pharmaceutical Departments or Departments for Ensuring Drug Supply. Lists of required signatures were drawn up, application forms created, and licenses issued. In progressive regions (like Samara), nearly all comers received licenses. In others (e.g., Chuvashia), the process was tortuous and often unsuccessful due to justified or unjustified hostility to the applicant, a reluctance to accept the role of private enterprise in health care, or incompetence. When they began processing license requests, lower-level bureaucrats may have realized that the system could be streamlined, or perhaps that they failed to check for something important. If they shared their observation with their supervisor, there may have been an effort to correct the problem, or it may have been ignored. The poorer the quality of the instructions and procedures provided to lower-level officials by their agencies, and the more ineffective the bottom-up feedback mechanism from rule-implementer to rule-designer, the greater the incentive for lower-level officials to modify the rules of the game in a way that allows them to make their work easier, more efficient, or more lucrative.

The issuing of pharmaceutical licenses to private firms was a new procedure, and we can assume it took time for local systems to be perfected. Each region had some leeway to develop its own version of the process, and each developed its own formal rules. Within each bureaucracy, officials implementing formal rules also developed informal rules; together these rules constituted procedures, some of which worked better than others. Along the way, bureaucrats in some of the less tightly run organizations were able to use the lack of clarity in procedures and monitoring to carve out revenue-producing niches for themselves. In this view, ad hoc reforms introduce slack and instability into a bureaucracy, thus creating greater opportunities for corrupt officials. This outcome may happen even if initial reforms are not explicitly written to create rent-seeking opportunities.

Winners Take All?

Theoretically, one could imagine a bureaucracy in which reforms were well organized and well implemented from the start. In this scenario, the leadership of a given organization accurately assesses the task at hand, develops appropriate rules, and is able to monitor low-level officials in a way that produces intended results. This may have happened in a few places. But the overwhelming body of literature on Russian reforms leans toward the view that they have not produced the expected results.[16] This is not surprising given that many of the problems presented by the transition from the communist system were totally unfamiliar to those charged with implementing them. In major transitions with many coincident policy changes, confusion and flawed procedures are almost inevitable. Political leaders are overwhelmed with major decisions that need to be taken, and often cannot adequately supervise the implementation of those already resolved. Doubts over the meaning of new rules, and over the means of executing these instructions make it difficult to monitor lower-level bureaucrats. If they are aware of changes in regulations, officials at the regional or municipal level may be unable or unwilling to implement them. Their hesitance may stem from ideological opposition, the feeling that current rules or political leaders are temporary, or frustration at the complexity of the task they have been assigned. Inefficient controls open the door for private rent seeking by bureaucrats at all levels. Moreover, the de facto freedom of Russia's emerging federalism invited organizational rent seeking by agencies cut off from stable central funding. The most common observable proof of this attitude was the creation by many bureaucracies of daughter firms whose services agency clients (firms or individuals) were obliged to use in order to receive required bureaucratic signatures or stamps.[17]

Bureaucrats and bureaucracies who manage to exploit rent-seeking opportunities at the beginning of the transition period have an incentive to use their control over formal and informal rules to inhibit attempts to rectify ambiguities and mistakes in the original reforms. Joel Hellman (1998) presented this argument in his seminal article, "Winners Take All." Focusing on those "in a position to arbitrage between the reformed and unreformed sectors of the state economy," Hellman described how the winners in the early transition would resist further reforms in order to protect the "rent-seeking opportunities [that arose] from price differentials between the liberalized sectors of the economy and those still coordinated by non-market mechanisms" (219–20). State enterprise managers who sold their subsidized inputs (e.g., oil) abroad at world prices, and commercial bankers who invested cheap government credits in high-interest money markets were the prototypical winners in the Hellman model.

This analysis can also be applied to bureaucratic behavior to explain the difficulty of institutional reform. A public official at any level of a bureaucracy who has used reforms to carve out a profitable niche for him or herself will not have an incentive to implement later reforms that eliminate this niche. The extent to which the bureaucrat can block future reforms will depend on his formal authority and the degree to which informal rules diverge from the formal ones. If changes in formal rules need not be reflected in changes in informal rules, then reforms can be announced, even codified, and ignored. This will be particularly easy if the management of the local bureaucracy resists reforms that reduce revenue-generating opportunities for the local office itself.

There are significant differences between this analysis of stalled reform and the one articulated by Hellman. First, he concentrates on the policy-making process, and on the political constituencies that support or oppose reform policies. My version looks at bureaucracies and the policy-implementation process. The implications of having resistant winners within government institutions are even more serious than those discussed by Hellman. Whereas one can include transition losers in elections and policy making, it is difficult to integrate them into policy implementation.[18] Second, this framework implies that a transition may be stalled not only by the failure to adopt reforms, but also by bureaucratic unwillingness to implement adopted reforms. Even if the winners are restrained at the policy-making level and additional reforms are passed, winners within bureaucracies may render these policy improvements ineffectual. The ramifications of this hypothesis are discouraging: Effective reform requires not only political will and support of the executive and legislative branches of government—a challenge in and of itself—but also good coordination and control over implementing agencies. The Russian experience suggests that the autonomy of government organizations in the regions may be even harder to reign-in than that of policy-making ministries in Moscow. Finally, when Hellman does consider rent seeking by well-placed officials, it is in the context of the entrenched communist elite in state enterprises and ministries who arbitrage between the subsidized state sector and the free market (1998: 229). In Russia, steady reductions in subsidies means that there are no longer many opportunities for exploiting state monies in this manner. And yet there are many instances of both highly placed and lower-level officials benefiting from partial reforms. Their rents do not come from arbitrage. They are generated by conflicts of interest, administrative barriers, and petty corruption.

Grand Corruption in the Russian Pharmaceutical Markets

This chapter thus far has focused on how transitions can engender rent-seeking opportunities for low-level officials and underfunded agencies. But to understand the mechanism by which early winners in a transition prevent further reforms, one needs to look beyond petty corruption and legal (though obstructive) administrative barriers. Grand corruption involves the abuse of public office by high-level officials with access to state funds. In an atmosphere of bureaucratic freedom and uncertainty, firms may find it possible and profitable to capture local regulatory authorities. This strategy will be most appropriate for larger firms that compete for state orders. In this study, it will involve distributors that are competing to fill government orders for essential drugs and medical equipment.[19] The techniques used by captor firms are similar across sectors, however, and it is instructive to briefly review how the phenomenon emerged in the pharmaceutical industry after 1991.

Early in the Russian transition, prescient entrepreneurs identified the most lucrative economic sectors (such as banking and exportable raw materials) and managed to gain control over ministries in charge of sectors they liked. In locations with assets or markets of interest, these businessmen recognized that certain regional bureaucracies could provide them with advantages over their competitors. (This was more true for bureaucracies related to specific sectors, such as the Ministry of Energy, than for agencies with broader roles like tax collection.) Placing their representative near or at the top of important federal and regional bureaucracies allowed these entrepreneurs to capture some of the key regulators of their industry and to lobby the remaining parts of the government for benefits "from within." Private interests pressured President Yeltsin and various governors to appoint "the right person" for official positions by noting the resources they had or could provide in past and future elections. These vanguard entrepreneurs had the money and credits desperately needed by national, regional, and municipal politicians. Funds were offered on the condition that this assistance would be remembered when the time came to staff a new administration. This was the classic tactic used by entrepreneurs to capture the parts of the federal and regional government that were important to them.[20]

Larger, more profitable industries were carved out first, and smaller sectors were ignored.[21] But as the juicier segments of the economy were allocated to the most aggressive, attention gradually shifted to remaining opportunities in smaller markets like the pharmaceutical industry.[22] The Health Committee is the most important bureaucracy for firms in the health care sector, and it is the one typically subject to capture by local firms. By summer 2002, when interviews were conducted in four regions, key positions in the regulatory apparatus in each city had been "acquired" by local firms openly using their influence to direct health care funds from the regional budget to their companies.

Capture took different forms in different regions. In the Republic of Mari El, the son of the head of the government ran a small firm that won profitable government orders in tenders (e.g., for a contrast dye used in X-rays).[23] In Samara, the head of the Health Committee centralized government orders so that they all passed through Pharmbox, a semiprivatized distributor whose shares in 2001 "fell into the hands of people close to the governor."[24] In Ufa, the republican Ministry of Health used Bashpharmacia, a semiprivatized distributor with over 250 of its own pharmacies, to make as many government purchases as possible and pressured hospitals to do the same. A distributor eager to win more tenders himself characterized the competitions as "closed and semiclosed (with the result known in advance)."[25] The director of a large retail chain pointed out that unlike in Samara and Volgograd, most of the Bashkir market was not from government purchases. As a result, "bureaucrats didn't crawl into this market. They split up the petrochemical industry."[26] In Volgograd, no single company had yet managed to capture the bulk of budget orders, though a strident competition was taking place. The conflict between municipal and regional authorities was expressed through competition between Volgopharm (the preferred city distributor) and Kominfarm (the preferred regional distributor).

Prospects for Reform

Once the regional and municipal governments have been carved up among economic interests, is there any possibility for reforms? Officials within an organization are unlikely themselves to eliminate extra procedures or inefficiencies that produce personal or institutional revenues. Potential sources of change will be exogenous to the agency: disgruntled clients or social groups, a new local manager with a fresh approach, or a crackdown by administratively superior entities. The individual or organization able to reverse a propensity for corruption within an agency will need to display credible enforcement capabilities. Let us consider whether or not any of these three sources of change is likely to alter the incentives of Russian bureaucrats.

Reform could be stimulated by forces outside of the government. In Hellman's model, integrating the losers in the transition process is the best means of restraining entrenched winners. While civil society remains largely ineffective in Russia, businesses have been more and more vocal in their demands for a reduction in administrative barriers. Local companies not favored by captured government bureaucracies could be a source of opposition to grand corruption. The growing number of professional associations suggests that firms do see benefits in collectively pressing for reform. In the pharmaceutical industry alone, three large lobbies were created in 2002 to push for improvements in the legislative environment.[27] In time, these may represent enough aggregate economic power to force mayors and governors to take their concerns into account and eliminate the open bias of regulatory bureaucracies.[28]

However, reforms initiated by regional leaders appear improbable at present, given that the top levels of their administrations are increasingly captured. A displeased regional governor can remove a corrupt health committee official, but he or she will rarely be replaced with a competent and honest professional. The selection of top officials for industry-specific bureaucracies is thoroughly dominated by political and economic concerns. Lobbies of firms not strong enough to co-opt regional leaders find it nearly impossible to trigger regional change on their own.

They have, however, found the federal government and the Putin government to be more receptive to their complaints. In response (and to fuel economic growth), reforming legislation has been pushed through the parliament at a fast clip.[29] New laws have pruned taxes, reduced the number of activities requiring licenses, simplified registration systems, and introduced other measures to encourage small- and medium-sized businesses. On the ground, the effect of these reforms has been limited, though a recent survey did find slight improvements in areas tackled by recent reforms (CEFIR and World Bank 2003).[30] In a reversal from the Yeltsin years, the Putin administration has been pushing regional leaders to submit to the authority of the federal government. Agencies have been pressured to implement reforms, in part through better monitoring by federal ministries, and also by inciting fear of the *verticale*, an expression alluding to the consolidation of administrative power in the administrative branch of government. (Ironically, interviewed firms complained that the *verticale* was also being used to justify the anti-competition measures that often result from capture.)

In the absence of more strident anticorruption movements from above or below, one can expect bureaucrats to continue extracting rents where possible. At the highest levels of state bureaucracies, leaders continue to be "nominated" by interested firms who cannot be ignored by hungry politicians. The managers of cash-poor agencies encourage their subordinates to supplement their budgets by charging firms additional official and unofficial fees. At the lowest levels, bureaucrats take their cue from their leaders, and conclude that petty corruption is acceptable. Greedier leaders of bureaucracies may even organize the rent seeking in a way that gives them some of the dividends of low-level corruption, perhaps by forcing officials to pass up a commission from what they collect in bribes.[31]

Conclusions

This chapter has used the Russian pharmaceutical markets to illustrate a framework that explains how transitions affect corruption. Simultaneous economic and political transitions produce confusion and uncertainty among public officials. If they are also characterized by decentralization of authority and weakening supervisory relationships, rent-seeking schemes can flourish. Policy makers may pursue their self-interest and adopt policies that allow them to exploit state assets or authority for personal gain. Unanswered questions about how to implement new rules—and about how an agency is to survive in the post-transition society—can drive officials to create their own schemes for survival. An organization trying to generate rents to survive in an atmosphere of inconsistent funding can foster an internal corporate culture in which officials also exploit their personal authority for personal rents. The civil servant who has used reforms to carve out a profitable niche for himself and his organization has an incentive to block later reforms that eliminate this niche. Effective reform requires not only good policy making, but also effective policy implementation.

The elaboration of this preliminary analysis highlights three sets of questions that remain unanswered. First, how do bureaucratic leaders influence the behavior of individual bureaucrats and their likelihood of engaging in corruption? The formal and informal ways in which leaders transmit their attitude toward corruption need to be identified with a greater precision. Second, how does culture affect the willingness of bureaucrats and private actors to enter into a corrupt transaction? Anecdotal evidence would lead one to believe that corruption is much worse in Russia now than it was under the Soviet regime. At the same time, much has been written about the system of *blat* that encouraged people to use a highly personalized approach to problem solving with and within bureaucracies. How does the legacy of relations with bureaucrats under communism influence current strategies of individuals and firms? Is there something about Russian culture that would make it more vulnerable to corruption, or do other variables (e.g., bureaucratic incentives, regional factors, institutional design) better explain variation in corruption? And finally, to what extent has corruption and capture had a negative effect on the development of the pharmaceutical industry in Russia? Fighting to maintain even the basic elements of the Soviet-era health care system has proven to be one of the most difficult aspects of Russia's transition. Corrupt officials in health care bureaucracies may be putting additional stress on an already weakened and crumbling system. Exposing the role of corruption in this sector would be a crucial step forward on the long road to rebuilding a viable public health care system.

Notes

1. A third party, the state (the principal) whose interests are violated by the self-serving public official (or agent), is also involved in the corrupt transaction, but will not be discussed here.
2. The regions were chosen to maximize variation in political and economic conditions. This was done by ranking all 89 Russian regions according to per capita income (adjusted for the cost of living) and according to how extensively they implemented market reforms. Progress in reforms was measured through proxies like the share of the workforce employed in the private sector and small enterprises, the degree to which price controls on food and electricity tariffs have been eliminated, and cumulative per capita FDI for 1999–2001. Samara emerged as high income/high reform; Volgograd was low income/high reform; Bashkortostan was high income/low reform; and Mari El was low income/low reform. Interviews by the author or a research assistant were held in the capital of each region. A survey of 267 pharmacy directors in these cities (plus Moscow and a small town in Samara oblast) was also comissioned but is not directly relevant for this chapter.
3. The expression "capture" is used loosely in much of the noneconomic literature. The definition offered here is specific but still less precise than a classical economic definition. A formal definition would require proof that a policy maker adopted a decision that would not have been approved by the polity, in exchange for benefits personal or political (Levine 1998).
4. The more time-consuming and complicated the regulatory requirements, the higher the likelihood of the firm employing a "specialist" to carry out the task. Vadim Radaev quotes a Russian registration specialist as saying that a regular person would never register his company himself "because it is impossible for a normal being. It is possible only in case he/she will treat registration as an ultimate goal in his whole life" (2002: 291).
5. In many countries, bureaucrats may actually buy potentially lucrative positions. A series of World Bank studies in Albania, Georgia, and Latvia in 1998 found that the price of obtaining "high-rent" positions is well known among public officials and the general public. In Latvia, ministerial positions are purchased more often than in Albania and Georgia, whereas the latter countries see more purchasing of the offices of customs officials, tax inspectors, natural resources licensers, judges, investigators and prosecutors, ordinary police, and local officials (Kaufmann et al. 1998: 3–4).
6. These administrative bodies may be called committees, ministries (in republics), or departments. Despite having different names, at any given territorial level they are administratively equivalent and will be called health committees for the sake of simplicity.
7. The Trade Inspectorate, part of the Ministry for Economic Development and Trade, is also very active in some regions.
8. The local office of a federal bureaucracy has a considerable degree of independence from the local government. There are instances, however, in which a branch office will have to react to initiatives taken by the regional or municipal government. A city government can create a new organization, the existence of which is not anticipated in federal or regional legislation and ministerial branch offices at the municipal level may begin to require that firms demonstrate adherence to the new entity's policies. In mid-2002, e.g., Kursk became the third Russian city to create a municipal Center for the Quality and Certification of Drugs. All pharmaceutical companies were required to make available the certificates they received to a special section of the local Internal Affairs Department (the local branch of the Ministry of Internal Affairs, or MVD). See www.pharmindex.ru/newsdetails.asp?id=1642.

9. The influence of leadership on the behavior of lower-level officials was made clear in interviews in a number of cities. In one region, bureaucrats and distributors repeatedly mentioned that the regional Health Committee chair's preference for a single distributor was a clear sign that health care monies could be channeled for private gain. According to these sources, until this official arrived, the city's pharmaceutical markets had been open and competitive. After the chairperson's consolidation of state orders, market participants reported that other local officials appeared much more willing to limit competition and give unmerited preferences to certain firms and not others. Barbara Geddes provides poignant examples from Brazil of how good leaders improved and bad leaders damaged bureaucracies such as the National Development Bank (1994: 62–3, 75).

10. The most obvious example is the creation of the State Property Committee, which was in charge of privatization.

11. Two examples illustrate continuing reorganizations of Russian bureaucracy: In January 2002, the Fire Department, part of the Ministry of Internal Affairs, was transferred to the Ministry for Extraordinary Situations. In March 2003, Putin announced that the State Communications Agency (FAPSI), which had been spun off of the KGB in 1991, would be disbanded and its resources divided between the Federal Security Service (FSB) and the Defense Ministry. In the same breath he said he signed a decree disbanding the Tax Police and incorporating its functions into the Interior Ministry, and shifting the Federal Border Service into the FSB. See MChS website (www.emercom.gov.ru/v010_h6.shtml, entry for January 2002 and Simon Saradzhyan "President Rethinks How FAPSI Will be Split up," *The Moscow Times,* March 27, 2003.

12. The Ministry of Finance reports that in 2002 the federal government spent 26.3 billion rubles on health care, while regional and local budgets spent a total of 215.2 billion rubles. Sergei Shishkin (1998: tables 1 and 2) estimated that in 1997 the 2.2% of the federal budget allocated for health care expenditures accounted for 10% of public health funding. At the regional level, budgets (on average) devoted 14.8% of their expenditures to funding 71% of overall public health spending. The compulsory insurance premium providing the remaining 19% of funds spent on health care.

13. The revenue referred to here includes legal charges for services rendered in accordance with revenue-generating regulations as well as corrupt payments from regulated to regulator. Although Radaev carefully contrasts rents and bribes, the transition literature often refers to both forms of revenue as rents and to the behavior of bureaucrats (in both the legal and illegal form) as rent seeking, both involving the exploitation of assets under one's control. Bribe taking is rent seeking by an agent—by an official collecting funds for himself—whereas collecting monies for an agency budget represents rent seeking by a principal.

14. The head of a department in the Volgograd oblast SES explained, "in accordance with Ministry of Health rule, we can [collect resources] from sponsors or subsidies." Although specialists do not conduct private consultations with companies, firms can ask for toxicology, diagnostic, chemical or radiographic analyses, and SES will sign a consulting contract with them. Source: Interview with head of a department of Volgograd Oblast SES, July 2002.

15. The cost of the certification process varies. Protek, the largest distributor in Russia, estimates that it pays over ten times more for certification in expensive regions than in cheaper ones. Source: Interview with Protek Moscow-based manager and head of a regional subsidiary, May 2002.

16. Vadim Volkov (2004) vividly illustrates this point with his description of how bankruptcy law is used to facilitate armed takeovers of companies. Shleifer and Treisman attribute "the stagnation syndrome" to the ongoing competition between levels of government, which contributed to uncertainty within state institutions (2000: 90).

17. A 2002 monitoring survey of small firms found that 20% of those applying for licenses and certificates reported that their applications would not have been considered had they not used the services of an "intermediary with close ties to the local administration" (CEFIR and World Bank 2003).

18. Susan Rose-Ackerman's chapter in this volume discusses the ways in which outsiders can be brought into policy implementation as a means of increasing government accountability. The Hungarian and Polish experiences indicate that incorporating outsiders into the regulatory process is possible but difficult.

19. Pharmacies do not compete for state purchase orders.

20. The most obvious example of this approach was the appointment of Vladimir Potanin, the head of the Unexim banking group and winner of the Norilsk Nickel loan-for-shares tender, as deputy prime minister after Yeltsin's oligarch-financed reelection in 1996. Potanin's mission was explicitly acknowledged to be the preservation of the shares-for-loans distributions (which could have been reversed if the government had repaid the relatively small loans it received as payment).

21. An exception was made if a close relative or friend of a local administration official was particularly interested in a specific sector. In Kursk, e.g., pharmacies were privatized more quickly than in other regions because Governor Rutskoi's son wanted to create a private pharmacy monopoly.

22. Pharmaceutical firms in Samara (which declined to be publicly identified) noted that the sector's margins paled in comparison with the car manufacturing and chemical industries. Governor Titov, it was argued, was liberal and independent, and thus limited capture to a few sectors, retaining a competitive economic environment in others. Source: Telephone interview with director of Samara distribution company in May 2002. In Ioskar-Ola, the capital of the Republic of Mari El, the same point was made from a territorial perspective: Mari El was so small (with some 800,000 residents), that there were few rents to be gleaned from capturing its tiny markets.

23. Interview with deputy general director of a Mari El distribution company, July 2002.

24. Interview with the general director of a large Samara retail organization, May 2002.

25. Interview with the director of the Bashkortostan daughter company of a national distributor, September 2002.

26. Interview, September 2002.

27. In November 2002, 1,100 firms participated in the first congress of the League of Russian Pharmaceutical Workers (Pharmindex, November 28, 2002 at (www.pharmindex.ru/newsdetails. asp?id=2251). Earlier in the month, five of the largest domestic producers announced that they would create an Association of Russian Pharmaceutical Producers (Pharmindex, November 14, 2002 at (www.pharmindex.ru/newsdetails.asp?id=2190). This came only five months after the largest domestic and foreign producers and distributors had formed the Union of Professional Pharmaceutical Organizations "to improve the normative legal base regulating the pharmaceutical market" (Pharmindex, June 18, 2002 at (www.pharmindex.ru/newsdetails.asp?id=1671).

28. Kliamkin sees this as the only potential constituency for reform, but believes that small and medium-sized businesses are still too weak and dependent on local bureaucracies to play an independent role in local politics (2002: 22).

29. Since 2000 new joint stock company laws, a new Land Code, a new Labor Code, and significant judicial reforms have been adopted. See Alex Nicolson's article "Legislative Changes Set a Fast and Furious Pace," *The Moscow Times* January 23, 2003.

30. In the pharmaceutical industry, reforms have been driven by crises. Studies indicate that some 10% of the drugs sold in Russia are counterfeits. This has prompted the Ministry of Health to create a new Pharmaceutical Inspectorate. It also led to a revision of pharmaceutical licensing procedures in summer 2002. In Saint Petersburg, confusion over the new rules led to a halt in licensing from August to October 2002 until a special "exclusive" subcommision was set up, staffed by former employees of a local firm, Farmakor. Farmakor competitors have since complained that it is taking them much longer to get their licenses than before (see Elena Shushunova's article "Litsensiz razdelila pharmatsevtov" (A License Divided Pharmaceutical Specialists), *Kommersant'* Petersburg edition January 2003, No. 7, p. 20.

31. Organized corruption within government agencies is a problem in Russia, though proof is naturally hard to come by. A large World Bank study concluded that corrupt networks are now the norm in Russia. Each network has three elements: a commercial or financial structure, a group of bureaucrats to protect them, and a tie with law enforcement officials (Satarov 2002: 8). Anecdotal evidence of bureaucracies penetrated by corruption appears periodically in the press. In February 2003, e.g., the head of the Moscow Traffic Police announced that most of the division heads of the traffic police had been fired for corruption ("Itogi proverki rukovodstva GIBDD Moskvy: pochti vse uvoleny" [The Results of a Review of the Moscow Traffic Police Leadership: Almost Everyone has been Fired], *Rosbusinessconsulting*, February 2003 at http://top.rbc.ru/index.shtml?/news/incidents/2002/12/24/24141459_bod.shtml).

References

CEFIR (Center for Economic and Financial Research) and World Bank. 2002. *Monitoring of Administrative Barriers to Small Business Development in Russia, Round 1*. Summary of results at www.cefir.ru.

———. 2003. *Monitoring of Administrative Barriers to Small Business Development in Russia, Round 2*. Summary of results: www.cefir.ru.

Geddes, Barbara. 1994. *Politician's Dilemma: Building State Capacity in Latin America*. Berkeley CA: University of California Press.

Hellman, Joel S. 1998. "Winners Take All: The Politics of Partial Reform in Postcommunist Transitions." *World Politics* 50: 203–34.

Hellman, Joel, Geraint Jones, and Daniel Kaufmann. 2000. *Seize the State, Seize the Day: State Capture, Corruption and Influence in Transition*. World Bank Policy Research Paper 2444, Washington DC: World Bank.

Johnson, Simon, Daniel Kaufmann, John McMillan, and Christopher Woodruff. 2000. "Why do Firms Hide? Bribes and Unofficial Activity After Communism." *Journal of Public Economics* 76: 495–520.

Kaufmann, Daniel, Sanjay Pradhan, and Randi Ryterman. 1998. "New Frontiers in Diagnosing and Combating Corruption." *PREM Note* 7, Washington DC: World Bank.

Kliamkin, Igor. 2002. "Bureaucracy and Business in Russia." Paper presented at the CERI (Center for International Studies and Research) Conference, Paris, November 14, 2002.

Levine, Michael E. 1998. "Regulatory Capture." In P. Newman (ed.), *New Palgrave Dictionary of Economics and the Law*, Vol. 3, pp. 267–71. London: MacMillan Reference Limited.

Moody-Stuart, George. 1997. *Grand Corruption in Third World Development*. Oxford: Worldview Publishing.

North, Douglass C. 1990. *Institutions, Institutional Change and Economic Performance*. Cambridge UK: Cambridge University Press.

Radaev, Vadim. 2002. "Corruption and Administrative Barriers for Russian Business." In S. Kotkin and A. Sajó (eds.), *Political Corruption in Transition: A Skeptics Handbook*, pp. 287–311. Budapest: Central European University Press.

———. 2004. "How Trust is Established in Economic Relationships When Institutions and Individuals are not Trustworthy: The Case of Russia." In J. Kornai, B. Rothstein, and S. Rose-Ackerman (eds.), *Creating Social Trust in Post-Socialist Transition*, pp. 91–110. New York: Palgrave Macmillan.

Roeder, Philip G. 1993. *Red Sunset: The Failure of Soviet Politics*. Princeton NJ: Princeton University Press.

Satarov, Georgy A. 2002. *The Diagnosis of Russian Corruption: A Sociological Analysis*. Moscow: INDEM Fund.

Shishkin, Sergei. 1998. "Priorities of Russian Health Care Reform." *Croatian Medical Journal* 39: 298–307.

Shleifer, Andrei and Daniel Treisman. 2000. *Without a Map: Political Tactics and Economic Reform in Russia*. Cambridge MA: MIT Press.

Shleifer, Andrei and Robert Vishny. 1993. "Corruption." *The Quarterly Journal of Economics* 108: 599–617.

Solnick, Steven. 1998. *Stealing the State*. Cambridge MA: Harvard University Press.

Volkov, Vadim. 2004. "The Selective Use of State Capacity in Russia's Economy: Property Disputes and Enterprise Takeovers, 1998–2002." In J. Kornai, B. Rothstein, and S. Rose-Ackerman (eds.), *Creating Social Trust in Post-Socialist Transition*, pp. 126–147. New York: Palgrave Macmillan.

CHAPTER EIGHT

The Missing Incentive: Corruption, Anticorruption, and Reelection

IVAN KRASTEV AND GEORGY GANEV

Anticorruption campaigns in post-communist democracies are running out of steam. There is a silent consensus that the war on corruption has failed to obtain the expected results. "Though still in the early stages of development, the experience of anticorruption programs to date has produced mixed results.... Ambitious anticorruption campaigns in several countries have floundered at the implementation stage. Key structural reforms have been blocked by powerful vested interests. In some cases, politicians have hijacked the anticorruption agenda and used it to attack their rivals," stated a World Bank report (World Bank 2000: 15). "The political economy of anticorruption initiatives has proven complex and difficult" (31). The conclusion reached is that "a serious anticorruption program cannot be imposed from the outside, but requires committed leadership from within, ideally from the highest levels of the state. While pressure for reform can come from below, any effective program must be supported from the top" (30).

Why anticorruption programs are not getting support from "the top" is the central question of this essay. It is not a study of anticorruption policies. It is a study of incentives. The "highest levels of the state" do not support anticorruption efforts (1) because they have incentives to be involved in corruption, or (2) because they do not have incentives to initiate anticorruption campaigns even when they do not have incentives to be involved in corruption. These two hypotheses are distinctively different. What interests us is the second hypothesis. We adopt the perspective of the government and not of the individual politician as the focus of research. We define the government as a vote maximizer. In the framework of our study the self-interest of the government is to be reelected.

Why post-communist governments have incentives to be involved in corruption is a problem that was the subject of several studies (see, e.g., della Porta and Vannucci 1999; Sajó 2002). In our essay we only refer to these studies. "Do democratic governments in post-communist Eastern Europe have incentives to launch anticorruption campaigns?" is the question that really interested us.

The assumption behind the present anticorruption policies endorsed by the World Bank is that successful anticorruption campaigns increase the chances of democratic governments to be reelected. When it "sells" its anticorruption policy, the World Bank relies on the self-interest of governments and not on their high morality. That is why the current failure of the anticorruption programs has contributed to the lack of political will and to the institutional weakness of the governments in transition countries. The possibility that uncorrupt governments do not have incentives to launch anticorruption campaigns was never discussed.

This essay tests that silent assumption. The result was unexpected: It turned out that translating successful anticorruption policies into electoral advantage is a principal difficulty. The launching of anticorruption campaigns does not improve the reelection chances of the government, regardless of the fact that society is in favor of anticorruption politics and that the government sincerely implements anticorruption policies.

We do not elaborate on the different definitions of corruption in this essay.[1] We accept that corruption is an abuse of public office for private gains (Heidenheimer 1999; Rose-Ackerman 1999). We view it as a result of "a network of illegal exchanges" (della Porta and Vannucci 1999: 20–1). And to the extent to which political corruption is at the center of our study we follow Claus Offe who defines political corruption as the "selling and buying of public decisions" (see Offe this volume).

We study corruption and anticorruption primarily as political/electoral resources. We do not focus on the individual corrupt act. We consider the personal enrichment of corrupt politicians as a side effect of the decision of political parties to adopt corruption as a necessary instrument for winning elections.[2] In the making of their electoral strategies it is up to politicians to evaluate the exact value of corruption and anticorruption as political resources. In democratic politics corruption is a mechanism to raise campaign money and to control loyalties that can be critical for electoral success (della Porta and Vannucci 1999: 22–3).

The loans-for-shares scheme that was implemented in Russia in 1995 is the most powerful illustration of the functioning of corruption as an electoral resource. In fall 1995 public opinion polls indicated that the reelection of President Yeltsin was a mission impossible. His approval ratings were desperately low; the rejection of his politics and personality were overwhelming. In order to get reelected Yeltsin was searching for a powerful political constituency to support his bid. This is where loans-for-shares schemes came in. In the words of Chrystia Freeland "the loans-for-shares deal was a crude trade of property for political support. In exchange for some of Russia's most valuable companies, a group of businessmen—the oligarchs—threw their political muscle behind the Kremlin.... The complicated two-step plan implicitly bound the economic fortunes of the future oligarchs to the political fortunes of the Yeltsin administration.

In the autumn of 1995, the businessmen received stakes in Russia's most valuable companies only in trust. The final, formal transfer of ownership would not take place until the autumn of 1996 and in 1997—after the presidential elections. When he signed the decree, the Kremlin chief bought himself the constituency which a year later would guarantee his reelection" (Freeland 2000: 162, 173).

But corruption can have a high political cost. A growing number of governments lost reelection as a result of devastating corruption scandals (Blankenburg 2002). Generally, voters do not like corrupt politicians. It is voters' perception of corruption as a social evil that makes not only corruption but also anticorruption a political resource. In a country where the public does not perceive corruption as morally wrong anticorruption is not such a resource. This is the weakness of the anticorruption campaigns in some African countries (de Sardan 1999). At the same time, the stronger the moral rejection of corruption the higher the risks of corruption-centered politics and the stronger the incentives for anticorruption politics. Polling data in Bulgaria in the last decade indicate that the increase in public concern with corruption leads to an increase in support for the opposition parties regardless of which party is in power and which is in opposition.

In asking whether noncorrupt governments have incentives to launch anticorruption campaigns, we define a noncorrupt government as a government that is not seeking reelection through corruption-centered politics. A noncorrupt government in this sense means neither incorruptible government (nobody dares to think about it), nor clean government or honest government. It refers to a government that is convinced that it cannot be reelected through a corruption-related strategy and has consciously decided not to rely on such a strategy. The government estimates that raising party funds and buying political support through corruption will be politically more costly than not raising this money. In the classical case a noncorrupt government is a government that comes to power after several governments relying on corruption schemes failed to be reelected.

Launching an anticorruption campaign reflects the decision of a government to mobilize anticorruption sentiments as an electoral resource. An anticorruption campaign is not simply a mix of anticorruption policies. An anticorruption campaign is a governmental strategy that defines corruption as the major problem faced by the country and formulates the reduction of corruption as the major policy objective of the government. In our specific case the campaign includes the implementation of a World Bank designed set of anticorruption policies and the use of anticorruption rhetoric to justify policy decisions of the government. In this sense the implementation of the anticorruption policy package in the absence of anticorruption rhetoric does not qualify as a campaign.

The question this essay explores is whether noncorrupt governments have incentives to launch anticorruption campaigns as means for reelection. In other words, do noncorrupt governments have an interest in defining corruption as the major problem of their country and to use anticorruption rhetoric as a pillar of their reelection strategy?

The argument is developed as a case study of one country—Bulgaria. The limited validity of the findings prevents us from coming to any general conclusion. But we believe that isolated cases can help produce radical rethinking of the existing policy paradigms.

The Case

The June 17, 2001 parliamentary elections were a breaking point for the Bulgarian political system. The results were surprising, shocking, and exotic. National Movement Simeon II, a political party that had been founded by Bulgarian ex-king Simeon Saxe-Coburg-Gotha just three months prior to the elections won a majority in the Bulgarian Parliament (Barany 2002). It won a majority in every age, education, and income group and in every region of the country with the exception of the regions with a compact Turkish population. The internationally praised Union of Democratic Forces (UDF) government of Ivan Kostov was bitterly defeated. According to many observers, the UDF government's corruption was the most convincing explanation for the electoral revolution/restoration of the former king (Barany 2002).

Corruption cleanups and promises of a politics of morality were central elements of the king's election victory. The new government formed in July 2001 was composed of political newcomers. None of the ministers had former governmental experience. None was connected with the political machines of the traditional parties. None had any record of corruption.

The situation that emerged on the day after the Bulgarian elections came close to a perfect opportunity for the implementation of a successful anticorruption campaign. It fits what the World Bank defines as "a window of opportunity" (World Bank 2000: xxviii, 69). Almost all components needed for a successful anticorruption campaign were present. There was a corrupt country. There was an election promise to clean up the system. There was a new reformist government that was a crusading outsider to corrupt politics. The new government was not a hostage of its own party machine because there was practically no party behind it. There was a carefully designed anticorruption policy package prepared by the international donors waiting to be implemented. There was an active anticorruption NGO community consolidated in an umbrella organization called Coalition 2000.

Bulgaria was a dream case not only for starting an anticorruption campaign; it was also a dream opportunity for empirically testing the chances for success of such a campaign. Since 1998 the Center for the Study of Democracy and Vitosha Research, an independent polling agency, had conducted 15 different polls tracing the anticorruption attitudes in the country. The method used was face-to-face interviews. Twelve of the surveys were based on the same questionnaire that allowed the construction of a detailed picture of the dynamics and specifics of the corruption reality in Bulgaria and the support for anticorruption politics. Three of the surveys studied a sizable sample of specific social groups—politicians, public officials, and businessmen.[3] The surveys culminated in the construction of several indices through which to monitor the corruption reality in the country. The closer the value of an index is to 10, the more negative is the assessment of the evaluated aspects of corruption in Bulgaria. Index numbers closer to 0 indicate an approximation to the ideal of a "corruption-free" society. The indices that are most interesting for us are:

- Index of corruption pressure: It measures the spread of attempts of employees in the public sector to directly or indirectly put pressure on citizens to give monetary gifts or services;
- Index of corruption practices: It reflects the level of personal participation of respondents in different forms of corrupt behavior (e.g., paying a bribe);
- Index of the perceived spread of corruption: It registers citizens' subjective assessments of the spread of corruption through society;
- Index of corruption expectations: It represents citizens' personal expectations about the future spread of corruption and its perspectives.[4]

The first two indices can be viewed as trying to measure corruption reality, to capture how many times bribes were demanded and/or offered. The last two represent public perceptions about the phenomenon. It needs to be recognized here that the measurement of both corruption reality and corruption perceptions is problematic, and the four indices may systematically deviate from the true values they are trying to measure. More specifically, it is natural for measurements of corruption reality to have a downward bias due to a tendency for respondents to public surveys to underreport corrupt acts they have experienced, and for measurements of corruption perceptions to have an upward bias due to a habit to use corruption as an explanation for various events and processes. At the same time, if these biases are relatively stable through time, the changes in the indices should reflect reality without much bias. As figure 8.1 shows, in the case of Bulgaria the two sets of variables differ significantly not only in their levels (which is to be expected as a result of the biases in their measurement), but also in their dynamics over a period of almost five years.

Between April and June 2002 the Open Society Foundation in Bulgaria in collaboration with the Centre for Liberal Strategies and Alfa Research conducted a "State of Society" survey combining representative public opinion survey with anthropological fieldwork in the country.[5] The research goal was to reveal citizens' interpretations of the meaning of transition: who won, who lost, and what happened to winners and losers. The survey was especially interested in anticorruption attitudes and anticorruption discourses, as a mechanism used by the respondents to rationalize their transition experience.

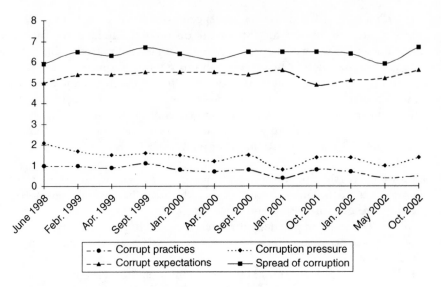

Figure 8.1   Bulgaria: Coalition 2000 Corruption Indexes
Source: Corruption Indexes of Coalition 2000, 2002.

These two massive blocks of data form the empirical basis of this study. We try to answer the question: Did the newly elected Bulgarian government have incentives to seek reelection through anticorruption campaigns?

The limitations of the suggested approach are significant. In order to use the data to study the incentives of the government to launch an anticorruption campaign we presume that the dynamics between reported corruption experience and corruption perceptions will remain the same after starting an energetic anticorruption campaign. Our focus on the government and not the individual politicians as vote maximizers also invites uneasy questions. The fact that Bulgaria has a party government elected through the system of proportional representation makes such an assumption legitimate, but it still can raise problems. Theoretically we cannot exclude the possibility of a noncorrupt government composed of corrupt politicians who do not use corruption as an electoral resource but use it simply as a means for personal enrichment.

The major justification for our approach is the intuition that in order to convince a prime minister to start an anticorruption campaign, you need to convince his election strategist. And the strategist will not miss the chance to read the existing empirical data on the subject.

We first draw up a fictional conversation in the office of the prime minister where an advocate of initiating an anticorruption campaign (e.g., a World Bank expert) and an opponent of such a campaign (e.g., an election strategist) are exchanging views. We then reflect on the dynamics of the anticorruption sentiments through the perspective of social constructivism and draw some conclusions.

The Prime Minister's Dilemma

It is one of those rainy days when governments wished they were honest. The date of the meeting is obscure because most questions asked are the same as the ones that were the most relevant in late summer 2001 but some of the empirical data presented cover later periods. So, we do not specify when the meeting takes place.

Let us imagine that the prime minister (formerly a king) has gathered the members of his cabinet, and the purpose of the meeting is to decide whether the new Bulgarian government should build its reelection strategy on an anticorruption campaign. Let us also imagine the following: There are two points of view—the proponents and the opponents of an anticorruption campaign; the speakers are closet social scientists; the prime minister is not only an ex-king but also an ex-dean of a social sciences department; the prime minister is sick of normative arguments and insists that their decision should be based on the available empirical data.

There are many more things to imagine in constructing a fictional conversation in the Bulgarian Oval Office. But there is a basic limitation: The government can only rely on the resources controlled by the executive power and its parliamentary majority. The government cannot rely on an efficient and impartial judicial power as an ally in the war against corruption. The European Union (EU) Report on the state of judicial reform in Bulgaria confirms that such an assumption is realistic (European Commission 2002). The pressure of the international community will also be omitted from the discussion. The incentives created by the EU accession process could have a critical weight in any government's decision to start an anticorruption campaign, and the signals coming from the EU could have a decisive impact on voters' behavior. But to make our major argument stronger, we omit these factors.

Another important assumption is that the World Bank's anticorruption policy package works. Let us imagine that implementing these policies will lead to a reduction in the actual levels of corruption and will have positive effects on the economy. Of course, some of the anticorruption policies suggested by the World Bank may be wrong and misconceived. There is a growing literature criticizing different elements of the anticorruption policy package (Stiglitz 2002; Easterly 2001). But this essay is not about policies. It is about incentives. That is why we imagine a working anticorruption package that results in an actual decrease in the levels of corruption.

One might say that all these assumptions and limitations make this essay an unreliable guide to the real functioning of Bulgarian politics after June 2001. But our purpose is not to be Virgil in the inferno of Bulgarian politics. What we are interested in are the policy implications of the elusive nature of corruption.

Let us now summarize the discussion in the prime minister's Oval Office. It is sanitized of emotions and details. The goal is to present the main arguments in a concise and clear form. The arguments of the opponent of an anticorruption campaign are presented at greater length because they are new to the ministers and because they are closer to the views of the authors.

Why Should Governments Launch Anticorruption Campaigns?
The Economic Argument

Recent literature on corruption[6] has reached several conclusions about the effects of corruption on the economy and on the economic state of society, using both theoretical arguments and empirical studies of various samples of countries. The advocate of launching an anticorruption campaign, who treats them as almost established facts, makes extensive use of some of these conclusions.

First, corruption hurts economic growth. It does so by hurting investments and by distorting the allocation of resources toward inefficiency. Corruption means that the rules of economic activity are arbitrarily imposed, that property rights are insecure, and that the administrative capacity to provide services is low, which translates into a highly uncertain business environment (World Bank 1997: 18–20). Uncertainty raises the costs of private investment and hurts the growth of productive capacity. At the same time, corruption impedes the effectiveness of public investment (Tanzi and Davoodi 1998)—it leads to higher public investment outlays combined with lower productivity of these investments. Corruption also hurts prospects for foreign direct investment, especially in Bulgaria, which is poor in natural resources that could attract investors despite corruption (World Bank 2000: 23, note 2). On the other side, corruption decreases the efficiency of resource allocation by introducing severe distortions into the price system (Shleifer and Vishny 1993: 599–617) and also, by creating incentives for lower budget revenues and higher budget expenditures, creating an unsustainable fiscal position (Tanzi and Davoodi 1998; World Bank 2000: 21–2), which results in high inflation and again in lower effectiveness of the price system. The impact on the price system results in a misallocation of resources toward suboptimal uses. Ultimately, low investments and poor allocation of resources spell low growth in the long run.

Second, corruption not only hurts the long-term welfare of people, but it does so in an unfair way. The costs associated with corruption fall mostly on the weakest and most vulnerable groups in society. Corrupt societies experience more poverty and higher inequality than noncorrupt ones. This is due not only to lower growth, but to the fact that corrupt governments get effectively financed through regressive, rather than progressive taxes, that they cannot effectively establish and maintain social safety nets, and that they divert resources away from investment in human and social capital, both of which are important for reducing poverty and inequality (Gupta et al. 2002; World Bank 2000: 20–1).

Third, corruption is a factor for the erosion of trust in institutions, and from there of the social fabric in general. Corruption leads to lower budget revenues and to higher but much less productive budget expenditures, which justifies people thinking that they are paying more for less. Moreover, it is mostly the poor and the disadvantaged who pay the bill, but get almost nothing from the services that they are in fact financing. Logically, this leads to a very low level of public trust in state organs and in political leaders, thus further reducing the capacity of the state to provide welfare enhancing services (Shleifer and Vishny 1993; Gupta et al. 2002; Tanzi and Davoodi 1998; Tanzi 1998; World Bank 2000: 21–2).

The conclusion that can be drawn from the literature on anticorruption is that a successful anticorruption strategy will result in a better performing economy that means higher growth, higher and more fairly distributed incomes, and will raise the capacity of the state to provide efficient public services and further improve the well-being of society.

Ultimately, the logic of the economic argument is that the government's incentives to launch an anticorruption campaign are rooted in the understanding of the damaging economic effects of corruption. If corruption is defeated, these damages will disappear, people will feel their lives improve, and will vote accordingly.

The Political Argument

The economic argument demonstrates the advantages that any government can have from reducing corruption. But it does not address the problem of why the government should employ anticorruption rhetoric and why it should focus its efforts on convincing the public that corruption has been reduced. The vacuum left by the economic argument is filled by the political argument. Those making the political argument do not discuss the damage that corruption does to democracy as a form of government (Rose-Ackerman 1999; della Porta and Vannucci 1999). Rather, the argument focuses on the importance of corruption as an electoral issue. The results of recent surveys demonstrate that in the public views corruption is one of the three basic problems the country faces (see table 8.1). So, it is unrealistic to play down corruption as a political issue. It is not only corruption but also the public's perception of the country's being corrupt that can hurt the reelection chances of the government.

The very nature of post-ideological politics increases the importance of corruption as an electoral issue. The decline of ideology led to the rise in the importance of the personal integrity of those in power. The EU accession process significantly limits the policy choices any "reasonable" government should follow in the period of transition, thus increasing the importance of the moral image of the government still further.

In a sense some influential elite groups (such as journalists and civil society activists) portray corruption in terms of what Cohen called "moral panic" (1972). A "moral panic" is said to exist when a particular condition comes to be defined as a threat to societal values and interests and when its

Table 8.1 Main problems faced by Bulgaria

	Sept. 1999	Jan. 2000	Apr. 2000	Sept. 2000	Jan. 2001	Oct. 2001	Jan. 2002	May 2002
Unemployment	64.6	65.3	71.3	67.8	67.5	64.0	68.9	71.5
Low income	50.2	50.6	48.9	49.0	46.0	45.4	32.9	45.2
Poverty	37.1	41.2	41.9	41.5	39.4	46.9	42.7.	40.3
Corruption	*38.5*	*37.5*	*40.1*	*37.5*	*36.5*	*45.6*	*47.0*	*39.3*
Crime	32.4	27.9	28.9	25.7	51.7	36.3	32.9	30.2
Healthcare	16.0	14.6	14.1	14.0	5.1	11.9	17.2	19.9
High prices	21.9	18.9	19.4	22.4	16.3	15.7	20.9	16.8
Political instability	15.4	13.1	13.8	17.0	18.2	12.0	13.1	14.1
Education	3.8	2.9	2.3	2.1	0.8	2.6	1.8	4.4
Environmental pollution	5.0	4.3	2.4	2.7	3.0	3.3	1.5	2.2
Ethnic problems	4.0	1.4	1.9	1.7	0.9	1.6	1.4	1.3

nature, consequences, and solutions are presented by influential elites in ".a stylized and stereotypical fashion" (Pavarala 1996: 134).

There are two additional practical arguments in favor of an anticorruption campaign that are specific to the present Bulgarian government. An anticorruption campaign can strengthen its image as the government of political novices who were not involved in the great redistribution of the last decade. Being in power for the first time, the government is perfectly positioned to attack and expose the corruption of previous governments thus undermining the electoral chances of the opposition insofar as it represents the parties of the previous governments.

More importantly, there were public expectations that the government would undertake decisive steps against corruption. In September 2001 the corruption expectation index changed in a positive direction regardless of the fact that both corrupt practices and corrupt pressures went in the opposite direction. This change can be explained only as a direct result of the June election. The index on the moral acceptability of corruption also demonstrates that public opinion is not inclined to trivialize the existence of corruption (see figure 8.2, which shows the index of moral acceptability of corruption with 0 meaning corruption is declared absolutely unacceptable, and 10 meaning it is found acceptable). On the contrary, corruption is perceived as a moral evil. There is a strong majority that is not ready to tolerate corruption. Anticorruption politics could be a major electoral resource.

Why Should the Government Not Launch an Anticorruption Campaign?

The presentation by the opponent of an anticorruption campaign was a surprise to most of the ministers. He did not question any of the arguments of the proponent of the anticorruption politics. He made only one point: The realm of corruption and the realm of anticorruption sentiments are

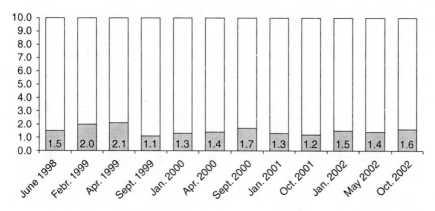

Figure 8.2   Bulgaria: acceptability of corruption in principle
Source: Corruption Indexes of Coalition 2000, May 2002.

two parallel worlds and governments cannot change short-term perceptions of corruption even if their anticorruption policies succeed in reducing actual corruption.

In his view, in electoral terms a success in the war against corruption means that people are convinced that corruption has significantly decreased and that the prospects of eliminating corruption have increased. In other words, the success of an anticorruption campaign in the language of our study means that the anticorruption campaign should produce visible changes in the index of perceived spread of corruption and in the corruption expectations index.

The major argument of the opponent of anticorruption campaigns and the major argument of this essay is that even the successful implementation of anticorruption policies is unlikely to produce such a change. The evidence is that the actual decline in the level of corruption measured by the corrupt pressure and corrupt practices indices fail to correlate with a significant decline in the perceived spread of corruption and corruption expectation indices. If votes are based on perceptions of corruption rather than on personal experience, this presents a problem for democratic reformers.

The assumption of those advocating anticorruption campaigns is that the public will "feel" the actual reduction of corruption, and the government will be politically rewarded. This assumption has never been tested. The reading of the existing Bulgarian data on the corruption attitudes of people does not support this assumption.

Figure 8.3 shows scatter plots of the observation points of corrupt practices and perceived spread of corruption indices (on the left axis) and the observation points of corrupt practices and corrupt expectation indices (on the right axis) for the 12 surveys performed by Vitosha Research. The graphic evidence suggests that the corrupt practice index does not correlate either with the perceived spread of corruption index or the corrupt expectation index.

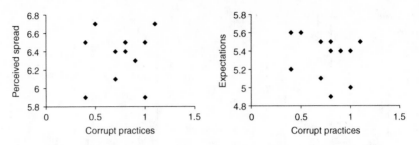

Figure 8.3 Effect of corrupt practices on perceived spread of corruption and corrupt expectations

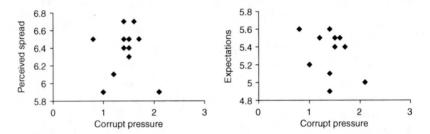

Figure 8.4 Effect of corrupt pressure on perceived spread of corruption and corrupt expectations

Table 8.2 Results of simple OLS regressions of corruption "perception" on corruption "reality" variables

Variable regressed on	*Perceived spread of corruption*				*Corruption expectations*			
	Practices	*Practices (lagged)*	*Pressure*	*Pressure (lagged)*	*Practices*	*Practices (lagged)*	*Pressure*	*Pressure (lagged)*
Coefficient	0.141	−0.171	−0.042	−0.127	−0.202	0.338	−0.243	0.240
t-statistic	0.385	−0.495	−0.161	−0.564	−0.642	1.121	−1.150	1.228
Adjusted R^2	−0.084	−0.082	−0.097	−0.073	−0.056	0.025	0.028	0.048

The data also indicate that the corruption pressure index does not correlate with the perceived spread of corruption index or corruption expectation index (see the scatter plots linking the corruption pressure index with the two perception indices in figure 8.4).

The statistical link between the two sets of variables is very weak, which is exactly the opposite of what the advocates of anticorruption campaigns imagine. This is demonstrated in table 8.2, which shows results from simple OLS regressions of variables measuring perceptions of corruption (perceived spread of corruption and corrupt expectations) on variables that aim at describing the corruption reality and acts (reports of corrupt practices and corrupt pressure). The dynamics of the corruption reality variables have no explanatory power for the dynamics of the corruption perception variables even with a lag of one observation.

In other words the opinion of the people on the spread of corruption in the country and their expectations on the further spread of the phenomenon are not formed on the base of their personal experience. Neither bribes they were asked to pay, nor bribes that they gave or that were given to them shaped their opinion on the spread of corruption.

Different interpretations of this unexpected result are possible, but the most obvious one is that when citizens judge the spread of corruption in the country, this is not a judgment of the level of administrative corruption that they encounter in everyday life, but it is a judgment of the amount of political corruption.

The basic problem that arises from our initial findings is that the public has difficulty "learning" that corruption has decreased and perceptions are weakly correlated with experiences. This finding is also confirmed by looking at a cross-section of individual respondents' data. If the full panel of observations is taken into account, the correlations between the two corruption reality and the two corruption perception variables are between 0.1 and 0.2.[7]

In this sense the legitimate question is whether the public can learn about the reduced level of corruption through the media if it cannot learn through personal experience. This is an essential question in deciding whether to go or not to go for an anticorruption campaign. It is obvious that in an environment of low trust in institutions, the public will not "trust" government when it claims success in reducing corruption. It is also obvious that if the government makes the reduction of corruption its priority, the opposition will have more incentives to attack the government for being corrupt and to claim that corruption has increased (which is what is actually happening in Bulgaria these days). Can the media be the channel through which the truth about the levels of corruption will reach the public?

The empirical data suggest that there is a strong correlation between the number of corruption-related publications in a certain period and increases in the index measuring the perceived spread of corruption. That means that the more the media writes about corruption the more people tend to believe that the level of corruption in their country has increased. The logical question is how the content of published articles influences this finding. The fact that there is a competitive media market in Bulgaria that does not have a visible ideological bias, and the fact that this market is dominated by foreign-owned media could be a precondition that informed citizens will get the truth even if the opposition or other enemies of the government make false accusations trying to discredit government policies. But is media competition a safeguard for truth?

Empirically it is simply impossible to test how many of the major corruption scandals that hit the front pages revealed real cases of corruption and in what proportion they represent the clever use of corruption accusations for political or business purposes. The nonfunctioning judicial system makes such a test a nonoption.

But the question of whether media competition neutralizes media bias is not confined to the coverage of corruption. So we adopt the argument constructed in Shleifer's and Mullainathan's recent article "Media Bias" (2002). They distinguish two different types of media bias. One of them, which they refer to as ideology, reflects a news outlet's desire to affect readers' opinion in a particular direction. The other one, which they refer to as spin, reflects the outlet's attempt simply to create a memorable story, thus selling more copies. The authors examined a theoretical model of competition among media outlets in the presence of these biases. What they demonstrated is that whereas, under their model, competition eliminates the effect of ideological bias, it actually exaggerates the incentives to spin stories. In other words, if the media market is dominated by spin bias, as is the case in Bulgaria, Shleifer and Mullainathan's results would suggest that competition will increase the incentives of news outlets to report stories in a way that meets the expectations of their readers.

The conclusion of this analysis is that a governmental anticorruption campaign will increase and not decrease the number of corruption-related stories and that media competition instead of correcting the antigovernmental bias and the fake nature of some corruption accusations will tend to exaggerate this trend. In other words the position of the media will be that any story that possibly could be a corruption story will be told as a proven corruption story. And that any story that was initially covered as a corruption story will tend to continue to be covered as a corruption story. More explicitly, media competition will side with corruption accusations even when the facts proving these accusations are of a doubtful nature.

The case of the "the corrupt executive director of Bulgartabak" is a powerful illustration of the effects of spin bias. In fall 2001 the new Bulgarian government decided to appoint a new executive director to Bulgartabak, the Bulgarian tobacco company. Bulgartabak is a big state-owned enterprise, which was scheduled for privatization in 2002. The government's decision to make this appointment was based on its desire to limit the temptation for inside dealings in the critical year when the enterprise was going to be privatized. It was a logical decision. The enterprise was known as a source of illegal party financing of more than one party. The government's choice for executive director was a young Bulgarian whose entire career had been with multinational companies outside of Bulgaria. His previous work had nothing to do with the tobacco industry. The appointment provoked sensational interest when information was leaked to the press that the new director had negotiated a Western-type salary, many times higher than the salary of the previous director.[8] For a month the government denied that such a salary was negotiated.

A month later representatives of one of the partners of Bulgartabak and candidate buyers of the enterprise wrote a letter to the prime minister accusing the executive director of asking for a 500,000 dollar bribe in a confidential meeting in a notorious restaurant. The accusers reported that they had had the conversation taped and were ready to give the tapes to the prosecutor. For several weeks the media covered the case extensively, openly favoring the accusing side. As a result of the media pressure, the director was replaced. This story could be an example of the important role of the media in revealing corruption cases. But it could also serve as an example of how spin bias works to the disadvantage of the government.

The story has its other side. The accusing party turned out to be very close to a well-known Russian businessman who was expelled from Bulgaria as a threat to national security; he never gave evidence for his accusations. The famous tapes that recorded the corrupt offer were never presented to the prosecutor.

Is, then, the Bulgartabak director a classical case of a corrupt official or is he a classical victim of a kompromat campaign whose aim was to oust the unfriendly director? The question looks difficult to resolve, but the public unanimously made up its mind. The investigation was closed for lack of evidence, but public opinion pronounced its sentence: The director's resignation was a confession from the government that their man was corrupt. For the government, the removal of the suspected director was the only way to prove that it had been serious in its decision to fight corruption. In the words of Akos Szilagyi "you cannot argue with kompromat, nor can you refute it. There is only one adequate response to kompromat, i.e., counter-kompromat" (2002: 219).

Making our argument stronger, we claim that the government's focus on corruption increases the incentives of the opposition to attack the government for being corrupt. Shleifer's argument demonstrates why in the Bulgarian media environment the government has little chance to defend itself. The fact that it takes years for any libel suit to be settled only strengthens this conclusion. The anticorruption campaign can easily turn into a kompromat war.

In short, the government does not have real instruments to change the indices of the perceived spread of corruption and of corrupt expectations, which, we assume, are precisely the indices that have to change if the government is to be reelected. This is the major finding of our reading of the empirical data. As we pointed out earlier the world of corruption perceptions and the world of corruption are two parallel worlds. What matters are the policy implications of this unexpected finding.

What is the Problem With Anticorruption Campaigns?
The Social Constructionist Perspective

Governments' disincentives to undertake anticorruption campaigns are related to the elusive nature of the corruption as a policy issue. This finding suggests the need for additional reflection on the nature of corruption and corruption perceptions in transition.

Recently, the debate on the "special nature" of corruption as a social problem took the form of a debate on the measurability of corruption

(Sik 2002; Krastev 2002). The construction of the Transparency International (TI) corruption perception index gave rise to a new generation of studies on the effects of corruption (Lambsdorff 1999). In these studies TI perception indices were treated as hard data. But what do we measure when we measure corruption? Do we measure the number of bribes per person in a country? Do we measure the number of people being involved in corrupt transactions? Do we measure the volume of money that circulates in corrupt exchanges? Do we measure which levels of political power are captured by special interests? But in the final analysis, the major problem with measuring corruption is its secret nature—all parties involved in a corrupt transaction have an incentive to hide it.

The measurement debate turned anticorruption studies away from another important aspect of corruption's elusiveness and away from the problem of how corruption has been constructed as a policy problem in different societies. Whose definition of the causes, culprits, and solutions of the corruption problem has been accepted? Who wins and who loses in the definitions war? It should not be surprising that "groups with conflicting interests and stakes in the system have varied perspectives on the nature of the problem and compete with one another to impose their particular constructions and influence the public discourse on the subject" (Pavarala 1996: 19).

Governments and international donors have defined corruption primarily as an institutional problem and have assumed that the public accepts the same definition of the causes and cures for the corruption phenomenon. But the consensus on the causes, effects, and solution of corruption turned out to be an illusionary one. In judging the success of anticorruption campaigns, the average citizen adopts his own perspective on the causes of corruption, its effects, and what constitutes successful anticorruption politics. And his perspective is not an institutional one. The definitions endorsed by the public are more broadly moralistic than narrow legalistic, and they tend to be more individual-centered than institutional. The public is more interested in fixing the responsibility than in analyzing the phenomenon.

In this respect only the social constructionist point of view can explain the fact that the corruption perception index does not reflect changes in the reported level of corruption. The critical problem is how to interpret the misrepresentation of the corruption phenomenon in Bulgaria. The nature of this misrepresentation is more important for designing anticorruption strategies than the actual levels of corruption.

The empirical data collected by Vitosha Research covered not only the corruption perceptions of the population as a whole, but in three occasions the agency has also studied the corruption perceptions of sizable samples of public officials, politicians, and businessmen. What is interesting for us is to understand how these four groups—the public, the politician, the public official, and the businessman—define the causes of corruption. What is the dynamic of their explanations, and whose definitions are winning the day?

In this respect we can distinguish between three basic constructions of the causes of corruption: (1) corruption is an institutional issue, and it can be reduced by institutional changes—withdrawing the state from the economy, more transparency and accountability, introduction of new legislation; (2) corruption is an economic phenomenon, it is the result of inadequate wages and weak incentives for honesty in the public sector; (3) corruption is a political problem—it is an instrument for politicians to enrich themselves at the expense of the majority of the population, and it is rooted in the selection of the political elite. Almost no one views corruption as a cultural problem. It is not surprising that the public, politicians, bureaucrats, and businessmen each predominantly favor one of these constructions. Politicians promote the institutional view of the causes of corruption and push for institutional solutions. Public officials endorse economic explanation for the spread of corruption, referring to the low salaries of public officials and the political pressures on the bureaucracy. Their preferable solution is higher salaries and higher punishment. At the beginning of the monitored period they tended to support the economic explanation of the causes of corruption. With the acceleration of the privatization process in 1999, they turned to a different explanation—it arose from the nature and the project of the political elite. For the general public, the question of what causes corruption was replaced by the question of who benefits from corruption. The public's preferable solution is a change in the political elite, so that all other anticorruption policies are peripheral. This coincides with the public's criticism of the existing electoral system based on proportional representation and the constantly declining trust in political parties. The businessmen have no view in common. They recognize the institutional nature of the problem but are ready to blame politicians for the state of corruption. What is interesting is that all four groups view themselves as the primary victims of corruption.

In our view the fact that the political elite lost the definition war and failed to convert the public to see the institutional nature of the corruption phenomenon is at the heart of the cognitive split between the personal experience of corruption and the shaping of corruption perceptions. The government and the public are operating with two different definitions of the causes of corruption and its cures. To the extent that public opinion defines corruption as the very nature of exercising power, attempts of the government to convince the public of its efforts to clean up the system will fail to confront the accusations of the opposition that this government is even more corrupt than the previous one.

There are two cases that illustrate the policy implications of the public's definition of corruption. The Privatization Agency is traditionally ranked among the most corrupt institutions in Bulgaria. What is unexpected is that businessmen who are familiar with the work of the agency tend to view it less corrupt than the general public which is at an arm's length from it. Where does this discrepancy come from? If our interpretation of the meaning of the post-communist perceptions of corruption is correct, then business people judge the corruption of the privatization process, while the general public sees the Privatization Agency as the agent of corruption because privatization itself is perceived as one of the sublime manifestations of post–communist corruption. For the public, the Privatization Agency is corrupt not because its representatives take bribes and rig procedures, but because as an elite project, privatization is by definition identical with corruption. It is an instrument for the elite to steal from the public through the state.

The case of the customs office is even more striking. If the institutional view of the political usefulness of anticorruption campaigns is taken seriously, it has to rely on a link between institutional performance and perceptions of corruption. The Bulgarian Customs Agency provides a very indicative example. From the very beginning of the corruption surveys in 1997 respondents perceived the customs office as the most corrupt institution in the country. Assuming that improved institutional performance will be rewarded by lower corruption perceptions and that institutional performance depends on institutional incentives, in fall 2001 the king's government opted for the radical solution of putting the agency under the supervision of a foreign private company (the British company, Crown Agents). The media massively covered the governmental initiative.

It is too early to tell whether the new arrangement will lead to improved institutional performance by the Bulgarian customs. However, corruption surveys conducted both before and after Crown Agents took over in early 2002 indicate that the public perceptions about the level of corruption in the customs is positively, rather than negatively, correlated with the performance of the agency measured by total customs revenues (customs collect not only tariffs, but value added and excise taxes at the point of entry as well) as a percent of total imports. This is illustrated in figure 8.5 using six-month periodicity for 2000–02.

The fact that the periods of most successful institutional performance (in the first half of 2000 and in the second half of 2002) correspond to the

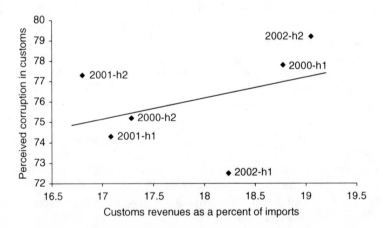

Figure 8.5   Customs performance and perceived corruption in customs
Source: Corruption Indexes of Coalition 2000; Bulgarian Customs Agency news releases; own calculations.

highest level of public perception about corruption in the customs is especially telling. Obviously, the Bulgarian public did not define corruption primarily as an institutional problem.

Reading the data leads to the conclusion that it is highly unlikely that the public infers the level of corruption based on institutional performance. Again, it is much more likely that, for the public, the problem with corruption is the problem with the elite, with the shared belief that "politicians are crooks" and with the criminalization of politics as public activity. The results of the "State of Society" survey in a different way confirmed these findings. The survey portrayed Bulgaria as a classical "us versus them" society where the vast majority of people experienced the time of transition as a time of economic and status loss.

In trying to rationalize the loss of income and social status, different social groups formulate different claims on the definition, consequences, and preconditions for corruption. The losers from the reforms tend to define corruption as the very essence of the exercise of power. This explains some important differences in citizens' perception of the causes of corruption. The majority of losers view the causes of corruption in the nature and the projects of the power elites. In the view of the losers the transition is a zero–sum game where they are the victims of a huge conspiracy. For them, transition is the period when elites have abandoned their social responsibilities. This definition of the nature of the transition explains why the majority of citizens defined politicians and criminals as the real winners of the change and why they defined people like themselves as the real losers (see tables 8.3 and 8.4).

Table 8.3 Which groups have won the most from the changes? (Open-ended question)

	Percent
Politicians	55.3
Mafiosi, crooks	36.8
Businesspersons, traders	18.3
Restitution beneficiaries	6.7
Former party leaders	5.2
The rich	5.0
Customs officers	4.9
Enterprising, proactive and resourceful people	3.7
Bankers, insurers	3.6
Doctors	3.3
Lawyers, judges, prosecutors	2.7
The corrupt	2.6
Millionaires "on credit"	2.5
Pushy, unscrupulous people, opportunists, schemers	2.4
Managers of enterprises	1.7
People close to the power-holders	1.3
Communists	1.3
Cunning, adaptable people	1.0

Source: Alpha Research, State of Society 2002.

Table 8.4   What social groups are the biggest losers from the changes? (Open-ended question)

	Percent
Ordinary people	36.8
Workers	21.3
Pensioners	20.3
Village residents	9.2
Poor people	7.6
Unemployed	7.0
Middle class	6.5
Farmers	4.6
Young people, students	4.3
Employed	4.0
Teachers	3.7
Educated, university degreed, intellectuals	3.4
Roma	2.4
Children	1.8
Undereducated	1.7
Public servants and municipal administrators	1.7
Businessmen	1.5
Industrious	1.3
Medicals	1.1

Source: Alpha Research, State of Society 2002.

This situation is not specific to Bulgaria. In their comparative study of the social psychological objectives on the way to a market economy in Eastern and Central a group of Hungarian sociologists have demonstrated that

> The public, after the collapse of state socialism in 1989–90, was shocked by the abruptness and depth of the transition and took shelter behind moral ideas thought to be safe. But from that vantage point, the economic transition seemed even more repugnant. Looking at the transition in terms of justice, trustworthiness, and confidence, people discerned corruption, untrustworthiness, injustice, and undeserved enrichment by a new elite, whereas in most cases, nothing had really happened beyond the normal functioning of the market (Csepeli et al. 2004: 216).

The public, after the collapse of state socialism in 1989–90, was shocked by the abruptness and depth of the transition and took shelter behind moral ideas thought to be safe. But from that vantage point, the economic transition seemed even more repugnant. Looking at the transition in terms of justice, trustworthiness, and confidence, people discerned corruption, untrustworthiness, injustice, and undeserved enrichment by a new elite, whereas in most cases, nothing had really happened beyond the normal functioning of the market.

Losing the war on the meaning of the transition, the political elites have come under siege. In the opinion of the public the economic transition is perceived as a zero-sum game where the enrichment and success of some people could be attained only at the expense and loss of others.

This explanatory interpretative scheme came just at the right moment for those who perceived themselves as losers, because they could explain their own failure by the undeserved enrichment of the others.

In this sense the index of the perceived spread of corruption reflects the lost war on the meaning of transition and the lack of legitimacy of the new market rules much more than the actual level of bribery. And this makes it an inappropriate policy objective.

Conclusions

The interpretation of the dynamics of the politics of corruption perceptions in Bulgaria invites unexpected conclusions. The findings of this essay could be read simply as a Bulgarian pathology. They could be read as an example of the particular nature of corruption perceptions in the transition countries. But our results could also be viewed as an example of a general problem with anticorruption politics.

Our most obvious policy conclusion is that noncontextual policy advice creates enormous risks for the political process in the host country. In the case of Bulgaria the idea of launching an anticorruption campaign looks unattractive to "the highest levels of government" because initiating such a campaign does not contribute to the reelection of the government. The assumption that noncorrupt governments have incentives to initiate anticorruption campaigns turned out to be a wrong one. Anticorruption campaigns contribute to the delegitimization of the elites and to the destabilization of the political system. Noncorrupt governments do not have incentives to start anticorruption campaigns because they do not have the chance to convince the public that they are successful in fighting corruption. The popular perception of corruption reflects the dynamics of the public's dissatisfaction with the current state of affairs much more than the actual levels of bribery. The consequence is that institution-based anticorruption campaigns were swayed by other features of the transition. The findings of this essay suggest that it would be more productive to pursue anticorruption policies for their own sake, avoiding anticorruption rhetoric as a major justification for reform policies.

Notes

1. For more on definitions of corruption see Heidenheimer (1999).
2. della Porta and Vannucci (1999) have demonstrated that the rise of the "business politicians" who abuse power for personal enrichment was the result of a decision by the political parties to make selling public decisions the core of party activity.
3. See Vitosha Research's website: www.vitosha-research.com.
4. For fuller details see www.anticorruption.bg/index_eng.php.
5. See report at www.osf.bg/sos.
6. A concise summary can be found at World Bank (2000: 18–24).
7. We are grateful to Vitosha Research for this information.
8. The Centre for Liberal Strategies has a project tracking specific corruption-related cases, including media coverage. See www.cls-sofia.org.

References

Barany, Zoltan. 2002. "Bulgaria's Royal Election." *Journal of Democracy* 13: 141–55.

Blankenburg, Erhard. 2002. "From Political Clientelism to Outright Corruption—The Rise of the Scandal Industry." In K. Stephen and A. Sajo (eds.), *Political Corruption in Transition. A Sceptic's Handbook*, pp.149–66. Budapest: Central European University Press.

Cohen, Stanley. 1972. *Folk Devils and Moral Panics: The Creation of the Mods and Rockers*. London: MacGibbon and Kee/St. Martin's Press.

Csepeli, György, Antal Örkény, Mária Székelyi, and Ildikó Barna. 2004. "Blindness to Success: Social Psychological Objectives Along the Way to a Market Economy in Eastern Europe." In J. Kornai, B. Rothstein, and S. Rose-Ackerman (eds.), *Creating Social Trust in Post-Socialist Transition*, pp. 213–40. New York: Palgrave Macmillan.

Easterly, William. 2001. *The Elusive Quest for Growth: Economists' Adventure and Misadventures in the Tropics.* Cambridge MA: MIT Press.

European Commission. 2002. *Regular Report on Bulgaria's Progress Towards Accession*. Brussels: The European Commission.

Freeland, Chrystia. 2000. *Sale of the Century. The Inside Story of the Second Russian Revolution*. London: Little, Brown and Company.

Gupta, Sanjeev, Hamid Davoodi, and Rosa Alonso-Terme. 2002. "Does Corruption Affect Income Inequality and Poverty?" *Economics of Governance* 3: 23–45.

Heidenheimer, Arnold J. (ed.). 1999. *Political Corruption: A Handbook*, 5th ed. New Brunswick NJ: Transaction Publication.

Krastev, Ivan. 2002. "A Moral Economy of Anticorruption Sentiments in Eastern Europe." In Y. Elkana, I. Krastev, E. Macamo, and S. Randeria (eds.), *Unraveling Ties—From Social Cohesion to New Practices of Connectedness*, pp. 99–117. Frankfurt—New York: Campus Verlag.

Lambsdorff, J. Graf. 1999. *Corruption in Empirical Research—A Review*. Paper presented at the 9th International Anticorruption Conference (IACC) at Durban, South Africa, October 10–15. Available at www.transparency.org/iacc/9th_iacc/papers/day2/ws1/d2ws1_jglambsdorff.html.

Pavarala, Vihod. 1996. *Interpreting Corruption. Elite Perspectives in India*. New Delhi—Thousand Oaks—London: Sage Publications.

della Porta, Donatella and Alberto Vannucci. 1999. *Corrupt Exchanges. Actors, Resources, and Mechanisms of Political Corruption*. New York: Aldine de Gruyter.

Rose-Ackerman, Susan. 1999. *Corruption and Government: Causes, Consequences and Reform*. New York: Cambridge University Press.

Sajó, Andras. 2002. "Clientelism and Extortion: Corruption in Transition." In K. Stephen and A. Sajó (eds.), *Political Corruption in Transition. A Sceptic's Handbook*, pp. 1–22. Budapest: Central European University Press.

de Sardan, Jean-Pierre Olivier. 1999. "A Moral Economy of Corruption in Africa." *Journal of Modern African Studies* 37: 25–52.

Shleifer, Andrei and Robert Vishny. 1993. "Corruption." *Quarterly Journal of Economics* 108: 599–618.

Shleifer, Andrei and Sendhil Mullainathan. 2002. *Media Bias*. NBER Working Paper No. 9295: National Bureau for Economic Research, Cambridge, MA. http://papers.nber.org/papers/w9295.

Sik, Endre. 2002. "The Bad, the Worse and the Worst: Guesstimating the Level of Corruption." In K. Stephen and A. Sajó (eds.), *Political Corruption in Transition. A Sceptic's Handbook*, pp. 91–114. Budapest: Central European University Press.

Stiglitz, Joseph E. 2002. *Globalization and Its Discontents*. New York: W.W. Norton & Company.

Szilagyi, Akos. 2002. "Kompromat and Corruption in Russia." In K. Stephen and A. Sajó (eds.), *Political Corruption in Transition. A Sceptic's Handbook*, pp. 207–31. Budapest: Central European University Press.

Tanzi, Vito. 1998. "Corruption Around the World: Causes, Consequences, Scope, and Cures." *IMF Staff Papers* 45: 559–94.

Tanzi, Vito and Hamid Davoodi. 1998. "Corruption, Public Investment, and Growth." In H. Shibata and T. Ihori (eds.), *The Welfare State, Public Investment and Growth*, pp. 41–60. Tokyo: Springer-Verlag.

World Bank. 1997. *Helping Counties Combat Corruption. The Role of the World Bank*. Washington DC: World Bank.

———. 2000. *Anticorruption in Transition: A Contribution to the Policy Debate*. Washington DC: World Bank.

PART III

Transition to Democracy

CHAPTER NINE

Transition to Corporate Democracy?

RUSSELL HARDIN[*]

In the study of the current East European transitions from communist autocracy to liberal democracy, there are two distinct questions we should ask. First, what does it take to make the democratic transition? Second, what will the transition lead these nations into? The answer to the first query seems to be a lot less difficult than what political theorists of many persuasions have supposed. Some of the East Europeans did it or are doing it with remarkable quickness. The answer to the second query is much harder. In part, it is the question of whether these polities will turn out to be like the liberal democracies of the West. This is a more complex question than it might seem for the reason that the democracies of the West, as will be exemplified for present purposes by the United States, are themselves far from any liberal ideal that one might think they represent. They can increasingly be characterized as corporate democracies, in the sense spelled out later.

The reasons for the Western failure to be more nearly ideal are that the ideal is virtually impossible to achieve because it does not fit the actual motivations of real citizens or elected officials. Among the biggest incentive problems is the radical divergence between incentives in the economy and incentives in politics. The political state can create and destroy individual and corporate wealth. Business therefore plays a very heavy role in politics. Hence, it is partly the combination of democracy and market economics that wrecks the liberal vision. There are also epistemological and incentive problems that afflict voters. In the face of these problems of democracy, one cannot be optimistic (Hardin 2002b).

I wish to lay out the liberal model, address its problems in real-world application, and then turn to an examination of the moves toward liberal democracy in the East. I will generally assume that the model for both liberal politics and market economics (also liberal in historical usage) is principally concerned with the welfare of citizens. I will not go very deeply into analyzing the possible measures of welfare but will suppose only that certain simple measures, such as GDP per capita and a small number of civil liberties are adequate for a first pass.

If we suppose that the ideal liberal government would be concerned with the welfare of its citizens, we immediately face the problem of how to motivate our governors to be essentially benevolent toward us. The Qing government of eighteenth-century China defined its role as "benevolent governance" (Rowe 2001: 447). Of course, its benevolence was in the cause of its view of how the society should be organized and what roles the people of various statuses should play in that society. It was surely also true that the agents of that government looked upon the government as in their interest. European kings similarly did not need arrogantly to claim "L'état c'est moi" to believe and act as though their own interest largely mirrored the interests of their peoples.

The central problems of contemporary American liberal democracy are the scale of the electorate with its consequent problems of representation and of citizens' knowledge of politics (Hardin 2002b). Some of the East European nations might be able to manage these problems because their scale is substantially smaller, although it seems unlikely that a polity of millions—even if it is only a few millions—can avoid these problems. These nations also may prove to have an advantage in the coherence of their parties, although this is not yet clear. So far, their party systems are often in shambles (Carothers 1999). The American parties have lost their former definition as essentially Left and Right, in the traditional American sense, on fundamental economic policy and are now relatively ill defined. This fact complicates the problem of citizens' understanding, because party identification of candidates has less meaning than it had before the coalescence of views in favor of mostly letting the market run on its own without much central management (Hardin 2000; 2004). Many East European parties seem to agree on a similar economic policy, although they sometimes do not preach what they practice.

To set the stage, I will first discuss the problems of contemporary American democracy and then turn to a standard set of claims about how liberal democracy is organized as partially the product of a vibrant civil society. Some writings on civil society suggest that the East European political transitions would be potentially quite difficult, and yet some of those transitions seem, on the contrary, remarkably quick and likely successful. Indeed, the level of hostile, divisive politics in many of these nations is possibly below that of the United States during its first decade or so, when extra-constitutional action against political opponents was relatively common. For example, the grossly unconstitutional Alien and Sedition Acts of 1798 were intended to allow the imprisonment of political opponents. In one historian's view, American public political discourse during the 1790s earned the epithet "paranoid style" (Morgan 1994: 11).

A related issue is the Hobbesian problem of political transition. The central problem of such a transition in Thomas Hobbes's view is its threat to social order. He insists that even agitating mildly for reform threatens to destroy government and bring back anarchy (Hobbes [1651] 1968: 380). Against traditional Hobbesian views in political philosophy, the transitions in East Europe have been surprisingly easy. In particular, of course, there has been virtually no problem of fundamental social order in many of these nations. There has been a general rise in criminality in some nations, perhaps especially in Russia with its quasi mafia and its armed takeovers of newly privatized firms (Volkov 2004).[1] But normal criminal law has not been particularly defective—as contract law has been in many of the nations (see, e.g., Radaev 2004b). Moreover, grand social theorists—who evidently fail to look at their own societies—claim that social order depends on a broad consensus on values. Contrary to such claims, order in the Eastern nations has been sustained from long before the transitions, through the transitions, and on into the present. It would be hard to argue that there has been a steady consensus on values throughout these periods.

A short-term conclusion from much of the discussion that follows is that the current Eastern transitions belie many standard views in political theory, views that often are thought to rest on substantial experience in many diverse contexts. Some of these views should now be laid to rest for failing the tests posed by the Eastern examples. The two most important, related but not identical, theses are that democratic society requires a value consensus (Durkheim [1893] 1933: 226–9 and passim; Parsons [1937] 1968: 89–94; and many communitarians, such as Etzioni 1993; but see Hardin 1999: ch. 1, 1995: ch. 7), or that it requires the existence of various elements of civil society (Tocqueville [1835 and 1840] 1966; Putnam 1993, 2000; Arato and Cohen 1992). Thousands of pages have been written on these theses, the bulk of which makes claims of the virtual necessity for one or the other of these if democratic society is to cohere or to work well. For example, it is widely claimed that, without civil society, and especially its intermediary organizations, democracy is not richly viable. Jean Cohen speaks of the "symbolic dimension of civil society and the role it plays in generating consent . . . and, hence, in integrating society" (Cohen 1999: 214).

Corporate Democracy

In the era of democratic representative government, it would be wrong to say that elected officials and bureaucrats see government as theirs in quite the same way as the Qing rulers or as French monarchs saw theirs. But the elected officials have become a separate class, as argued from the early twentieth century, and many of their actions seem to serve their specific interests as office-holders, sometimes in conflict with the interests of their constituents or the citizenry (see Hardin 2003b). In part, their interest is simply hanging onto office and power, but it is also to benefit themselves financially (including in their later careers) and with perquisites that would come otherwise only to the most powerful officers of large corporations or to the extremely wealthy. For example, Andras Sajó slyly remarks: "Government sleaze is often completely legal but still unethical, for instance, taking a vacation to Madagascar and claiming the trip was intended to study how that country's public administration operates" (1998: 38). One would like to see an accounting of the public costs of such benefits for being a corporate democrat. Those costs are as little public as certain parts of the extravagant emoluments of corporate CEOs. Many of these benefits would have come to earlier aristocratic governors through their family fortunes rather than from the public finances. In the United States, however, such costs are staggered by the scale of often sleazy campaign finance.

Adolph Berle and Gardner Means note that the rise of the corporate form of organization of private firms broke the link between ownership and management, thus opening the possibility of conflicts of interest between owners and professional managers (Berle and Means 1932: 119–25 and passim; see also Means 1959). Berle and Means propose three legal forms that property in the corporate form might take. The first is analogous to pure property rights, with managers acting wholly as agents of those who own the stock of the corporation and who retain the full rights of ownership of property. The second is analogous to what we have seen in many corporations historically, including many in recent years during the extraordinary stock bubble of the 1990s. This form creates "a new set of relationships, giving to the groups in control powers which are absolute and not limited by any implied obligation with respect to their use." Through their absolute control of a corporation, the managers "can operate it in their own interests and can divert a portion of the [corporation's income and assets] to their own uses," and we face the potential for "corporate plundering" (Berle and Means 1932: 354–5). We have seen recently just how massive the conflict between managers and owners in these two contending models of property can be, with managers of many high-flying firms in the United States looting the firms while very nearly bankrupting certain owners, such as those whose retirement funds were virtually liquidated in the subsequent collapse of the firms.

Their third form of corporate control perhaps reflects the fact that they were writing in the heyday of beliefs in the superiority of communism or socialism over capitalism (Stein 1989). They supposed that the corporate form would develop into what would now be called a socially conscious institution. This wildly optimistic expectation is at odds with their hard-headed analysis of what had already developed in corporate governance. They quote Walter Rathenau's 1918 view that the private "enterprise becomes transformed into an institution which resembles the state in character" (Berle and Means 1932: 352). Ironically, they and Rathenau were right for reasons contrary to what they thought. Corporations have not become more like states in working partly for the public interest; rather, the state has become more like the corporations whose ownership and management is starkly separated.

In a reversal of Rathenau's argument, representative government is a form of organization in a sense analogous to the corporate form of enterprise management. Elected officials act as "professional" managers on behalf of the citizenry who "own" the nation. For the most part, these officials police themselves, if they are policed at all, with citizens having only an occasional say, primarily at times of elections. Sajó notes, "the fundamental myth of parliamentary popular sovereignty today, namely, that the members of [parliament] represent the people or the nation cannot be sustained" (1999: 118). The officials are co-owners along with the citizens, but their rewards from management often far transcend anything they can gain as their share of the general good produced by government, just as the corporate managers of Tyco, WorldCom, and Enron gained far more from looting these firms than from the genuine increase in value of the stock they owned. Indeed, they manipulated the market valuation of that stock through accounting misrepresentations in order to enrich themselves, as Berle and Means (1932: 296–7) virtually predict. Such corporate managers were policed by corporate boards whose members they appointed, and many of these boards were also paid in stock options.

In principle, elected officials are subject to greater control, but in practice they are apt to be policed only by their opponents in power unless their behavior becomes egregious. Even if I greatly disapprove of my party's representatives, for example, any action I might successfully take to replace them in office is not likely to benefit alternatives within my party, but candidates from an opposing party, candidates of whom I would be likely to disapprove even more than I disapprove of my party's incumbents. Democrats who voted for Ralph Nader, a guaranteed loser, are rightly charged with having helped put George W. Bush in the presidency. I am very nearly stuck with my party, so long as its office-holders are not egregiously awful and self-serving to the detriment of me and my fellow citizens.

If presidents Andrew Johnson (1865–69), Richard Nixon (1969–74), and Bill Clinton (1993–2001) had had majorities of their own parties in control of Congress, they very likely would not have faced serious impeachment proceedings.[2] It was only the anomaly of so-called mixed government in the United States that put them at risk. During the attacks on Clinton, for example, the interests of most Democratic national legislators, as Democrats, were to defend him, and the interests of Republicans, as Republicans, were to attack him. Of course, it could just happen to be true that almost all Democrats thought his offenses inadequate for removal from office while almost all Republicans thought those offenses adequate. In the case of Andrew Johnson, one of the Radical Republicans who opposed him would have taken the office of president if Johnson had been removed and would have elevated many others of his party to positions of national power. Separating personal interests from the positions all these people took would be very difficult, but it is hard to believe that their personal interests as office-holders were not a major factor.

What might set legislators apart from the citizens who elect them is that they become competent at politics and even legislation and governance through the specialization of their roles, and they develop resources to help them stay in office. Our representatives even tend, in Bernard Manin's characterization, to become aristocratic in that they must have relatively high levels of competence and achievement to attain and hold their offices (Manin 1997: ch. 4). As the American constitutionalist Benjamin Rush, writing as Nestor, says, government cannot be done well by people who "spend three years in acquiring a profession which their country immediately afterwards forbids them to follow" (Nestor 1786; see Hardin 1999: 225). Moreover, actual elected officials clearly do not represent their constituents in the sense of being like them. There are, for example, few working-class representatives in modern democratic governments, and lawyers are grossly overrepresented in U.S. legislative bodies. The representation of groups must often be through so-called active representation by people who themselves do not directly share the interests of the groups they represent. For example, Senator Ted Kennedy of Massachusetts often represents the interests of union members and the poor although he has no experience of either group in his own life.

An obvious but painful implication of this account is that representatives are enabled to take advantage of citizens. This is true not merely in the manner of Silvio Berlusconi, who has used his official power to enact laws that specifically benefit him financially. For example, he proposed and pushed legislation to allow a change in the venue of his trial for bribery so that the trial would go before a court more likely to be friendly to him (Bruni 2002, 2003). To do this, of course, he had to get general legislation passed, although no one is likely to suppose he cared at all about the generality of the legislation.[3] It is true more fundamentally that legislators take advantage of citizens in the sense that, without such overt actions as Berlusconi's, the elective personnel of government can be parasitic on the larger society, making many of them wealthier than they could have been in any other activity available to them, giving themselves prerogatives far beyond their ordinary emoluments, and securing themselves and often even their relatives in power. They commonly support legislation in large part in return for support from the specific beneficiaries of the legislation rather than supporting legislation because it would be generally good for the economy. Through such devices, which help to keep them personally in office, they become an aristocratic class apart from the society they both govern and represent in a sense well beyond Manin's.

Even the slightest Madisonian or Humean view of human nature yields this implication. Roberto Michels ([1911] 1949) claims that the internal democratic government of political parties—especially European socialist parties of his time—produces an aristocracy with great power over the rank and file members. This claim is true more generally of democratic government, although the latter may typically be subjected to greater scrutiny that might impede some of the worst excesses of oligarchic power. In Michels's famous slogan, "Who says organization says oligarchy." Perversely, who says elective representative democracy evidently also says oligarchy.

In the Manin and Michels theses of an aristocracy of leadership, it is not the individual elected officials but the class of them that is problematic. As John C. Calhoun says, "The advantages of possessing the control of the powers of the government, and thereby of its honors and emoluments, are, of themselves, exclusive of all other considerations, ample to divide... a community into two great hostile parties" (Calhoun [1853] 1992: 16). As a class, the political aristocracy is parasitic on the society that they ostensibly serve and that has the power of election over them. Although some representatives may be very well grounded in their constituencies, the reference group for many representatives is far more likely to be their fellow "aristocrats" than their electorates so long as they attend to certain issues of great salience to their constituencies. The supposedly powerful citizenry with its power of election over officials does not have the power to refuse to elect all of them; it can only turn out the occasional overtly bad apple. In the United States, it seldom has the temerity to overcome incumbents' advantages.[4] Edmund Burke thought citizens should be deferential to their aristocratic leaders. Few people would argue for such social deference today although there is pervasive deference to the power of elected officials and to their celebrity, which is a peculiarly ugly aspect of modern democracies, perhaps uglier and more pervasive in the United States than in other advanced democracies.

Note, as an aside, that family connections per se increasingly contribute to political success in, at least, the United States. In the presidential election of 2000 each major party had a candidate who was a scion of an old political family. The brother of the current president is governor of the third largest state and is often mentioned as the possible next Republican candidate to succeed his own brother. In the Senate and House of Representatives, there are later generations, siblings, or spouses from the Chafee, Pelosi, Kennedy, Udall, Bentsen, Sununu, Murkowski, Dole, and Clinton families. In governorships there are later generation representatives of the Taft, Romney, and Bush families. In 2002 in an extraordinary abuse of his power, newly elected Governor Frank Murkowski of Alaska appointed his own daughter to fill his vacated Senate seat (Kurtz 2003). Americans who have deplored the inheritance of political leadership in some communist states should look at their own system of inherited political power and privilege.

Calhoun spent the last two decades of his life defending slavery and the prerogative of the southern states to maintain slavery. The minority that his writings generally defend was the minority of southern states and their representatives in the national government against the majority of antislavery states and their representatives. Some of his central arguments, however, are more generally compelling in the abstract and when applied to many other issues. He argued the case that officials use their offices to serve their private interests nearly a century before Berle and Means made the analogous case for the governance of the modern corporation. Although the corporate form of organization had precedents in the seventeenth century, the first important manufacturing firm organized that way—with a significant number of stock-holders, all of them minority stock-holders—was the first of the large New England textile mills, organized in Waltham, Massachusetts, in 1813 (Berle and Means 1932: 10–11). This company followed the virtual invention of modern representative government in the U.S. Constitution of 1787 by a quarter century so that, in a sense, the corporate form of control with few managers and large numbers of owners was pioneered by the U.S. government, which has remained the world's largest corporate entity while thousands of substantial private corporations have come and gone.

The Eastern European democracies are similarly well on the way to corporate democracy. One might argue that substantial fractions of the politicians of the past have continued in office because they have the human capital to debate, speak in public, organize, and mobilize. In addition they have the social capital of connections to the larger class of those influential in politics, which is primarily other politicians. These people are part of the aristocracy of rulers selected within the Communist Party who quickly shifted to become an aristocracy by election. Much of the human capital that they had developed under the old system was useful for campaigning and gave career politicians an advantage over many of the "amateurs" who entered politics de novo in the liberalizing moment.

Some of the amateurs, such as Vaclav Havel most notably, were sufficiently charismatic and sufficiently clean of any association with communism that they succeeded politically. Havel survived a long time by standing virtually outside politics and letting such people as Vaclav Klaus take the burden of responsibility—and sometimes the blame—for actual policies. Lech Walesa in Poland quickly lost his charisma because of his dirigiste behavior and his heated partisanship. His democratic mantra cloaked an autocratic spirit. He could not transfer his extraordinary organizational talents to the world of active politics in the new liberal order. Behind all such people, however, there stand large numbers of people who have redefined themselves as democrats, but who are clearly corporate democrats. The Manin thesis has applied to the Eastern European societies from the earliest days of their liberal transitions.

A remarkable feature of the corporate democrats is that they could translate their professional lives into successful roles in the transitional and later society. Hence, theirs is a profession that allowed even those over 50 years of age to continue to prosper, whereas in the broader societies those over 50 generally suffered substantial losses of status and prosperity as a result of the upheavals of 1989. The human capital and organizational roles of the over-50 losers were reduced in importance in the new world of economic liberalism, and they were too old to develop the talent for new careers.

Civil Society and Social Order

A grand claim in our time is that we need "civil society" in order to have successful liberal, democratic government (Putnam 2000; Arato and

Cohen 1992). The presumed elements of civil society are varied, but they commonly include some version of a limited normative consensus, the existence of intermediary groups that help to integrate individuals into the political order while helping them maintain their relatively particular identities, and—commonly within the intermediary groups—opportunities for discourse over social and political issues. Related to these three elements are several associated themes, not all of which would be common to all exponents of civil society.

The notion of a normative consensus is often associated with a supposition or claim that social order is constituted by a social contract. The assumption of a social contract is incoherent for a modern or for any more or less pluralist society (see further Hardin 1999: ch. 4). Discussion of intermediary groups often has the flavor or explicit character of communitarian claims. Interestingly, however, the intermediary groups are seen as supports for personal autonomy in the face of pluralist politics whereas for John Stuart Mill and many others political participation in such politics contributes to autonomy. And the claims for discourse generally are grounded in a theory—perhaps only implicitly—of democratic participation.

Discussions of civil society are both normative and causal. The normative claims are that we will be better people and that we will constitute better polities or societies if we have civil society. This sometimes sounds like nothing more than a definitional claim, but it is also sometimes a causal claim such as those Mill and others make for a connection between liberal democracy and personal autonomy and development. But the most challenging and potentially interesting of the claims of exponents of civil society is the grand causal claim that we need it if we are to cohere politically and socially (Putnam 1993, 2000). If this is true, then Russia and some of the East European states should not so readily have developed relatively democratic polities. In the Soviet Union, highly developed networks of friends substituted for the public, organized activities of civil society. Such networks are still active, perhaps especially in black-market dealings (see Ledeneva, 1998, 2004), but they have largely been displaced by the market for standard dealings.

For some writers on civil society, normative consensus is crucial for social cohesion, as in the visions of Émile Durkheim ([1893] 1933: 226–9 and passim) and Talcott Parsons ([1937] 1968: 89–94). A directly contrary sociological vision is that societies prosper when they succeed in creating institutions that manage conflicts over which there is (and perhaps can be) no consensus (Dahrendorf 1968). What are the actual facts on consensus in real societies? In the United States, throughout its history, it is hard even to imagine what normative consensus there was that was of political significance although there has been a limited pragmatic consensus on legal order and open commercial relations. In its early decades the new nation was deeply divided on issues of religion, slavery, region, the political franchise, small-farming versus commerce and plantation-farming, residual aristocratic versus radically democratic leanings, and, perhaps most fearfully, propertied wealth versus poverty.

The original U.S. constitutional consensus covered the very limited concerns of such constitutionalists as Alexander Hamilton and James Madison. The consensus was limited in two ways. First, it was limited to means, not larger purposes. The constitutionalists concurred principally in transferring the power to regulate trade from the states to an overarching federal government (Hardin 1999: 241–8). Second, it was limited to only a politically critical part of the society of the time. It rolled under the slaves and the Anti-Federalists, whose interests and values were in direct conflict with the means on which the constitutionalists coordinated, and it ignored women. After the initial constitutional era, the lack of significant normative consensus has continued. Even the limited pragmatic consensus on commerce broke down during the decades around the Civil War and faltered during the Great Depression. The consensus on keeping religion largely out of politics has collapsed in the perversely religious era of George W. Bush. It would take artful manipulation of the facts to argue that England, France, India, or any other major democratic society has enjoyed a normative consensus on which to build its social and political order.

Defense of civil society is a program at the level of ideas, not at the level of description of actual societies. Civil society might have benefits for political liberalism, but it is evidently not necessary. Even at its most gloriously political moments in 1989–91, Czechoslovakia did not have a sweeping civil society. It merely had far more political discussion than most societies proportionately have. The bulk of the population had been orderly under Nazi and communist government and continued to be orderly under liberal democratic government. They took little part in either the government or the politics of their nation. They were economically productive throughout although entrepreneurial activity and market-oriented production increased dramatically after 1989, primarily because the new regime allowed it. Many of the entrepreneurs had no part in the politics of 1989— indeed, many of them were abroad until after 1989. Many of the entrepreneurs in China after 1989 were, oddly, the people whose political prospects had been severely reduced by the regime's harsh suppression of the Pro-Democracy movement. Richer political life was not a source of economic success but an alternative to it.

The claim that civil society is needed is far too grand. Various kinds of networks might help in organizing political participation, but insofar as participation merely means the activities of the mass populace, which are primarily voting, networks may not be crucial. It is only for mobilizing the people who might constitute the core of a party that extant networks might matter, as argued later for the origins of the proto-political party called Democratic Russia. Democracy seems to have been established quickly and even vibrantly in some of the Eastern nations (for Bulgaria, see Fish and Brooks 2000; for Mongolia, see Fish 1998; for Poland, see Sztompka 1999; for Russia, see Gibson 2001; for general optimism, see Krygier 1999; and for a mixed review overall, see Carothers 1999). Apart from but related to the quasi-authoritarianism of many of the nations, the biggest failing is arguably the dismal quality of political parties in most of the nations (Carothers 1999). They are not the creation of civil society institutions. Many of them are the opportunistic political equivalents of what is called the big grab in the privatization of many state enterprises in these nations (Hellman 1998; Hoffman 2002; Sergeyev 1998: 149).

A fundamentally important fact about the East European transitions after 1989, no matter how difficult they might seem to be, is that they did not need first to create institutions for mere social order. Institutions for basic social order were in place before, during, and after the transition from communism to a liberal order. Strangely, perhaps, those institutions did not need to be crafted to fit each of these three conditions, but could be essentially the same in, say, 1980, 1989–93, and now in the present. Some of the uses to which those institutions were put earlier were eliminated later and many of the personnel changed, as would have been true merely from demographic succession but as was sometimes hastened by the dismissal of certain administrative personnel. A similar story can be told of police and citizen obedience to law from before the Nazis, during the Nazi regime, and after World War II. Any claim that legal order depended on an overall national consensus is belied by such histories.

If a substantial part of a populace is coordinated on some institution, practice, or norm, that is commonly sufficient to make it in the interest of virtually all to go along with that institution, practice, or norm. For example, when enough of us drive to the right, the rest of us will want to drive to the right also, no matter what preferences we might have in the abstract. A constitution and its government do not require universal support, they require only virtually universal acquiescence. If enough do acquiesce, others may be coerced and the government will prevail (Hardin 1999: 3). This is not a claim that we all or most of us must share some value that keeps us orderly, as in the seeming argument of H. L. A. Hart (1961: 88; see Hardin 1985), but only that we be coordinated on some order. What keeps most of us coordinated is that any individual deviant would be readily brought into line by the inability of one or even a substantial minority of us to recoordinate the rest of us.

During all the stages in the past few decades in East Europe, from communism to transition and on to post-communism, many people would have gone along with social order without any commitment to supporting the overall regime beyond acquiescing in its order. Creating social order de novo, as in a violently anarchic society such as medieval Iceland or various African states such as, at the extreme, Somalia, is likely to be radically harder. What order there is in such cases is apt to be local and to be subject to being overrun by other communities or ragtag armies whose chief occupation might be plunder. None of the East European transition states faced any such difficult problem of establishing order—not even Yugoslavia after the rise of the destructive regimes of Slobodan Milosevic and Franjo Tudjman. Hence, for these nations, reference to Hobbesian resolution of the problem of social order is misplaced unless it is intended to refer to distant past history. For Somalia, there is need today for a Hobbesian resolution. In comparison to Somalia, the fact of continuous order in the nations of East Europe suggests the limited truth of Hobbes's view that any government is better than none, because any government brings at least order, without which little personal prosperity or economic productivity is possible.

Networks, Norms, and Trust During Transition

Compare the forms of desirable social organization in East European societies under communism and Soviet hegemony to the forms under the later developing liberal regimes. In the Soviet societies one would want to develop or enter into small, closed networks, each focused on a single issue or matter; or one would want to rely on a very small closed community of people with whom one shared many interests (Ledeneva 1998, 2004; Sajó 1998: 42). I would want to keep my life as private from others as possible, and, therefore, I would want to keep each network informed only about its own subject matter. And because trust is the three-part relation—A trusts B with respect to X—each network would be about a particular matter X, with little or no expectation that one would trust the members of the network with respect to matters other than X. Norms in defense of individuals in ways that might go against state policy were undermined in the worst days of the former Soviet system, in which even one's children might be informers.

In a liberal, market organization of society, there would be little need for the economic networks that were used to find goods during the Soviet era because the market handles allocations of material goods. There might still be uses for such networks in, for example, arranging admission to schools and universities and finding jobs. Access to these and many other benefits might be manipulated by special networks, as is still true of market societies in general.[5] But, as a rule, one would want open networks with overlaps among networks within the business world in order to facilitate cooperation. These might be so far-reaching that they could not always reliably be regulated by informal social norms and incentives but might require legal or political institutions to back them up. Such institutions would be especially necessary for regulating relations between firms or others when their interactions are not part of an ongoing network of relations. For example, I might wish to hire your firm to build a house for me even though I have no prior interactions with you or your firm and might expect to have no further interactions with you once my house is built. For such a potentially high-risk exchange—high because the values at stake are large even if there is not much problem of reliability—I will want to have institutions to back me up in the event of conflict with you over our exchange.

In the life of citizens under autocracy, it was necessary to develop capacities for secrecy and for handling often senseless, Byzantine bureaucracy, elements of which still persist (Aberg 2000: 313; Rose 2000). Such capacities are often useful for living in the most developed liberal societies, but not so pervasively as in the former Soviet world. It was not necessary and may not even have been possible to develop capacities for speaking in public and debating, or for mobilizing others for political action and organizing more generally. The extensive role played by intellectuals, primarily from university faculties and, in Russia, from the Soviet Academy of Science (Hayoz and Sergeyev 2003), in the early political transitions may be explained in part by the fact that such people had long had professional forums in which to develop these capacities in contexts that did not challenge their regimes. They could quickly translate their talents to the new forum of liberal politicking. They also were parts of relatively extensive networks in their intellectual fields, and they could mobilize each other fairly easily through these networks.

The activities of these scientists suggest the kernel of truth in the thesis concerning the benefits of civil society. It was those already accustomed to debating and gathering who were organizing politically by 1988 and who created the proto-party, Democratic Russia (Hayoz and Sergeyev 2003). (The law did not allow multiparty politics until 1991.) In Russia, the academics have evidently failed to translate their prior trust networks into political power (ibid.), perhaps in part because the basis of their initial networks was too restricted to scientific purposes and could not readily be expanded to include others on different bases. In particular, apart from commitments to some civil liberties, they may not have been in political agreement. The greatest of them was arguably Andrei Sakharov, a Nobel laureate in physics and a charismatic public figure, who was elected to the Congress of People's Deputies shortly before he died in 1989.

Again, the central economic problem in the Eastern transitions was not ordinary order but the absence of state institutions for regulating private businesses and the general failure of the state to regulate market economic relations. Mafia organization has been one "solution" to very uncertain and risky situations not governed by, for example, the law of contracts when the risks do not come from the state per se, but the state fails to help manage the risks. The Mafia substitutes for the state in some degree but by exacting high costs from businesses. Such a communal solution does not work well when the source of risk is the state. As the mafia exemplifies, effective networks need not be beneficial to broader interests, they can also be harmful. If they are organized by economic interests, they can be "rent-seekers depleting the public treasury and inhibiting economic growth" (Bruszt and Stark 1998: 129). Or they can organize themselves for a pervasive system of corruption (Rose-Ackerman 1999: 97). In much of the former Soviet world, in which clientelism was already highly developed from the past, the extant clientelist networks have continued to play major roles, "notwithstanding the inefficiencies of the resulting give-and-take that corrupts the morale of democracy and the logic of the market" (Sajó 1998: 41).

This is a much more general problem because there are many instances of transitions from one form of social regulation to another, from closed small networks to larger open networks, from communal norms to networks or vice versa. There are geographical constraints on what is possible in transitions that are purely social in the sense that they are managed by informal social norms rather than by powerful regulatory organizations. We cannot easily build norms or communities quickly across dispersed collections of people. We may therefore require institutional structures to mediate between potential partners in cooperation. In the East European transitions, the major problem was not social order but rather the creation of institutions for handling the new market economy and, with less difficulty perhaps, the creation of institutions for handling the new democratic political system.

Liberalism Piecemeal

In part because modern societies are pluralist, the various aspects of social, political, and legal order that are needed to lead them to prosperity can be created piecemeal, they need not be created all at once. For all the Eastern European societies, the creation of social order long preceded the move around 1989 to political liberalism and market economics. So far, in many of these nations, it appears that political liberalism can take root at least as fast as or even faster than market economics. Economic liberalism arguably came before political liberalism in England and other European nations at the dawn of the liberal era. Economic liberalism grew up through many steps and was seemingly an unintended consequence of various drives to serve interests. It was enabled to grow by the weakness of states at the time. Political liberalism was virtually invented, and, in part, it was invented to protect civil liberties, especially with respect to religious practice (Creppell 2003).

With the partial exception of Bulgaria and Russia, the East European nations do not face the transition to religious toleration and the separation of church and state that northern European nations went through (although Turkey probably does face that problem despite eight decades of secularism). One of the most beneficial legacies of 40–75 years of communism in the various Eastern nations may be the end of deeply divisive religious conflict. With that conflict out of the way, East Europeans can focus on essentially welfare values. These are de facto the values of individual choosers. The protections of civil liberties that East Europeans want might essentially be the same as those in Western democratic nations. Unlike the case of religion, your exercise of your civil liberties need not conflict with exercise of mine.

The Eastern nations are involved from 1989 in what we may call rational choice political philosophy (Hardin 2003a), not in traditional value debates. Rational choice political philosophy and economic theory in the tradition of Bernard Mandeville, Hume, Adam Smith, and Mill are both fitted to the individual's concern with own-welfare. It is not theoretically required that individuals have a dominant concern with own-welfare, but it is factually true that, for many individuals, own-welfare is a central concern and for some it is the chief concern. Other values can be brought into the political sphere but, so long as these are also the values of individuals, they can fit within the vision of rational choice political philosophy.

The similarity in the two cases of contemporary Eastern Europe and the earlier developments toward rational choice political philosophy is that much of the invention of political liberalism was driven by concern to stop state interventions into the economy, as in the granting of royal patents, the regional exclusion of outsiders from various trades, and demographically restrictive poor laws. Smith wanted liberal government in order to keep government out of the economy, so that it might be as successful as a liberal economy could be (Hardin 1999: ch. 2). In part, this meant, as Madison supposed in his design of much of the U.S. Constitution, the creation of weak government, especially was too weak to interfere in the economy (Hardin 2002a).

Sentiments in Eastern Europe, Russia, and the former Soviet Republics often seem to favor strong government in order to manage the transition to liberalism in the economy and in politics. The stance of the current Chinese government might be characterized as the view that strong government can best manage the economic transition. (Critics might argue that strong government's main claim is that it can keep certain people in power.) The account of Vadim Radaev (2004a) implicitly challenges this view. He notes that entrepreneurs in Russia avoid using the state to help them in their relations with other businesses. Appealing to state authorities is seen as an effort to break down a competitor or potential partner. Perhaps part of their concern is that they wish as much as possible to keep the state at arm's length. These entrepreneurs, unlike many politicians and maybe even citizens, do not want strong government involvement in their activities.

A fundamental element of liberalism is individualism. This is important because it fits with incentives that motivate productivity. Perhaps even more important, it runs against familism (Hardin 2002c: 98–100, 105, 176; Banfield 1958). Hence, it breaks tendencies to focus on subsistence of families and to focus instead on individual prospects for prosperity. Strangely, the latter focus may finally be the best way to secure family prosperity far beyond mere subsistence. Although Soviet communism probably interfered with the development of open trust relations in the larger society and led individuals to protect themselves through very restricted network relationships, it may also have broken the hold of kin over individuals' lives. Here, the negative side of individualism—what it breaks—is a common element of both Soviet and liberal visions. This is true primarily, perhaps, because industrial economies cause massive demographic shifts that shatter familial economic organization.

The positive side of individualism is entrepreneurship and self-seeking, which is much more readily asserted once state hostility to it is past. For the creation of a market economy it is not essential that everyone be a Smithian homo economicus driven by such self-seeking, but only that many be. If enough are, then there will be productivity for the market rather than for familial consumption, and this creates at least the seeds of a capitalist society.

Similarly, if enough are driven by such desires, there will be withdrawal by some from dependence on the state and its collective provision of goods. Hence, in both Smith's England and the contemporary Eastern European nations, there is a strong payoff from individualism in the creation of a dynamic economy that is relatively free of familial or state control.

Note that only a small number of people might be involved in the initial moves to capitalist behavior. Hence, as noted earlier, capitalism is now and was historically created piecemeal, not whole cloth. It grows faster in some contexts than in others, and it might especially grow faster in a nation that is already industrialized and already relatively individualistic and monolingual than it did in its early days in England and parts of other nations in Europe. Its rise was spread over a few centuries in England. In part, it took so long because there was no common language for the workforce. Early factories (which were very small, with less than 100 workers) standardized the language of the workers (Gellner 1987: 15). Achieving a common language came before capitalism in many of the transitional societies (there are minority languages in most of the Eastern nations), which could therefore be transformed far more quickly than preindustrial England could be.

Capitalism arguably first gained hegemony in the United States under Madison's constitution, which was designed to create a government that was weak in ways that would make it unable to interfere massively in the economy but strong in its capacity to block interference in the economy by the state governments. Although 80–85 percent of American society at the time of the constitution was engaged in farming—and necessarily not much more than subsistence farming for most—the plantation South and the nascently industrial North were relatively capitalist, with a hideous, but initially small, part of the southern capital in the form of slaves, as though they were mere tools. Insofar as parts of the economy were not capitalist, they were virtually forced to live by market incentives under the constitution. In essence, some of the Eastern European nations today have constitutionalized capitalism to a similar degree, not by declaring it the form of the economy but by enabling it by not deliberately constitutionalizing alternative forms.

Typical practices in the old Soviet-style economy are virtually the opposite of practices in what is often called the Toyota system of production (Milgrom and Roberts 1992: 4–6, 1993). Workers and managers in the Soviet system engaged in hoarding, shirking, and the use of blat (side payments or bribes) to get things moving. The Toyota system relies on the "just-in-time" system, which means having virtually no stock on hand (antihoarding), and on engaging workers on the assembly line to take responsibility for catching mistakes and for keeping the production underway (antishirking). And, of course, in the Toyota system there is no reliance on side payments other than the general rewards of promotion in the company. "Without inventories to buffer the disruptions caused by defective products and broken machines, Toyota engineers had to work to improve the reliability of every step of the process. The same changes that reduced the number of interruptions in the production process often reduced the number of defects in Toyota's cars as well" (1992: 5). Quality was an unintended by-product of trying to operate on less capital.

For the Toyota system to work, there must be very efficient markets for everything Toyota needs. All inputs arrive at the final assembly plant "just in time" to be installed. Moreover, the parts must be so precisely manufactured that they are interchangeable, so that the door that arrives this morning fits the next car in the line without any need for special tinkering or matching doors to bodies. Finally, every car has a destination in the market when it is assembled—there is no inventory of cars. Not even General Motors, once it learned directly from its partnership with Toyota, could readily replicate the Toyota system. It has taken many years of developing different parts of the supplier market, ending relationships with many long-time suppliers that could not make the transition, and intervening in the production processes of many suppliers to get them to make parts that are precisely cut to fit.

In the Eastern European transitions, the efficiencies of the Toyota system (or even of the slack in earlier General Motors system) could not be created quickly. The difficult and numerous tasks of making the transition include altering the motivations of workers and managers to treat their firm's goals as well matched to their own personal goals (of prosperity through reward for contribution to the firm's success), altering the generally sloppy practices that justified hoarding in the past, and relying exclusively on wage and productivity incentives rather than side payments to get things done. To move to the Toyota system requires, roughly, that all suppliers move essentially to that system. It even required the development of new institutions, such as Federal Express, which could reliably ship parts for the just-in-time system. If Toyota had to rely on the U.S. Postal Service or traditional freight lines, it would begin hoarding at least a few days' supply of many parts, and its efficiency would decline. Toyota is central planning with the discipline of brutal competition.

The transition must be pervasive, it cannot be made by one firm alone. It can, of course, only be made piecemeal, each firm in its turn, and those firms in international markets might have to move faster or go under. During the transition, it is necessarily the case that overall efficiency cannot compare to the efficiency of the Toyota system even in the best reorganized firm. General Motors—which did not have to deal with problems of blat and probably did not face massive shirking by workers and managers—was still slow to make the transition to the Toyota system because its entire network of suppliers came along only piecemeal. In the early years, lower wages in the Eastern firms might allow for competitiveness, but otherwise they could not be competitive because they could not be as efficient as Toyota in their pervasively inefficient economies.

Early liberalism in the West had two distinct poles: protection of the civil liberties of individuals against the state and protection against state intrusion into economic relations. The rise of these two concerns was complex and the histories of the two concerns are quite different, but the core issue of both concerns was protection against the state (Hardin 1999: ch. 2). Smith expresses the value of economic liberalism very well, and Mill expresses that of political liberalism even more forcefully. Both these thinkers were fundamentally individualist in their outlook, and it was their individualism that grounded their political views. They were also basically welfarist in their justifications for their views and, for perhaps different philosophical reasons, they both supposed that individualism was necessary for general welfare. As is true of most standard political vocabulary, liberalism has taken on a variety of meanings. All that is meant here is the basic concerns of Smith and Mill: The state should not control business or personal activities unless its intervention is to prevent harm to others from the activities of firms or individuals.

The Toyota example is relevant in some ways to the political problem. One could retell the story of the transition to the Toyota system as a story of the development of new forms of human and social capital, as argued earlier for the transition to political liberalism. That transition requires the development of the human and social capital for open democratic politics if it is to last and be genuinely democratic at the level of the citizenry or of political parties.

We might even suppose that the much-touted openness of the civil society is useful to business in that it prods faster adaptation. The conspicuous tendency of industrial firms in a given industry to locate near each other can be explained by their shared need for a pool of talented workers (see, e.g., Stinchcombe 1965). For example, if I want to build a steel factory, I should locate near yours because then I will have an initial pool of workers from which to draw. In the American financial industry, which is extremely concentrated in lower Manhattan (even after September 11, 2001), talented people from many firms might often lunch together and share insights. Because moving from one firm to another would not require the expense of moving their homes, personnel can switch firms fairly easily. Your firm might see itself as losing when you take your talents off to a competitor, but the intellectual capital of the industry overall rises through the sharing from one firm to another. Therefore, your firm stays in Manhattan and faces the higher incidence of one-at-a-time costs of losing its personnel to competitors while receiving the offsetting benefit of its own capacity to attract personnel and intellectual capital from those competitors. The net exchange must generally be beneficial.

Concluding Remarks

In the short term, the greatest gift of the Eastern European transitions arguably was the debilitation of government for at least a brief period after 1989. A very high cost of that debilitation in Russia was to enable the big grab during privatization of formerly state-owned enterprises and the substantial inequality that has followed in some nations (Hellman and Kaufmann, this volume). Managers and others took control of formerly state-run enterprises and established the grounds on which they could become rich, even in some cases fabulously wealthy. There is no claim of justice that can be made in defense of the grab. One might distort the libertarian arguments of Robert Nozick (1974) to see the grab as essentially carried out in a state of nature in which ownership is to be established, so that all those who followed some minimal rules were entitled to what they claimed. Short of such an artful argument, however, the grab is easily characterized as highly unjust in its implications.

Nevertheless, the very fact of the grab suggests why the weakness of government was in certain ways a good thing. Through that grab, state control over the economy was broken fairly substantially and very quickly. In East Europe after 1989, there was probably little hope of creating constitutions as weak as the American constitution was in its early years. Indeed, some of the present constitutions there are merely—often heavily—amended versions of the prior, very strong constitutions. Hence, the brief window of weak transitional government was perhaps the nearest these nations could come to the Madisonian ideal. It was weak government, not weak constitutions that reduced the future potential of government to regain control over the economies of these nations.[6]

Over the somewhat longer term of a bit more than a decade since 1989, the East European parties have followed the pattern of American and many West European parties of recent decades (Hardin 2000) in that they have increasingly adopted the simple economic policy of letting the economy largely run itself. The Madisonian vision in the United States is Hayekian (Hardin 2001), although few Americans can articulate the arguments of Friedrich Hayek in the way that many in the East can. (I recently heard a Russian government official give, over dinner, an extended and nuanced account of the intellectual history of Hayek.) The Left–Right dimension of economic policy has lost most of the meaning it had in American and much of Western politics until recently. In the West, the Left–Right dimension is internal to the capitalist system. Relatively tight fiscal policy and hostility to government regulation of business are policies of the Right; relatively loose fiscal policy and support for broad welfare programs are policies of the Left.[7] In this sense, the Republican Party was on the Right and the Democratic Party was on the Left. Now both parties follow relatively pro-business tight money policies and pro-welfare policies on some issues—although Republicans may be more interested in the welfare of the wealthy and of certain corporations and Democrats in the welfare of the poor and unions.

The Left–Right terminology can be confusing in the Eastern context. Indeed, parties in the East sometimes win elections by proposing a reversion to central control and populist economic policies against the relatively laissez-faire neoliberal policies of the incumbent government. Once elected, they then follow those laissez-faire policies themselves, much as many seemingly anticapitalist parties in Latin America have, upon election, adopted or continued strong neoliberal economic policies (Stokes 2001).

There are real issues at stake in choosing among the parties, but positions
on economic policy are far closer together than they were historically in
Western democracies.

The East European and Latin American votes suggest that the
Left–Right distinction is still sufficiently alive in popular political imagination for politicians to appeal to it. Voters, however, might not know what
positions on that dimension mean for policies. For example, they might
summarize their allegiance to a Left or Right party by saying it supports
workers and the poor or it supports business. Occasional voters might even
suppose that there is a Left–Right issue of easy versus tight money supply,
but it is asking a lot to expect many voters to grasp the supposed causal
implications of such policies. Argentines know they were recently victims
of massive losses in the value of their bank accounts and other financial
holdings, but they could no more explain why the policies had such effects
than can many high-powered economists. They and many East Europeans
might, however, be able to demonize a politician who works for one or the
other monetary policy.

Notes

* I wish to thank Bruce Ackerman, Alberto Diaz-Cayeros, April Flakne, János Kornai, Susan
Rose-Ackerman, and Alexandra Vacroux for acute written comments on this chapter. I also wish to
thank participants in colloquiums and a conference at the Collegium Budapest, and James Fearon
and colleagues of the Thursday faculty lunch seminar at Stanford University for discussions of the
chapter.

1. Legislation to authorize such moves was passed in 1998, a couple of years after the first forcible
takeover (Alexei Miller, in conversation at the Collegium Budapest, November 25, 2002).

2. Johnson had been elected with Abraham Lincoln, but his background was not in the Republican
Party, whose radical wing controlled Congress at the time of his impeachment and trial. He was not
removed because the vote in the Senate missed the required two-thirds majority by one vote.

3. After the new legislation, Berlusconi's appeal to have his bribery case moved to another court (and
therefore substantially postponed) was denied by the courts (Bruni 2003).

4. Consider the 2002 congressional elections in the United States. Only four incumbents in the House
of Representatives (which has 435 members, all of whom are elected at two-year intervals) lost to
non-incumbent challengers (a few incumbents lost to other incumbents because their districts were
changed to reflect demographic changes). Overall, 90% of all candidates won by margins of more
than 10% of the votes cast. When districts are redrawn by a state government after each decennial
census (as for the 2002 election), they are often gerrymandered to insure election of the candidates
in the state's dominant party. For data, see Richie (2002).

5. In a recently noteworthy case, Jack Grubman, who rates stocks with recommendations to buy or
sell, sought admission of his three-year-old twins into the prestigious preschool of the 92nd Street Y
in Manhattan. Their admission was arranged through a complex triangular set of deals. Sanford Weill,
the head of Citibank, Grubman's employing corporation, gave a $1 million gift to the school out of
bank funds. In return, Grubman gave a strong "buy" rating to AT&T stock. In return for that, Mike
Armstrong, head of AT&T and a member of Weill's board of directors at Citibank, helped Weill
defeat John Reed, his rival for power at the bank. None of these business leaders was out of pocket
for any expense, but the stockowners of their companies were cheated on behalf of these managers.
For sophistication, this three-way barter transcends anything we normally see in traditional barter
economies. The irony of it is that one of these sophisticates, Grubman, was arrogant or foolish
enough to write an email saying: "I used Sandy to get my kids into the 92nd Street Y pre-school
(which is harder than Harvard), and Sandy needed Armstrong's vote on the board to nuke Reed in
showdown. Once the coast was clear for both of us (i.e., Sandy clear victor and my kids confirmed)

I went back to my normal self" (Doran 2002; see also Greider 2002). A *New York Times* editorial ("The Pre-Kindergarten Connection," November 16, 2002) noted, tongue-in-cheek, that "you can go only so far in guarding against tainted research by erecting a wall between analysts and invest-ment bankers. This is especially true when an analyst knows that somebody on the other side of the wall holds the key to the right nursery school."

6. A substantial cost of the Russian grab was that it was kept for domestic grabbers only. The result has been a relatively autarkic economy in a time when the route to prosperity must be through the global economy. Autarky had been the ruin of the Soviet world before 1989 and of India under Nehru's awful policies and it arguably has been the cause of much of Russia's decline in economic productivity during the 1990s. Keeping the economy autarkic gave monopoly rents to the new owners of firms that need not become internationally competitive. Restricting buyers of the enter-prises to Russians also must have radically reduced the prices paid for them—to the cost of the Russian people. At one point, reputedly, "the equity of all Russian factories, including oil, gas, some transportation and most of manufacturing, was worth less than that of Kellogg or Anheuser-Busch [two American firms of modest size]" (Hoffman 2002: 205). The smaller states of East Europe had no hope of autarky and have been much more open to international entry into their economies (see further, Sajó 1998).

7. Carles Boix (1997) puts this somewhat differently. Left-wing governments spend physical and human capital; right-wing governments rely on business to maximize economic growth.

References

Aberg, Martin. 2000. "Putnam's Social Capital Theory Goes East: A Case Study of Western Ukraine and L'viv." *Europe–Asia Studies* 52: 295–317.

Arato, Andrew and Jean L. Cohen. 1992. *Civil Society and Political Theory*. Cambridge MA: MIT Press.

Banfield, Edward C. 1958. *The Moral Basis of a Backward Society*. New York: Free Press.

Berle, Adolph A. and Gardner C. Means. 1932. *The Modern Corporation and Private Property*. New York: Macmillan.

Berlin, Isaiah. 1992. *The Crooked Timber of Humanity*. New York: Vintage.

Boix, Carles. 1997. "Political Parties and the Supply Side of the Economy: The Provision of Physical and Human Capital in Advanced Economies, 1960–90." *American Journal of Political Science* 41: 814–45.

Bruni, Frank. 2002. "Protesters in Rome Accuse Berlusconi of Exploiting His Power." *New York Times* September 15, p. 1.9.

———. 2003. "Italy's Leader Balances Ambitions and Trials." *New York Times* February 16, p. 1.3.

Bruszt, Laszlo and David Stark. 1998. *Postsocialist Pathways: Transforming Politics and Property in East Central Europe*. Cambridge UK: Cambridge University Press.

Calhoun, John C. [1853] 1992. "A Disquisition on Government." In R. M. Loss (ed.), *Union and Liberty: The Political Philosophy of John C. Calhoun*, pp. 5–78. Indianapolis IN: Liberty Fund.

Carothers, Thomas. 1999. "Western Civil-Society Aid to Eastern Europe and the Former Soviet Union." *East European Constitutional Review* 4: 54–62.

Cohen, Jean. 1999. "Trust, Voluntary Association and Workable Democracy: The Contemporary American Discourse of Civil Society." In M. Warren (ed.), *Democracy and Trust*, pp. 208–48. New York: Cambridge University Press.

Creppell, Ingrid. 2003. *Toleration and Identity: Foundations in Early Modern Thought*. New York: Routledge.

Dahrendorf, Ralf. 1968. "In Praise of Thrasymachus." In R. Dahrendorf, *Essays in the Theory of Society*, pp. 129–50. Palo Alto CA: Stanford University Press.

Doran, James. 2002. "Grubman Inquiry Questions Nursery Board Members." *Times of London*, November 19.

Durkheim, Émile. [1893] 1933. *The Division of Labor in Society*. New York: Macmillan.

Etzioni, Amitai. 1993. *The Spirit of Community: Rights, Responsibilities, and the Communitarian Agenda*. New York: Crown.

Fish, M. Steven. 1998. "Mongolia: Democracy Without Prerequisites." *Journal of Democracy* 3: 127–41.

Fish, M. Steven and Robin S. Brooks. 2000. "Bulgarian Democracy's Organizational Weapon." *East European Constitutional Review* 3: 63–71.

Gellner, Ernest. 1987. *Culture, Identity, and Politics*. Cambridge UK: Cambridge University Press.

Gibson, James L. 2001. "Social Networks, Civil Society, and the Prospects for Consolidating Russia's Democratic Transition." *American Journal of Political Science* 45: 51–69.

Greider, William. 2002. "The Grubman." *The Nation*, December 16, pp. 5–6.

Hardin, Russell. 1985. "Sanction and Obligation." *The Monist* 68 (July): 403–18.

———. 1995. *One for All: The Logic of Group Conflict*. Princeton NJ: Princeton University Press.

———. 1999. *Liberalism, Constitutionalism, and Democracy*. Oxford: Oxford University Press.

———. 2000. "The Public Trust." In S. J. Pharr and R. D. Putnam (eds.), *Disaffected Democracies: What's Troubling the Trilateral Democracies*, pp. 31–51. Princeton NJ: Princeton University Press.

———. 2001. "Seeing Like Hayek." *The Good Society* 2: 36–9.

———. 2002a. "Liberal Distrust." *European Review* 1: 73–89.

———. 2002b. "The Street-Level Epistemology of Democratic Participation." *Journal of Political Philosophy* 10: 212–29.

———. 2002c. *Trust and Trustworthiness*. New York: Russell Sage Foundation.

———. 2003a. "Rational Choice Political Philosophy." In I. L. Morris, J. Oppenheimer, and K. Soltan (eds.), *Politics from Anarchy to Democracy*. Palo Alto CA: Stanford University Press.

———. 2003b. "Citizens' Knowledge, Politicians' Duplicity." In A. Breton, G. Galeotti, P. Salmon, and R. Wintobe (eds.), *Rational Obfuscation and Transparency in Politics*. Cambridge UK: Cambridge University Press.

———. 2004. "Representing Ignorance. Social Philosophy and Policy." Special issue of *Morality and Politics*. Presented at Bowling Green State University, Ohio.

Hart, H. L. A. 1961. *The Concept of Law*. Oxford University Press.

Hayoz, Nicolas and Victor Sergeyev. 2003. "Social Networks in Russian Politics." In G. Badescu and E. M. Uslaner (eds.), *Social Capital and the Democratic Transition*. London: Routledge.

Hellman, Joel. 1998. "Winners Take all: The Politics of Partial Reform in Post-Communist Transition." *World Politics* 50: 203–34.

Hobbes, Thomas. [1651] 1968. *Leviathan*. London: Penguin, C. B. Macpherson (ed.), Originally published, London: Andrew Cooke.

Hoffman, David E. 2002. *The Oligarchs: Wealth and Power in the New Russia*. New York: Public Affairs.

Krygier, Martin. 1999. "Traps for Young Players in Times of Transition." *East European Constitutional Review* 4: 63–7.

Kurtz, Howard. 2003. "Media Notes." *Washington Post* January 21.

Ledeneva, Alena V. 1998. *Russia's Economy of Favors: Blat, Networking, and Informal Exchange*. Cambridge UK: Cambridge University Press.

———. 2004. "Underground Financing in Russia." In J. Kornai, B. Rothstein, S. Rose-Ackerman (eds.), *Creating Social Trust in Post-Socialist Transition*, pp. 71–90. New York: Palgrave, Macmillan.

Manin, Bernard. 1997. *The Principles of Representative Government*. Cambridge UK: Cambridge University Press.

Means, Gardner C. 1959. *Power Without Property: A New Development in American Political Economy*. New York: Harcourt, Brace.

Michels, Roberto. [1911] 1949. *Political Parties*. New York: Free Press.

Milgrom, Paul and John Roberts. 1992. *Economics, Organization and Management*. Englewood Cliffs NJ: Prentice Hall.

———. 1993. *Johnson Controls, Inc—Automotive Systems Group: The Georgetown Kentucky Plant, Case #S-BE-9*, Stanford Graduate School of Business, Palo Alto CA.

Morgan, Edmund S. 1994. "Pioneers of Paranoia." *New York Review of Books*, October 6, pp. 11–13.

Nestor (Benjamin Rush). 1786. "To the People of the United States." *Independent Gazetteer* (Philadelphia) June 3 [in microfiche at Bobst Library, New York University].

Nozick, Robert. 1974. *Anarchy, the State, and Utopia*. New York: Basic Books.

Parsons, Talcott. [1937] 1968. *The Structure of Social Action*. New York: Free Press.

Putnam, Robert D. 1993. *Making Democracy Work: Civic Traditions in Modern Italy*. Princeton NJ: Princeton University Press.

———. 2000. *Bowling Alone: The Collapse and Revival of American Community*. New York: Simon and Shuster.

Radaev, Vadim. 2004a. "How Trust is Established in Economic Relationships When Institutions and Individuals are Not Trustworthy: The Case of Russia." In J. Kornai, B. Rothstein, and

S. Rose-Ackerman (eds.), *Creating Social Trust in Post-Socialist Transition*, pp. 91–110. New York: Palgrave Macmillan.

———. 2004b. "Coping with Distrust in Emerging Russian Markets." In R. Hardin (ed.), *Distrust*. New York: Russell Sage Foundation.

Richie, Rob. 2002. *Fair Elections Update: Election 2002 and the Case for Reform*. Washington DC: Center for Voting and Democracy, November 14.

Rose, Richard. 2000. "Uses of Social Capital in Russia: Modern, Pre-modern, and Anti-modern." *Post-Soviet Affairs* 16: 33–57.

Rose-Ackerman, Susan. 1999. *Corruption and Government: Causes, Consequences, and Reform*. New York: Cambridge University Press.

Rowe, William T. 2001. *Saving the World: Chen Hongmou and Elite Consciousness in Eighteenth-Century China*. Palo Alto CA: Stanford University Press.

Sajó, Andras. 1999. *Limited Government: An Introduction to Constitutionalism*. Budapest: Central European University Press.

———. 1998. "Corruption, Clientelism, and the Future of the Constitutional State in Eastern Europe." *East European Constitutional Review* 2: 37–46.

Sergeyev, Victor. 1998. *The Wild East: Crime and Lawlessness in Russia*. New York: Sharpe.

Stein, Herbert. 1989. *The Triumph of the Adaptive Society. Frank E. Seidman Lecture in Political Economy*. Memphis TN: Rhodes College, September 14.

Stinchcombe, Arthur L. 1965. "Social Structure and Organizations." In J. G. March (ed.), *Handbook of Organizations*, pp. 142–93. Chicago: Rand-McNally.

Stokes, Susan C. 2001. *Mandates and Democracy: Neoliberalism by Surprise in Latin America*. New York: Cambridge University Press.

Sztompka, Piotr. 1999. *Trust: A Sociological Theory*. Cambridge UK: Cambridge University Press.

Tocqueville, Alexis de. [1835 and 1840] 1966. *Democracy in America*, translated by George Lawrence. New York: Harper and Row.

Volkov, Vadim. 2004. "The Selective Use of State Capacity in Russia's Economy: Property Disputes and Enterprise Takeovers, 1998–2002." In J. Kornai, B. Rothstein, and S. Rose-Ackerman (eds.), *Creating Social Trust in Post-Socialist Transition*, pp. 126–47. New York: Palgrave Macmillan.

CHAPTER TEN

Attitudes Toward Democracy and Capitalism: A Western Benchmark

JOHN MUELLER

It is often lamented that people in post-communist countries commonly and routinely express distrust in, disappointment over, and even moral outrage at the way democracy and capitalism are playing themselves out in their countries. However, a key question is the classic one posed by comedian Henny Youngman when asked, "How's your wife?" His reply was: "Compared to what?"

In this essay, I would like humbly to suggest that, judging from the experience in advanced capitalist democracies, particularly the United States, distrust, disappointment, moral outrage, and cynicism about democracy and capitalism and their defining institutions are normal and will never really go away—or, probably even decline very much. Indeed, cynicism seems to be the quality people most quickly pick up when their country turns democratic and capitalistic.

Moreover, if corruption recedes, people will continue to claim that the political system is rotten to the core. And, as they become wealthier, they will respond by raising their standards and complaining that they are no happier than before—that is, in an important sense, things never get better.

The central cause for this condition, besides fundamental human nature, are the ministrations of reformers and other intellectual critics. For example, a fundamentally unrealistic perspective about democracy adopted by most reformers leads inescapably to the conclusion that democracy is necessarily and viscerally corrupt.

On the brighter side, a popular incomprehension about, and even contempt for, the way democracy and capitalism actually work does not seem to prevent them from functioning adequately.[1]

Attitudes Toward Democracy

Bismarck once observed, "If you like laws and sausages, you should never watch either one being made." It is a fundamental property—and perhaps defect—of democracy that citizens may watch laws being made, and when they do so they often compare democracy to some sort of idealized image and then reject the actual process with righteous disdain, even outrage, opaquely dismissing it as bickering and correctly, but uncomprehendingly, labeling it "politics as usual." Effectively, however, politics as usual is the same as democracy in action.

The problem, as John Hibbing and Elizabeth Theiss-Morse have aptly put it, is that people lack "an appreciation for the ugliness of democracy." In fact, "true democratic processes in any realistic environment are bound to be slow, to be built on compromise, and to make apparent the absence of clean, certain answers to important questions of the day." Yet, people want "both procedural efficiency and procedural equity," a sort of "stealth democracy" (1995: 18, 19, 157; see also Hibbing and Theiss-Morse 2002).

It could be argued, for example, that the health care debate in the United States in 1993 and 1994 showed democracy at its finest. A problem the voters had sensibly determined to be important was addressed and debated. President Bill Clinton had a solution, others in Congress had theirs, affected interested groups appropriately weighed in with theirs, and there were months of thoughtful and nuanced (if sometimes confusing and boring) discussion of this difficult topic. Admittedly, a solution (apparent or real) to this complicated concern was not smoothly worked out in two years of effort, but the problem did not have to be solved immediately, and there was plenty of time in the next years to come up with judicious remedies with this groundwork laid—something, indeed, that substantially happened. Yet voters, few of whom paid much attention to the substance of the often-tedious debate, dismissed it as "bickering," cried "gridlock," and often became angry and cynical (see Toner 1994). Not surprisingly, after this experience, the popularity both of the President and of Congress plummeted. Outraged at the unpleasant untidiness, the voters exacted punishment in the 1994 election. An analysis of exit polls in the election finds "no unifying theme" among the voters except for "an overall distaste for government." It suggests Clinton got the election's message, such as it was, when he concluded that the voters were saying "Look, we just don't like what we see when we watch Washington. And you haven't done much about that. It's too partisan, too interest-group oriented, things don't get done. There's too many people up there playing politics" (Berke 1994).

There seem to be two potential solutions to this problem, if problem it be. One, of course, is for law makers simply not to appear to do much of anything, and, indeed, in 1998 when the most visible accomplishment of the American Congress was to rename an airport, the popularity of the institution rose notably, if temporarily.[2] The other is to wait for one of those exogenous shocks economists are always identifying and hope it will have favorable consequences. The terrorist attacks of September 11, 2001, obviously did not change in the slightest the competence, ability, intellectual capacity, or level of corruption of the U.S. Congress, yet public approval of the institution abruptly jumped nearly 40 percentage points.[3]

This comparison suggests that it is anything but surprising to find that cynicism has flourished in the new democracies of Eastern and Central Europe where politicians deal daily with issues that are far more difficult. American politicians can agonize for months over raising the gasoline tax a few cents; politicians in the post-communist countries regularly have had to deal with changes that, however potentially beneficial in the long run, will necessarily cause enormous social disruption and pain. For example, in the early 1990s, politicians in Poland alone privatized more businesses than had previously been privatized in the entire history of the human race and created a banking system in less time than it takes in the West to train a bank examiner (Fischer and Gelb 1991: 99, 100).

Nonetheless, one analyst is shocked at a poll showing that 79 percent of the Romanian population feels politicians were "ready to promise anything to get votes" while 65 percent say politicians are more interested in strengthening their own parties than in solving the country's problems (Shafir 1993: 18). Another asserts that Russian voters have "lost their faith in all politicians" (Rutland 1994/95: 6). And another is concerned that only 62 percent of Macedonians trust their parliament (Hislope 2002: 36).

The implication, apparently, is that this condition is notably different in real democracies like the United States or Great Britain. In 1994, after a tumultuous political year, only 12 percent of Russians said they trusted their parliament, and only 6 percent said they trusted political parties (Rose 1994: 53). But in 1992, after decades of comparative political placidity, only 17 percent of Americans approved the job their Congress was doing (Patterson and Magleby 1992: 544) while a mere 14 percent said they were satisfied with the way things were going in the country and over 80 percent opined, "things have gotten pretty seriously off on the wrong track" (Mueller 1994: 281, 286). Further, a 1994 poll in the United States discovered only 10 percent willing to rate the "honesty and ethical standards" of congressmen as "very high" or "high," tidily placing them twenty-fifth on a list of 26, just ahead of car salesmen (McAneny and Moore 1994: 2–4). And a poll in Britain in the mid-1990s found that 73 percent of Britons considered the ruling Conservative Party to be "very sleazy and disreputable."[4]

Seymour Martin Lipset twice quotes with alarm a Hungarian analyst: "All the surveys and polling data show that public opinion in our region rejects dictatorship, but would like to see a strong man at the helm; favors popular government, but hates parliament, parties, and the press; likes social welfare legislation and equality, but not trade unions; wants to topple the present government, but disapproves of the idea of a regular opposition; supports the notion of the market (which is a code word for Western-style living standards), but wishes to punish and expropriate the rich and condemns banking for preying on simple working people; favors a guaranteed minimum income, but sees unemployment as an immoral state and wants to punish or possibly deport the unemployed" (1993: 51; see also 1994: 13–14). And Richard Rose argues, "An election produces a representative government if those elected are trusted representatives of those who voted for them.

The current Russian government is democratically elected but distrusted" (1994: 53). However much the same could be said for the United States at many points in its history. Rose continues, "the communist regime has left a legacy of distrust," but it seems clear that Americans managed to pick up the legacy without that experience. Indeed, in the post-communist context a healthy distrust of all politicians has probably helped, as Stephen Holmes suggests, to keep extremists from gaining much political ground (1996: 33–4). And concern that Hungarians yearn for a strong leader seems to imply that real democrats prefer weak ones. Yet, oddly enough, people campaigning in established democracies never seem to parade their weakness. Instead, they characteristically promise to be firm and decisive and to "get things done" as they explain as forcefully as possible their miraculous plans to rid the nation of all its ills with little or no pain.

Objectively, of course, things are probably worse in some post-communist countries—that is, their governments actually *are* more corrupt and less trustworthy than those in the West. However, experience in the West suggests that successful reform is unlikely to make much difference in public perceptions. The elaborate campaign finance reforms enacted in the aftermath of the Watergate scandal of the 1970s did not cause faith in politicians to rise in the slightest.

Similarly, effective efforts that reduce corruption are unlikely to reduce the cynicism that people casually express about the democratic process. Direct corruption has certainly been reduced in the United States over the last century, but cynicism about the process continues to flourish.

Thus, countries are exceedingly unlikely to be able to overcome this attitude by democratic development. The world's two oldest democracies—the United States and Switzerland—also boast the lowest turnout rates. Susan Rose-Ackerman points to apathy as a "danger sign" for democracies (2001: 563). If so, it is America and Switzerland that are in deep trouble, not the new democracies.

Sources of Attitudes Toward Democracy

The cynicism, disappointment, and moral outrage about democracy have chiefly arisen because there is out there an image of the perfect democracy, one that has been invented and sold over centuries by democratic theorists, idealists, and reformers. Some of them simply retreat into the vapor and conclude that democracy, as it turns out, does not really exist at all, but that it is just some sort of attractive, impossible dream. Thus, in February 1990, Czechoslovak President Vaclav Havel patiently explained to the Congress of the world's oldest democracy that the country it represented still had not made it and, actually, never would: "As long as people are people, democracy in the full sense of the word will always be no more than an ideal; one may approach it as one would a horizon, in ways that may be better or worse, but it can never be fully attained. In this sense you are also merely approaching democracy."[5]

Others press for reform, seeking to refashion democratic institutions and their human constituents to more nearly approximate the qualities called for in the theories and in the ideals that derive from some of the theories. As part of this effort, reformers have frequently tried to make the process more politically equal and to control the play of "special interests." They have also sought to elevate the human race to match such rarified images as the one projected by John F. Kennedy: "Democracy is a difficult kind of government. It requires the highest qualities of self-discipline, restraint, a willingness to make commitments and sacrifices for the general interest, and it also requires knowledge" (1964: 539).

Some of the reformers want nostalgically to return to an imagined past (e.g., Putnam 1995a,b; Sandel 1996). The implication is that trust and confidence in the United States have traditionally—that is, until the middle or late 1960s—been high. But quite a bit of data suggest that, although expressions of cynicism may have been relatively low in the early 1960s, the seeming increase in cynicism and distrust since that time is more nearly a return to normal levels. For example, the poll question, "If you had a son, would you like to see him go into politics as a life's work?" found a very low acceptability in the 1940s and 1950s, a rise in the mid-1960s, and a decline to 1950s levels since then.[6] A similar pattern was found is answers to the question, "Do you think most people can be trusted?" (Niemi et al. 1989: 303). Similarly, turnout rates reached a sort of peak in the early 1960s and afterward returned to more normal levels (Nardulli et al. 1996). And confidence in the U.S. Congress peaked in the mid-1960s before declining again (Hibbing and Theiss-Morse 1995: 34–5). More broadly, there is good reason to believe that political participation even in the "golden years" of American politics—the years before the Civil War—was, contrary to the usual supposition, marked mainly by apathy and political cynicism (Altschuler and Blumin 1997).

A key concern in all this is the Quixotic quest for equality. An extensive study on the issue of equality by a team of political scientists finds, none too surprisingly, that people in the United States differ in the degree to which they affect the political system. This variance in effectiveness, the authors then conclude, poses a "threat to the democratic principle of equal protection of interests" (Verba et al. 1995: 267, 314). Another analyst, reviewing their findings, makes a similar observation: "liberal democracies fail to live up to the norm of equal responsiveness to the interests of each citizen" (Mansbridge 1997: 423).

But this clearly expresses a romantic perspective about democracy, a perspective that has now been fully and repeatedly disconfirmed in practice. Democracies are responsive and attentive to the interests of the citizenry—at least when compared to other forms of government—but they are nowhere near *equally* responsive to the interests of each citizen. Indeed, democracy could be characterized as a system in which people are left (equally) free to become politically unequal—that is, to organize to pursue their own, if "special," interests. In the end, special interests can be effectively reined in only by abandoning democracy itself because their activities are absolutely vital to the form.

Most of the agitation against political inequality is focused on the special privileges business is presumed to enjoy. For example, concern is voiced that the attention of public officials can be differently arrested: "A phone call from the CEO of a major employer in the district may carry considerably more weight than one from an unknown constituent."[7] But if the business leader's access advantage to a time-pressured politician is somehow reprehensible and must be reformed, what about other inequalities—that is, why focus only on economic ones? A telephone call from a big-time political columnist is likely to get the politician's attention even faster than that of the CEO. Should the influential columnist hold off on his next column until the rest of us deserving unknowns have had a chance to put in our two cents in the same forum? Inequalities like these are simply and unavoidably endemic to the whole political system as, indeed, they are to life itself. It may be possible to reduce this inequality, but it is difficult to imagine a reform that could possibly raise the political impact of the average factory worker—or even of the average business executive—*remotely* to equal that enjoyed by some columnists.[8]

Democracy is fundamentally about giving people the right to pursue and promote their interests in a nonviolent manner. That is, the undisciplined, chaotic, and generally unequal interplay of special interests is democracy's whole point. But for many observers the pursuit of a special interest is tantamount to corruption, and thus by this popular view democracy is, always will be, and, indeed, *must* be corrupt. And, of course, if actual corruption, however defined, were to be eliminated, the reformers will want next to rid the world of the *appearance* of corruption.

It seems to me, thus, that democratic cynicism stems not as much from the inadequacies of people or of democracy as from the ministrations of the image makers: People contrast democratic reality with its ideal image, note a huge discrepancy, and logically become cynical about the process. If cynicism about the form is a problem, what may need to be reformed is not so much the system as the theory—and perhaps the theorists.

Thus, Rose-Ackerman contrasts a "system based on democratic principles" with one where the "government is a structure of mutual favor-giving that benefits those with the most resources and the biggest mutually-reinforcing networks of trusted friends and supporters" (2001: 552–3). But if that is the distinction, no system based on democratic principles exists now, has ever existed, or ever will. They *all* are mutually reinforcing networks of favor-giving. Consequently, we either have to abandon democracy as it actually exists or else abandon those "democratic principles" that have now clearly been shown in hundreds of years of practice to be hopeless, irrelevant fantasies. I vote for the latter approach.

Actually, this argument should be extended one notch. Rose-Ackerman's apt characterization not only fits all democracies, but also all nondemocracies. That is, all governments are mutually reinforcing systems of favor-giving, where people and groups pursue special interests. What differentiates democracy is that *all* specially interested people and groups, not just those who happen to be favored by the ruler or the ruling group, are admitted into the fray and permitted freely to seek to manipulate governmental policy to their benefit. Some interests in a democracy do enjoy special privileges, but this is nothing compared to the perks traditionally graced upon preferred groups like the army, the aristocracy, the Church, the landed gentry, riot-prone urban dwellers, or the nomenklatura in nondemocracies. In a democracy, interests that are not officially preferred have at least a fighting chance of undercutting favored interests and getting some of the gravy for themselves.

Attitudes Toward Capitalism

There is no particular reason to think that people in advanced capitalist countries generally understand the economic system any more than those who only recently have emerged from decades of communist anticapitalist propaganda.

For example, in polls conducted in 1990, the residents of capitalist New York tended to agree with those in still-communist Moscow that it is "unfair" for an entrepreneur to raise prices merely because demand increases, and New Yorkers were, if anything, *less* tolerant of economic inequality, *more* distrustful of "speculators," and *less* appreciative of the importance of material incentives (Shiller et al. 1991, 1992). And, although the overwhelming majority of economists insist otherwise, generous portions of the American public continue to hold downsizing to be bad for the economy, foreign trade agreements to cost domestic jobs, and gasoline prices to result mainly from the quest for profits by Big Oil rather than from the normal play of supply and demand (Brossard and Pearlstein 1996).

Thus, incomprehension about, and distrust of, capitalism seems to be extremely widespread in advanced capitalist countries. For example, when oil prices were high, as John D. Rockefeller found, wildcatters would go out and prospect and then accuse refiners of cheating them when the consequent glut caused prices to plummet (Chernow 1998: 197). Efforts to use government for protection from competition are standard business practices. Americans rate automobile salesman at the very bottom in honesty and ethics polls, even though the vast majority of car purchasers—upward of 90 percent—profess they are happy with their purchase.

Sources of Attitudes Toward Capitalism

These perspectives about, and the negative image of, capitalism seem to have a variety of sources.

Some of it arises from critics, like socialists and communists, who champion an alterative economic system—one, they propose, that is more humane and fair than capitalism. As part of their promotional activities, they have naturally criticized and caricatured the competition and have done so with great, and often highly effective, elan.

Another impressive source of negativism is storytellers. As Irving Kristol has rhetorically observed of capitalism, "what poet has ever sung its praises? what novelist was ever truly inspired by the career of a businessman?" (Kristol 1978: xi). Instead over the centuries writers have persistently disparaged it in broadside and in banner, in polemic and in poem, in tract and in novel, in movie and in folksong, for its supposed heartlessness, cruelty, vulgarity, and casual exaltation of debased human values.

More generally, there is also something of a natural, historic antipathy toward capitalists from intellectuals. In George Stigler's understatement, "The intellectual has been contemptuous of commercial activity for several thousand years" (1982: 32). For example, Plato pointedly consigned the trader to the lowest level in his ideal society (Machan 1996: 36).[9]

Another traditional enemy of capitalism and an effective source of anticapitalist propaganda has been the church. St. Augustine denounced money lust as one of the three principal sins (right up there with power lust and sex lust) (Hirschman 1977: 9). And Stigler identifies "a dislike for profit seeking" as "one of the few specific attitudes shared by the major religions" (1984: 150).

The hostility of those who exalt the aristocratic and martial virtues—chivalry, honor, nobility, glory, valor, martial heroism—has also been a problem for capitalism. For these critics, observes McCloskey, "Don Quixote's idiocies in aid of chivalry are uncalculated, but noble," and an "impatience with calculation is the mark of romance" (1994: 189).[10]

Greed has never been an easy sell, and capitalism is, in economist Paul Samuelson's words, an "efficient but unlovable system with no mystique to protect it" (McInnes 1995: 91). Mario Vargas Llosa agrees: "Unlike socialism, capitalism has never generated a mystique; capitalism was never preceded by a utopian vision" (Gallagher 1990).

But even taking that into account, capitalists, many of whom have been spectacularly effective at selling their own products and services, have not been terribly good—or often, it seems, even very interested—in selling the system as a whole. In fact, many capitalists essentially seem to believe much of the anticapitalist caricature. Some of this may derive from the fact that whereas in war, it is the winners who write the history, in business it is the losers who do so. This is because the winners are so busy making money they don't have time to reminisce while the losers have plenty of leisure and may spend much of it crying foul. As Alfred Marshall (1920) observes, traders or producers who are undersold by a rival often "are angered at his intrusion, and complain of being wronged; even though . . . the energy and resourcefulness of their rival is a social gain."[11] The alternative, of course, is to admit one's own failings or at least one's own bad luck. Blaming the winner, and positing nefarious motives and tactics, are often much more satisfying.

The Elusive Quest for Happiness

Whatever its problems, capitalism, when left alone, is pretty good at generating economic growth—as can be seen in several post-communist countries even in the short time they have been free to let the capitalist process enrich them. The experience in the West suggests, however, that a considerable expansion of economic well-being will not cause people to profess that they are happier. In fact, they are likely simply to complain more.

When people are asked about happiness and their personal concerns, economic matters—including such issues as the standard of living and housing—tend to be the most often mentioned. Not surprisingly, health also scores highly as do family and personal relationships.[12] Moreover, wealthier people are more likely to profess being happy than poorer ones in the same society, a relationship that holds even when other variables such as education are controlled.[13] However, when a country grows economically, the professions of its people as to their state of happiness do not similarly grow. There is quite a bit of longitudinal data from the United States, Western Europe, and Japan to indicate this (Campbell 1981: 27–30; Easterlin 1996: 136, 138; Smith 1979). American and Japanese data are displayed in figures 10.1 and 10.2. The Japanese data are particularly impressive. During much of the survey period Japan underwent economic growth that was not only spectacular in rate, but widely distributed among the population (Sullivan 1997). Yet, when asked if they were better off from the previous year, Japanese routinely answered in the negative.[14]

There seem to be several possible explanations for this curiously unhappy state of affairs about happiness.

Some people argue that people may use a relative standard, not an absolute one, when assessing their well-being. If everybody's wealth increases at more or less the same rate relative incomes remain the same, and so does happiness. There exists a "consumption norm," suggests

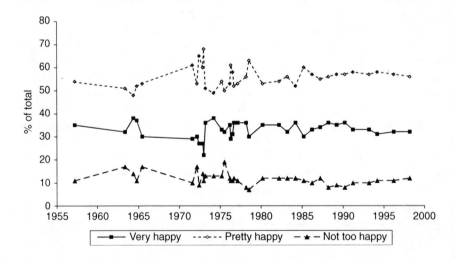

Figure 10.1   Happiness in the United States

Respondents were asked the following question: Taken all together, how would you say things are these days—would you say you are very happy, pretty happy, or not too happy?

Source: Niemi et al. 1989: 290 and Roper Public Opinion Center.

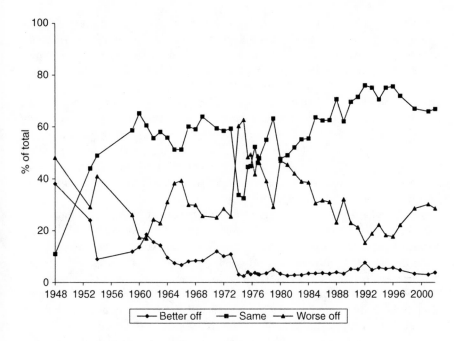

Figure 10.2   Household well-being compared to a year ago in Japan

Richard Easterlin, and one gauges one's happiness relative to this norm, not to the norm's absolute placement (1974: 111–16). But this cannot be the full explanation. After all, health is also an important component in happiness self-evaluations, and, while people may think of wealth in relative terms, they are unlikely to think of health in the same way. That is, people simply do or do not feel healthy, and whether other people are or are not in a similar condition is likely to be quite irrelevant to their judgment on this issue. Because health has been improving at least as impressively as income in places like the United States, happiness should be going up even if people adopt a relative standard with respect to the wealth component of the happiness calculation. But it is not.

Others suggest that nonmaterial concerns dominate perceptions of happiness (Campbell 1981). But it remains clear, as noted earlier, that economic and health considerations are of very considerable importance in personal assessments of happiness and well-being. And, because there have been enormous improvements in wealth and health in the United States and other surveyed countries, any failure of happiness to rise cannot be due to noneconomic factors unless it can be shown that these factors have greatly deteriorated over the same period of time—and they have not.

There is also the argument that material accumulation leads not to satisfaction, but to boredom and discontent (e.g. Scitovsky 1992: vi–viii, 4). Thus, a letter sent to the *New York Times* in 1998 from Latvia expressed worries that the youth in that country were being "worn down by grinding affluence" (January 5, A24). This perspective distrusts prosperity—a process in which people are bountifully and indiscriminately supplied at an attractive price with the things they happen to think they want. The concern is that, in a world that lacks danger and stimulating challenge, people will come to wallow in luxury and to give in to hedonism. In the process, not only do their minds rot, but they become dissatisfied and essentially unhappy.[15] There may be something to such concerns, but they would predict that happiness should actually decline in affluent areas, something that has not happened. Intellectuals who consider business to be boring, mindlessly repetitive, unsatisfying, or lacking in daring, courage, and imagination have never tried to run—much less start—one.

The chief reason for the phenomenon, it seems to me, is that improvements in well-being are effectively unappreciated. I have yet to run into an American over the age of 47 who regularly observes, "You know, if I had been born in the nineteenth century, I'd very probably be dead by now." Nobody really thinks in such terms, yet the statement is completely true—and, of course, I do not mean in the sense that just about everybody who happened to be born in that century is no longer with us, but that life expectancy in the United States as late as 1900 was 47.

It is commonly observed that people do not appreciate their health until they get sick, their freedom until they lose it, their wealth until it is threatened, their teeth until they ache. In other words, when things get better, we quickly come to take the improvements for granted after a brief period of often-wary assimilation: They become ingested and seem part of our due, our place in life.

Moreover, although some advances, like the end of the Cold War, can come about with dazzling speed and drama, many improvements of the human condition are quite gradual and therefore, are difficult to notice. Rosenberg and Birdzell observe that the remarkable transformation of the West from a condition in which 90 percent lived in poverty to one in which poverty was reduced to 20 or 30 percent of the population or less took a very long time: "Over a year, or even over a decade, the economic gains, after allowing for the rise in population, were so little noticeable that it was widely believed that the gains were experienced only by the rich, and not by the poor. Only as the West's compounded growth continued through the twentieth century did its breadth become clear" (1986: 6, also 265). Clearly, the same can be said for the massive improvements in life expectancy that have taken place over the last century and that have proved to be so easy to ignore.

The Functioning of Democracy and Capitalism

Thus, democracy and capitalism seem routinely to inspire in their constituents a curious incomprehension about, and appreciation for, the way they work.

Both in mature democracies and in new ones, I have argued, many still cling to a fuzzy, romantic image that, centuries of experience suggest, is quite fantastic. Democracy is not about active mass participation, enlightened citizen vigilance, heartwarming consensus, or majority tolerance, but the view that it ought somehow to be that way persists and inspires cynicism when real democracy is compared to such ideal images.

Similarly, the general view of capitalism—often even that held by capitalists when they trouble to generalize about it—can be quite cynical, suspicious, and uncomprehending. This view holds capitalism to be somehow vicious and reprehensible or at least devoid of virtue even though the daily business experience of people in advanced capitalist countries—where they are treated overwhelmingly with honesty, fairness, civility, and even compassion by acquisitive proprietors and deal-makers—constantly belies the negative image.

However, while political cynicism seems more nearly to be a constant than a variable quality in capitalist democracies, it is hardly a terminal problem. Long and extensive experience with the form suggests that Dionne is patently wrong when he argues that "a nation that hates politics will not long survive as a democracy" (1991: 355) as is Michael Nelson when he asserts that democracy "cannot long endure on a foundation of cynicism and indifference" (1995: 72).

Moreover, these faulty popular perspectives do not seem to have notably hampered the workings of either institution at least in advanced capitalist democracies. That is, although there probably ought to be *some* guiding minds at work for democracy and capitalism to be properly instituted and maintained, it does not appear necessary for people in general fully to understand them, or even to believe in them, for them to work. For societies aspiring to become democratic and capitalistic, that somewhat perverse message could be the most hopeful of all.

In the end, there may also be benefits to the endless and endlessly successful quest to raise standards and to fabricate new desires to satisfy and new issues to worry about. Not only does this quest keep the mind active, but it probably importantly drives, and has driven, economic development as well. Rosenberg and Birdzell suggest that it seems unlikely that a "self-satisfied people could move from poverty to wealth in the first place" (1986: 5), and David Hume observes that commerce "rouses men from their indolence" as it presents them with "objects of luxury, which they never before dreamed of," and it then "raises in them a desire of a more splendid way of life than what their ancestors enjoyed" (1955: 14).

By contrast, Easterlin puts a rather negative spin to all this when he applies the phrase, "hedonic treadmill," to the process and concludes, "each step upward on the ladder of economic development merely stimulates new economic desires that lead the chase ever onward" (1996: 153). The word, "treadmill," suggests an enveloping tedium as well as a lack of substantive progress. However, it seems clear that the "chase" not only enhances economic development but has invigorating appeals of its own. As Hume notes, when industry flourishes people "enjoy, as their reward, the occupation itself, as well as those pleasures which are the fruit of their labour." As part of this process, "the mind acquires more vigour" and "enlarges its power and faculties" (1955: 21; see also Murray 1988: ch. 7).

Moreover, there is no evidence that economic development exhausts the treaders, *lowers* their happiness, or inspires many effective efforts to turn back the clock. Professions of happiness may not soar, but, despite the anguished protests of some intellectuals, people do not seem to have much difficulty enduring a condition of ever-increasing life expectancy and ever-expanding material prosperity.

Notes

1. This essay develops and draws upon materials in Mueller (1996) and Mueller (1999).
2. For data see *Gallup Poll Monthly*, February 1998, p. 16. On this phenomenon more generally, see Hibbing and Theiss-Morse (1995: 36).
3. It also abruptly more than doubled the percentage of Americans who said they trusted the government to do what is right, leading some to question what, if anything, this question, so often cited and theorized about, actually measures. See Langer (2002).
4. *Harper's*, February 1995, p. 11. On this issue, see also Rose-Ackerman (2001: 537).
5. Address to a Joint Session of the United States Congress, February 21, 1990.
6. *Wilson Quarterly* Spring 1997: 121.
7. Verba et al. (1995: 13). See also Broder and Johnson (1996: 630–1). Without full explanation, Lindblom simply and casually labels this phenomenon "undemocratic" (1977: 169).
8. On this issue, see also Smith (2001: especially chs. 7, 8).
9. Interestingly, the intellectual's antibusiness mentality often infects the views even of economists and of putative defenders of capitalism. Adam Smith gloomily maintained that the "commercial spirit . . . confines the views of men" with the result that their minds "are contracted, and rendered incapable of elevation" (1896: 257, 259). John Maynard Keynes declared the capitalists' "money-motive" to be "a somewhat disgusting morbidity, one of those semi-criminal, semi-pathological propensities which one hands over with a shudder to the specialists in mental disease" (1963: 369). Joseph Schumpeter, somewhat along the lines of Smith, argued (erroneously it seems) that capitalism would, or had, become stiflingly bureaucratized so that "human energy would turn away from business" and "other than economic pursuits would attract the brains and provide the adventure" (1950: 131; see also McInnes 1995). On capitalism's supposed alienating and repressive effects on the human personality, see Hirschman (1977: 132).
10. Adam Smith concluded that capitalism could render a man "incapable of defending his country in war. The uniformity of his stationary life naturally corrupts the courage of his mind, and makes him regard with abhorrence the irregular, uncertain, and adventurous life of a soldier." And, ignoring or dismissing the issue of capitalist risk just like some of capitalism's most ardent opponents, he concluded that commerce "sinks the courage of mankind" with the result that "the heroic spirit is almost utterly extinguished," and the "bulk of the people" grow "effeminate and dastardly" by "having their minds constantly employed on the arts of luxury" (1896: 257–9). Tocqueville was so alarmed at the prospect of the decadence of plentitude that he advocated the occasional war to wrench people from their lethargy (Boesche 1988: 39). And Immanuel Kant once argued, "a prolonged peace favors the predominance of a mere commercial spirit, and with it a debasing self-interest, cowardice, and effeminacy, and tends to degrade the character of the nation" (1952: 113).
11. As he adds, a perspective like that can lead many to spend less time actually competing than seeking to reduce the risks of competition by guild or government regulation or through collusion and price-fixing (1920: 8).
12. Easterlin (1974: 90–6), mostly using data and analyses from Cantril (1965). On this issue, see also Murray 1988: ch. 4.
13. Diener (1983: 553). See also Campbell (1981: 241); Easterlin (1974: 99–104); Easterlin (1996: 133–5); Murray (1988: 66–8); Inglehart and Rabier (1986: 22–3). People in wealthy countries may

be happier on average than those in poorer ones, but the association is often weak and inconclusive. See Inglehart and Rabier (1986: 40, 44–50); Easterlin (1974: 104–8); Easterlin (1996: 138); but see also Veenhoven (1991: 9–12).

14. One study contends that a notable rise in happiness in England, France, the Netherlands, and West Germany took place between the terrible immediate postwar years and the 1960s or 1970s. Thus, the conclusion is, the wealth–happiness connection is subject "to the law of diminishing returns" (Veenhoven 1991: 19; see also the data for Japan in figure 10.2). At best, of course, this suggests that happiness will increase only when a country moves from misery to some degree of economic security and that little additional gain is to be expected thereafter. But, as Richard Easterlin notes, even this conclusion is questionable when one looks at data from Japan. By 1958, that country had substantially recovered from the war, but it still sported an income level lower than or equal to ones found in many developing countries today. Yet there was little or no increase in Japanese happiness ratings during the next 30 years (Easterlin 1996: 136–40; using data from Veenhoven 1993: 176–7; see also Inglehart and Rabier 1986: 44).

15. It is an old fear for successful capitalism, a fear voiced even by some of its champions. Adam Smith anticipated that through repetitive tasks workers would "become as stupid and ignorant as it is possible for a human creature to become" and be rendered incapable of exercising "invention" or "of conceiving any generous, noble, or tender sentiment" as they came to concentrate on repetitive tasks (1976: 782 [V.i.f]). Similarly, Alexis de Tocqueville was concerned that, when "the love of property" becomes sufficiently "ardent," people will come to regard "every innovation as an irksome toil," "mankind will be stopped and circumscribed," the mind "will swing backwards and forwards forever without begetting fresh ideas," "man will waste his strength in bootless and solitary trifling," and, though in continual motion, "humanity will cease to advance" (1990: 263).

References

Altschuler, Glenn C. and Stuart M. Blumin. 1997. "Limits of Political Engagement in Antebellum America: A New Look at the Golden Age of Participatory Democracy." *Journal of American History* 84: 855–85.

Berke, Richard L. 1994. "Victories Were Captured by G.O.P. Candidates, Not the Party's Platform." *New York Times*, November 10: B1.

Boesche, Roger. 1988. "Why did Tocqueville Fear Abundance? Or the Tension Between Commerce and Citizenship." *History of European Ideas* 9: 25–45.

Broder, David S. and Haynes Johnson. 1996. *The System: the American Way of Politics at the Breaking Point.* Boston: Little, Brown.

Brossard, Mario A. and Steven Pearlstein. 1996. "Great Divide: Economists vs. Public." *Washington Post*, October 15: A1.

Campbell, Angus. 1981. *The Sense of Well-Being in America: Recent Patterns and Trends.* New York: McGraw-Hill.

Cantril, Hadley. 1965. *The Pattern of Human Concerns.* New Brunswick NJ: Rutgers University Press.

Chernow, Ron. 1998. *Titan: The Life of John D. Rockefeller, Sr.* New York: Random House.

Diener, Ed. 1983. "Subjective Well-Being." *Psychological Bulletin* 95: 542–75.

Dionne, E. J., Jr. 1991. *Why Americans Hate Politics.* New York: Simon & Schuster.

Easterlin, Richard A. 1974. "Does Economic Growth Improve the Human Lot? Some Empirical Evidence." In P. A. David and M. W. Reder (eds.), *Nations and Households in Economic Growth: Essays in Honor of Moses Abramovitz*, pp. 89–125. New York: Academic Press.

———. 1996. *Growth Triumphant: The Twenty-first Century in Historical Perspective.* Ann Arbor MI: University of Michigan Press.

Fischer, Stanley and Alan Gelb. 1991. "The Process of Socialist Economic Transformation." *Journal of Economic Perspectives* 5: 91–105.

Gallagher, David. 1990. "Vargas Llosa Pans His Political and Intellectual Peers." *Wall Street Journal* April 6: A19.

Hibbing, John R. and Elizabeth Theiss-Morse. 1995. *Congress As Public Enemy: Public Attitudes Toward American Political Institutions.* New York: Cambridge University Press.

———. 2002. *Stealth Democracy: Americans' Beliefs About How Government Should Work.* New York: Cambridge University Press.

Hirschman, Albert O. 1977. *The Passions and the Interests: Political Arguments for Capitalism Before Its Triumph*. Princeton NJ: Princeton University Press.

Hislope, Robert. 2002. "Organized Crime in a Disorganized State: How Corruption Contributed to Macedonia's Mini-War." *Problems of Post-Communism* May/June: 33–41.

Holmes, Stephen. 1996. "Cultural Legacies or State Collapse? Probing the Postcommunist Dilemma." In M. Mandelbaum (ed.), *Postcommunism: Four Perspectives*, pp. 22–76. New York: Council on Foreign Relations.

Hume, David. 1955. *David Hume: Writings on Economics*, ed. Eugene Rotwein. Madison WI: University of Wisconsin Press.

Inglehart, Ronald and Jacques-Rene Rabier. 1986. "Aspirations Adapt to Situations—But Why are the Belgians So Much Happier than the French?" In F. M. Andrews (ed.), *Research on the Quality of Life*, pp. 1–56. Ann Arbor MI: Institute for Social Research, University of Michigan.

Kant, Immanuel. 1952. *The Critique of Judgement*. London: Oxford University Press.

Kennedy, John F. 1964. *Public Papers of the Presidents of the United States: John F. Kennedy, 1963*. Washington DC: United States Government Printing Office.

Keynes, John Maynard. 1963. *Essays in Persuasion*. New York: Norton.

Kristol, Irving. 1978. *Two Cheers for Capitalism*. New York: Basic Books.

Langer, Gary. 2002. "Trust in Government . . . to Do What?" *Public Perspective* July/August: 7–10.

Lindblom, Charles E. 1977. *Politics and Markets: The World's Political-Economic Systems*. New York: Basic Books.

Lipset, Seymour Martin. 1993. "Reflections on Capitalism, Socialism & Democracy." *Journal of Democracy* 4: 43–55.

———. 1994. "The Social Requisites of Democracy Revisited." *American Sociological Review* 59: 1–22.

Machan, Tibor R. 1996. "Business Bashing: Why Is Commerce Maligned?" *Jobs & Capital Winter*: 35–40.

Mansbridge, Jane. 1997. "Normative Theory and Voice and Equality." *American Political Science Review* 91: 423–5.

Marshall, Alfred. 1920. *Principles of Economics*. 8th ed. London: Macmillan.

McAneny, Leslie and David W. Moore. 1994. "Annual Honesty & Ethics Poll." *Gallup Poll Monthly*, October, pp. 2–4.

McCloskey, Donald. 1994. "Bourgeois Virtue." *American Scholar* 63: 177–91.

McInnes, Neil. 1995. "Wrong for Superior Reasons." *National Interest Spring*: 85–97.

Mueller, John. 1994. *Policy and Opinion in the Gulf War*. Chicago: University of Chicago Press.

———. 1996. "Democracy, Capitalism and the End of Transition." In M. Mandelbaum (ed.), *Post-Communism: Four Views*, pp. 102–67. New York: Council on Foreign Relations.

———. 1999. *Capitalism, Democracy, and Ralph's Pretty Good Grocery*. Princeton NJ: Princeton University Press.

Murray, Charles. 1988. *In Pursuit: Of Happiness and Good Government*. New York: Simon & Schuster.

Nardulli, Peter F., Jon K. Dalager, and Donald E. Greco. 1996. "Voter Turnout in U.S. Presidential Elections: An Historical View and Some Speculation." *PS: Political Science & Politics* 29: 480–90.

Nelson, Michael. 1995. "Why Americans Hate Politics and Politicians." *PS: Political Science & Politics* 28: 72–7.

Niemi, Richard G., John Mueller, and Tom W. Smith. 1989. *Trends in Public Opinion: A Compendium of Survey Data*. Westport CT: Greenwood.

Patterson, Kelly D. and David B. Magleby. 1992. "Trends: Public Support for Congress." *Public Opinion Quarterly* 56: 539–51.

Putnam, Robert D. 1995a. "Bowling Alone: America's Declining Social Capital." *Journal of Democracy* 6: 65–78.

———. 1995b. "Tuning In, Tuning Out: The Strange Disappearance of Social Capital in America." *PS: Political Science & Politics* 28: 664–83.

Rose, Richard. 1994. "Getting By Without Government: Everyday Life in Russia." *Daedalus* 123(3): 41–62.

Rose-Ackerman, Susan. 2001. "Trust, Honesty and Corruption: Reflection on the State-building Process." *Archives Européennes De Sociologie* 42: 526–70.

Rosenberg, Nathan and L. E. Birdzell. 1986. *How the West Grew Rich: The Economic Transformation of the Industrial World*. New York: Basic Books.

Rutland, Peter. 1994/95. "Has Democracy Failed Russia?" *National Interest* Winter, pp. 3–12.

Sandel, Michael J. 1996. *Democracy's Discontent: America in Search of a Public Philosophy*. Cambridge MA: Harvard University Press.

Schumpeter, Joseph A. 1950. *Capitalism, Socialism and Democracy*. 3rd ed. New York: Harper & Row.

Scitovsky, Tibor. 1992. *The Joyless Economy: The Psychology of Human Satisfaction*. Revised edition. New York: Oxford University Press.

Shafir, Michael. 1993. "Growing Political Extremism in Romania." *RFE/RL Research Report*, April: 18–22.

Shiller, Robert J., Maxim Boychko, and Vladimir Korobov 1991. "Popular Attitudes Toward Free Markets: The Soviet Union and the United States Compared." *American Economic Review* 81: 385–400.

———. 1992. "Hunting for *Homo Sovieticus*: Situational versus Attitudinal Factors in Economic Behavior." *Brookings Papers on Economic Activity* 1: 127–81, 193–4.

Smith, Adam. 1896. *Lectures on Justice, Police, Revenue and Arms*. Oxford: Clarendon.

——— 1976 [1776]. *An Inquiry into the Nature and Causes of the Wealth of Nations*. Oxford: Oxford University Press.

Smith, Bradley A. 2001. *Unfree Speech: The Folly of Campaign Finance Reform*. Princeton: Princeton University Press.

Smith, Tom W. 1979. "Happiness: Time Trends, Seasonal Variations, Intersurvey Differences, and Other Mysteries." *Social Psychological Quarterly* 42: 18–30.

Stigler, George J. 1982. *The Economist as Preacher and Other Essays*. Chicago: University of Chicago Press.

———. 1984. *The Intellectual and the Marketplace*. Cambridge MA: Harvard University Press.

Sullivan, Kevin. 1997. "Cost of Economic Equality Questioned." *Guardian Weekly* June 8, p. 17.

Tocqueville, Alexis de 1990. *Democracy in America*. Trans. Henry Reeve. New York: Vintage.

Toner, Robin. 1994. "Pollsters See a Silent Storm That Swept Away Democrats." *New York Times*, November 16: A14.

Veenhoven, Ruut. 1991. "Is Happiness Relative?" *Social Indicators Research* 24(February): 1–34.

———. 1993. *Happiness in Nations: Subjective Appreciation of Life in 56 Nations 1946–1992*. Rotterdam: Erasmus University of Rotterdam Department of Social Sciences.

Verba, Sidney, Kay Lehman Schlozman, and Henry E. Brady. 1995. *Voice and Equality: Civic Voluntarianism in American Politics*. Cambridge MA: Harvard University Press.

CHAPTER ELEVEN

And Now for the Bad News?

BRUCE ACKERMAN

Did the communists turn out to be half-right?
They were wrong about the dictatorship of the proletariat, but were they right in their critique of liberal capitalism?

1.

Russell Hardin and John Mueller certainly are not Marxists, but their diagnosis eerily confirms three crucial elements of the standard communist critique.

The first is *the moral bankruptcy of liberal individualism*. Capitalist democracy, the Marxist story goes, is a cold and cruel place, where private property owners ruthlessly pursue their self-interest in politics, without any concern for social justice or simple humanity.

Mueller enthusiastically agrees, except that he does not see anything wrong with it. Only a moralistic fool would take a different view. Democratic politics breeds cynicism because it is just plain silly to suppose that free people might sacrifice self-interest for the public good. The only good thing about democracy is that it allows every interest to compete for a piece of the action.

Russell Hardin is a bit more cautious. He recognizes that some actors might have larger political ideals in mind, but he does not take this possibility very seriously. Indeed, his larger analysis casts doubt on Mueller's pallid praise of democracy. Mueller is undoubtedly correct that interest groups are free to compete for a slice of the political pie but will the poor and the disorganized manage to get anything other than crumbs that drop from the table?

Hardin does not think so—for reasons that recall a second familiar Marxist critique. Call it *the illusion of bourgeois democracy*. Apologists for proletarian dictatorship conceded that voters in liberal democracies were free to choose between competing political parties. But they denied that this freedom provided more than an illusion of popular sovereignty. Voters might gain a passing moment of satisfaction when casting their ballots, but this happy feeling had almost nothing to do with the business of government. When it comes to power politics, the ballot box provides an illusory check on the conduct of the political class.

Hardin agrees. Voters simply do not have an adequate incentive to inform themselves about the issues or punish incumbents who fail to live up to their campaign promises. A leading proponent of rational choice theory, Hardin does not expect this to change any time soon. Philosophers might chatter about popular sovereignty, but serious thinkers should not take the notion seriously.

Which leads us to the final element of the Old Left critique. Call it the *betrayal of the masses*. Capitalist propaganda celebrating the right to vote might pacify the masses by giving them an illusion of control. But the political elite knows better and uses democratic ideology as a screen for pursuing its own interests.

Hardin, once again, agrees. But he is a bit uncertain about the precise manner in which the elites betray the masses. On the one hand, he suggests that the political class simply arranges affairs for its own advantage. This is a variation on Milovan Djilas's theory of a "new class" (1957). On the other hand, Hardin's text also suggests that the political class achieves reelection by providing special interest legislation for well-organized capitalist groups, who reciprocate with campaign finance. This is the more familiar Marxist notion of the state as the "executive committee" of the capitalist class. Of course, there is no need for Hardin to choose starkly between these two views. Maybe he thinks that both should be combined to provide a really plausible account of the causal dynamics of mass betrayal.

Whatever ambiguities remain, Hardin's bottom line is clear: Even more than Mueller, he thinks that cynicism is entirely justified about the everyday operation of liberal democracy.

2.

The communists believed that their three-part critique was preparing the way for revolution: Workers of the world unite, you have nothing to lose but your chains!

For both Hardin and Mueller, this is a nonsequitur. They believe that modern democracy is remarkably robust despite the mass cynicism generated by its routine operation. They both point to America as evidence to establish their point. For them, it is the classic case of selfish corporate democracy—and yet it has been remarkably stable.

My own writings take a different view. American government would never have sustained itself over the centuries without periodic citizen mobilizations that successfully renewed its moral foundations. Cynics and corporate democrats cannot satisfactorily account for the legislative achievements of the civil rights movement, the environmental movement, the feminist movement, to name just a few. The system also relies on political professionals to temper their self-interest by larger considerations of democratic legitimacy and the public good. Although there have been many failures, there have also been lots of genuine acts of statesmanship—enough to convince most citizens that the ongoing system is worthy of their support.

But this is not the place to continue this argument: If a couple of big books do not suffice, a few more pages will not be convincing (Ackerman 1991, 1998). Even if one assumes that Professors Hardin and Mueller are right in their analysis of American politics, they are still guilty of a nonsequitur when they use the American example to downplay the dangers of mass cynicism in the former communist world.

American workers have had generations to experience the benefits of a free-market economy. Even if they are only left with crumbs from the capitalists' table, these crumbs have mounted up to a considerable pile over centuries—making the income of the average American family the envy of the world. So if Americans are cynical about their system of democratic capitalism, they are understandably reluctant to kill the goose that lays the golden eggs. But the former residents of the "workers' paradise" have had no similar experience with democratic capitalism. For them, free-market economics is just a theory—and they have seen lots of economic theories fail to deliver the goods over the last century!

It is one thing for Americans to be skeptical about democracy while enjoying the fruits of capitalism; quite another, for citizens of the "second world" to lose their idealistic commitment to democracy without any compensation in the economic realm. Unless and until free-market economics actually delivers the goods to the post-communist world, American cynicism cannot serve as a relevant benchmark. To the contrary, a deeply skeptical post-communist public may well respond to a sustained period of economic failure by concluding that neoliberal politicians are not very different from their Leninist predecessors. The Khruschevs and the Kadars *also* claimed to possess an economic theory that promised a bright future to the next generation if flesh-and-blood humanity sacrificed its interests to the Truly Scientific Economic Model. If neoliberal politicians have merely switched the definition of True Economic Science but continue to demand severe economic sacrifice, why will not a skeptical public switch its support to the next demagogue who comes along promising both an end to sacrifice and a great leap forward into instant gratification?

Transition regimes will survive tough times only if lots of people reject a cynical view about democracy—either because they remain democratic idealists of the sort derided by Mueller or because the real-world political system is closer to the democratic ideals than the corporate democracy modeled by Hardin. To put my point in a single line: *Democracy needs committed citizens to survive crises.*

I think this is true in America, but it is especially true in transitional polities because they cannot rely on a tradition of success to induce skeptics to suspend their disbelief and reject demagogic threats to democratic survival.

Hardin and Muller hope to deflect this point by taking a particularly dim view of the command-and-control economies that characterized "real and existing socialism." Because these were dreadfully inefficient, they should provide a very undemanding benchmark to judge future capitalist success. Perhaps even a brutal form of capitalism, for all its injustices, will deliver more goods to the lower classes—or so they seem to suggest. If so, perhaps a cynical citizenry will keep their democratic faith even if the free market does not operate at American levels of entrepreneurial energy or economic efficiency.

I share their belief in the long-term success of the free market. But unless aggressive steps are taken to tax the rich and guarantee a decent social minimum, the process of trickle-down will sometimes be very slow—judging from the shocking decline in Russian life expectancies, Professor Mueller's cheerfulness about mortality rates strikes me as distinctly premature.[1] For the next generation or more, neoclassical economics is very much on probation in the transitional societies, even in regimes that have been much more successful. Short-term economic failures will threaten political regimes that cannot rely on committed citizens—men and women who are convinced that democracy is worthwhile for its own sake.

I have been looking to the political future, but I also disagree with Professor Hardin's diagnosis of the political present. In his view, the post-communist world has done a remarkably good job in making its move to liberal democracy. Taking this transition as an established fact, Hardin argues that it falsifies a host of political theories that emphasize the crucial role of a civic culture in sustaining democracy.

I read the data differently. Many countries in the communist bloc have plainly failed to make a successful transition—Belorussia, the Central Asian republics, Ukraine, Yugoslavia, to name just a few. Worse yet, the Russian Federation is hardly out of the woods—how will President Putin react if he thinks his political future is in doubt? Will he use authoritarian methods to crush his opponents? Will he deny them access to the mass media? Disrupt their rallies? Cheat in counting up the votes?

Hardin's optimism is based principally on the performance of the band of Central European and Baltic states slated for admission to the European Union in 2004, as well as those lining up as promising EU candidates over the next decade. But I draw different lessons from these transitions. For one thing, these countries do have a different civic culture from those further east. They experienced only 40, not 70, years of communism, and this meant that there were still some living memories of prewar systems of government. Although most of these systems were not fully democratic, they were not totalitarian either—allowing for some degree of party competition, free speech, and the like. This gave the transition-builders some half-remembered experiences to build on.

Even more important, communism was imposed on Central Europe by the Red Army, and during the 40-year period of occupation, both elites and masses were constantly using Western democracy as a reference point for their own dissatisfactions with Russian rule. When the end came in 1989, there was broad support for a return to European values. In contrast, communism further east was the product of a genuine revolution, and its disintegration has led to genuine bewilderment, with a renewed debate that resembles the nineteenth-century contest between Europhiles and Slavophiles. Hardin is wrong, then, to dismiss these deep cultural differences when accounting for the big differences in the relative success of Central Europe and the Baltic states.

A final difference is perhaps the most important of all—and that is the role of the EU in the process of transition. Call it the logic of perspective federation.[2] Admission to the EU promises a host of benefits to elites and masses alike. Militarily, EU membership is even more important than NATO in deterring the threat of future Russian aggression; economically, it promises regional subsidies, especially to agriculture, and access to a vast market; legally, it provides a stable framework for foreign and domestic investment; ideologically, it redeems the region's sense of European identity after a period of Russian domination; and finally, if things do not go well at home, citizenship in the EU will allow Easterners to move their families to the richer parts of the Union—an especially attractive exit option for those who can master foreign languages.

Citizens would be foolish to put this bundle at risk by backing a demagogic assault on democracy. This did not stop the Serbs, of course, but their disastrous example should deter many more such demagogic adventures. For example, I suspect that the Serbian disaster helps account for Vladimir Mečiar's failure to sustain his demagogic appeal in Slovakia. When faced with the prospect of a loss of their place on the gravy train to the EU, the majority of Slovaks quite sensibly recognized that a bit of nationalistic self-indulgence was not really worth the loss of a chance of a lifetime.

Even within this context, I do not agree with Professor Hardin's dismissive treatment of cultural values, or committed citizenship, to explain successful transitions—recall the first two factors differentiating Central Europe and the Baltics from the rest of the Soviet Union, which strike me as quite important. Nevertheless, the prospect of EU membership did have the happy consequence of putting overwhelming material benefits on the side of a successful transition. Because a single breach of basic democratic norms would lead to EU exclusion for a generation or more, a materialistic cost–benefit analysis does play a significant role in explaining the short-term success of these transitions.

What is harder for materialists to explain is the other side of the equation: Why should Western Europe admit the Easterners to their comfortable club? EU expansion is not a zero-sum game, but the Westerners are accepting very substantial costs for rather speculative gains. In the short term, they will be spending a lot of money on subsidies and such. Even more serious are the long-term dangers. If and when the Russians resume an aggressive military policy, the English or French will find their room for maneuver greatly limited. Though preceding generations of Western leaders were very reluctant to have their nationals "die for Danzig," they will be obliged to treat a Russian invasion of the Baltics, say, in a very different spirit. Once Latvians are fellow citizens of the EU, it will be very difficult indeed for England or France to turn their backs on the ground that the attack does not directly concern their countries' narrow self-interests. What *precisely* are the benefits to the Westerners that outweigh these short-term economic costs and long-term military dangers?

I do not think a materialistic explanation suffices. To make sense of EU expansion requires us to take a very noncynical view of the Westerners' commitments to liberal democratic values.

Consider the recent Irish referendum on the EU's admission of the ten new states from Eastern Europe and the Baltic. Under present EU arrangements, each member state can veto any such expansion, and Ireland's constitution put the decision up to its voters. Thus, a tiny group in the far West of Europe had a critical role to play in deciding the fate of the East. Moreover, it was perfectly plain to the Irish that expansion was not in their material self-interest, and this is why they voted No when the question was to put to them at an initial referendum.

And yet, in rejecting the ten Eastern states, were they not betraying the great liberal democratic ideals they shared with all right-thinking Europeans? Having gained so much from European integration during earlier decades, was it not especially mean-spirited for the Irish to deny their fellow Europeans the chance to share in the great Enlightenment hope of the twenty-first century?

What is this hope? That the great ideals of liberal democracy might not fare quite so poorly as they did in the nineteenth or twentieth centuries; that this time around, the Europeans might use their great Enlightenment heritage as material to build a better world for their children and for all humanity.

This is the sort of rhetoric that Professor Mueller despises as the work of intellectual idlers who blather about the Enlightenment rather than use their minds to make money. But it was this appeal to common European values that caused the Irish to change their mind and vote Yes at their second referendum. Suppose that the Irish had instead voted No a second time, following the dictates of their narrow self-interest. What would have happened next?

The first stage is pretty easy to predict. As a matter of EU law, the Irish rejection would have resulted in a complete mess. The EU would have been obliged to tell the ten applicants that they would have to wait quite a while—maybe a few years—before the legal groundwork might be prepared for another treaty of accession.

The analysis gets more interesting at the second stage—how would the ten applicant states have reacted to the postponement?

We have been betrayed. A bunch of selfish Irishmen has now opened up the political field in the applicant states to a host of nationalist demagogues. They have been waiting in the wings, eagerly prophesying the failure of the cosmopolitan European project—and now they have been given their chance!

Do the Westerners really want us after all? Or will they use the Irish vote as a convenient excuse to avoid the costs of enlargement forever? After this betrayal, can we hold the fort of democracy against the demagogues who will exploit it for all it is worth?

Professors Hardin and Mueller do not provide a conceptual space for the anxieties captured in this thought-experiment. According to Hardin, the transition to democracy is an unequivocal success, demonstrating the irrelevance of civic culture or common values to the enterprise. According to Mueller, only pointy-headed intellectuals and moralizing prelates should be surprised by cynicism about democracy. Sensible people know better than to trust their blather about liberal democratic ideals.

This bracing realism has its virtues, but it cannot account for the *shudder of anxiety* any sensible Central European would have experienced if the Irish had rejected EU expansion a second time, leading to a *genuine doubt* about the ultimate success of the democratic transition.

But the Irish did not betray Europe's Enlightenment dream. They joined a long list of political players, stretching back to Jean Monnet, who have managed to revitalize European ideals of liberal democracy after the shattering disasters of the World War II. These actors were not starry-eyed idealists, but many did temper their narrow self-interest by larger considerations—sacrificing quite a lot to push Europe down the path to union, and thereby deepening the collective commitment to Enlightenment ideals of liberty, equality, and democracy.

Hardin draws a mistaken lesson from the short-term success of the transition in the relatively narrow strip of post-communist territory represented by Central Europe and the Baltic states. This success does not suggest the irrelevance of collective values or civic culture. It suggests that one cannot assess the importance of these values without taking account of the larger interaction between the transitional countries and the larger European political community. Each of the transitional states contained groups of committed democratic activists, whose political activities have been immensely assisted by the prospect of EU entry. Quite simply, these activists were no longer faced with the daunting task of convincing their skeptical brethren that democracy was worthwhile for its own sake; they could combine their ideological appeal with the bread-and-butter benefits of potential entry into the EU. This has tilted the political game of local politics in their favor—to the point where Hardin can suppose that an appeal to values is entirely irrelevant to the transition's success. But once we ask why the EU decided to make the effort to tilt the local political game toward liberal democracy in the first place, the generative role of political values emerges with renewed force.

3.

Hardin and Mueller offer some good news and some bad news. Their good news is that democratic capitalism is remarkably robust, surviving despite massive cynicism about its moral value. So far as they are concerned, this means that the post-communist world may secure its future without undue concern about the puzzling process of creating a new generation of committed democratic citizens, capable of sustaining a vital civic culture.

The bad news is that the democratic capitalism they describe is morally reprehensible, eerily converging on Marxist caricatures.

A *democracy without a committed citizenry* is easier to achieve, but less valuable, than one might have thought.

There is only one problem. They have not given us good reason to accept their good news. Whatever the meaning of the American experience, it is an irrelevant benchmark for the post-communist world. Worse yet, the overwhelming majority of people in the "second world" have not yet made a secure transition to democracy, and those that have succeeded owe their success, in significant part, to the commitments of the larger EU to liberal democratic values. Democracy without a committed citizenry does not seem terribly robust.

That is the really bad news. The good news, if there is any, is that a democracy built by committed citizens looks morally attractive, in sharp contrast to the dismal swamps portrayed by Professors Hardin and Mueller.

They are right, of course, to caution against unrealistic expectations. There is absolutely no chance of returning to the classical world of Athenian democracy, and I would not want to live in Athens anyway—they killed Socrates, among many other stupid and evil things. But it is one thing to caution against unrealistic utopias; quite another, to lower one's expectations to the Marxist caricatures offered up by Hardin and Mueller.

Despite their suggestions to the contrary, most contemporary political and legal theorists reject both extremes and explore the vast conceptual space between cynicism and utopia. Without seeking to transform human nature, they have explored the social, economic, and cultural factors that seem to facilitate the operation of democratic systems throughout the world.[3] These studies certainly do not provide a blueprint for transition to democracy. They do provide grounds for cautious optimism—provided, and it is a big proviso, that political elites and ordinary citizens are willing to stand up for democratic values during the long and difficult period of institutional construction.

The moral challenges faced by democratic citizens during this period are many and complex. One problem is especially relevant to this volume's concern with honesty and trust. A democratic transition requires a lot of it, because lots of citizens will initially be skeptical about whether the new system deserves their commitment—after all, the preceding system has properly taught most of them to be very skeptical about loud protestations of political virtue. Nevertheless, most people *are* willing to be good citizens if they can be convinced that the system deserves their confidence. A key challenge, considered by many essays in this volume, is how a new system can earn its citizens' trust, and thereby build "cycles of political virtue"— in which the citizens become increasingly committed to the system as the system demonstrates that it is actually committed to their fair and decent treatment.[4]

It is also critically important to design institutions that give ordinary people a sense that they can make a real-world difference in the practical operation of liberal democracies. Here too, these volumes contain a range of innovative proposals that are worthy of serious attention.[5] Perhaps the intellectual energy represented by this work will help provoke constructive political activity in the years ahead.

Only time will tell. But if there is to be progress—especially in the vast area beyond the scope of the EU—it will require the serious political commitment of millions and millions of men and women. Societies cannot make a transition to liberal democracy without a committed citizenry. Undue cynicism, no less than excessive utopianism, can be a source of harmful illusions.

Notes

1. Russian men have experienced a tragic collapse in life expectancies since the end of communism. In 1989, average life expectancy was 64.2 years; in 2000, it was 59.0. The decline for women—from 74.5 to 72.2 years—was modest only by comparison. Sources: Statistical Collections of the USSR Central Statistics Department; USSR Goskomstat; Goskomstat of the Russian Federation, all at www.demoscope.ru/weekly/ssp/sng_e0.php.
2. I discuss this dynamic further in Ackerman 1997.
3. See, for e.g., the classic work of Robert Dahl (1971).
4. See Horne and Levi, Offe, Vacroux, and Krastev and Ganev, this volume.
5. See especially those of Susan Rose-Ackerman, this volume, and Bo Rothstein (2004). For my own efforts along these lines, see Ackerman and Fishkin (2004), on improving the quality of citizen deliberation; Ackerman and Ayres (2002), on campaign finance reform; Ackerman (1992) on liberal constitutionalism. See also Ackerman and Alstott (1999) on distributive justice. Many others are making important contributions, but this is not the place for a comprehensive bibliography.

References

Ackerman, Bruce. 1991, 1998. *We the People*. Vols. 1 and 2, Cambridge MA: Harvard University Press.
———. 1992. *The Future of Liberal Revolution*. New Haven CT: Yale University Press.
———. 1997. "The Rise of World Constitutionalism." *University of Virginia Law Review* 83: 771–97.
Ackerman, Bruce and Anne Alstott. 1999. *The Stakeholder Society*. New Haven CT: Yale University Press.
Ackerman, Bruce and Ian Ayres. 2000. *Voting with Dollars*. New Haven CT: Yale University Press.
Ackerman, Bruce and James Fishkin. 2004. *Deliberation Day*. New Haven CT: Yale University Press.
Dahl, Robert. 1971. *Polyarchy: Participation and Opposition*. New Haven: Yale University Press.
Djilas, Milovan. 1957. *The New Class: An Analysis of the Communist System*. New York: Praeger.
Rothstein, Bo. 2004. "Social Trust and Honesty in Government: A Causal Mechanisms Approach." In J. Kornai, B. Rothstein, and S. Rose-Ackerman (eds.), *Creating Social Trust in Post-Socialist Transition*, pp. 13–30. New York: Palgrave Macmillan.

AUTHOR INDEX

SUBJECT INDEX